EASY WAYS
TO EXPERT
WOODWORKING

ROBERT SCHARFF

EASY WAYS
TO EXPERT
WOODWORKING

NEW YORK
TORONTO
LONDON

McGRAW-HILL BOOK COMPANY, INC.

Published by the McGraw-Hill Book Company, Inc.

Printed in the United States of America

CONTENTS

CHAPTER **1**

Introduction to the radial-arm machine

WOODWORKING is the most lasting and also the most satisfying of all pastimes. This fact can be borne out by the ever-increasing popularity of this hobby. One of the most powerful appeals of wood to all workers is the ease with which it can be fashioned into useful products. It can be cut into any desired form and shaped, drilled, or sanded; as a matter of fact, it can be worked with a variety of wood-working tools.

Wood is also very flexible in application. It can be used in many different ways to produce many different items; in fact, there are over 6,000 known uses of wood, ranging from a toothpick to a structural member in an industrial building. The flexibility of wood and its ease of working have led to the development of versatile tools of many different designs and types, each of which enjoys one or more features to satisfy a specific need.

When selecting a power tool for your shop, the determining factor is not so much the many jobs it can do but primarily the end uses, that is, how it fits your particular needs. The tool that meets this requirement, yet is extremely versatile, is the radial-arm machine. Homecraftsmen and hobbyists are discovering that they can get professional scope and skill into their work with this machine.

As you can see by the table of contents, it is a complete workshop. It will saw, dado, and shape with complete accuracy. (These operations comprise basically 85 per cent of all homeshop work.) With the proper attachments added, it will function as a jointer, drill press, router, saber saw, lathe, sander (disk, belt, and drum), grinder, buffer, and polisher.

Principle of Operation. The radial-arm type of power tool is in effect a mechanical arm that features the easy dexterity of a human arm. In fact, it can actually duplicate all movements with unerring, controlled accuracy on every operation. When cutting lumber, for instance, the human element makes it impossible for even an expert carpenter to cut two boards exactly alike; but the mechanical arm, with its ball-bearing carriage riding on precision-machined tracks, guarantees accuracy on every cut. For further accuracy and safety, all work is done from the top of the material.

Flexibility with this tool means that the cutting member can be placed in any position throughout all three dimensions (length, width, and depth). This is possible because of the unique design allowing full maneuverability through a complete circle in any of three directions.

Without going into the why's and wherefore's of these different movements (they will be explained in detail in Chapter 2), let us see how three-dimension flexibility is possible with the motorized mechanical arm.

As shown in Fig. 1·1, the radial arm (*A*)—from which this type of machine derives its name—rotates 360 degrees for right- or left-miter cuts. You merely release clamp (*B*) and lift latch (*C*), then

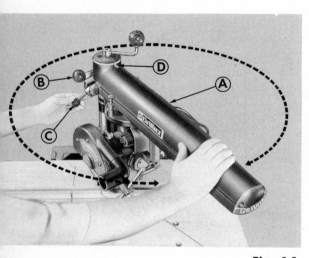

Fig. 1·1

easily swing the arm to any angle. The eye-level calibrated miter scale (*D*), shows you precisely the miter angle you want. The "built-in" stops at 0 and 45 degrees automatically locate these common angles. Also, you never shift the lumber for miters—the radial-arm machine puts the saw at the exact angle and you pull across for perfect cuts every time. An accurate measuring scale, on the right side of the arm, gives you instant measuring for ripping.

Figure 1·2 shows the shoulder action of the mechanical arm. As the arm is raised

or lowered, it measures for you. Each full turn of the elevating handle (*A*) lifts or lowers the arm (*B*) exactly ⅛ inch. One-half turn gives you 1/16 inch. This is a precision depth control.

The elbow action of the mechanical arm is illustrated in Fig. 1·3. The yoke, which holds the motor, is beneath the arm and rides freely on it. Release the yoke clamp (*B*) and lift the locating pin (*C*), then swing the yoke right or left. It automatically stops at all four 90-degree positions, giving you quick, positive adjustment for rip and crosscuts. The clamp (*D*) locks the saw in the desired rip position.

To see the wrist movement of the mechanical arm, look at Fig. 1·4. Pull out the clamp (*A*) and locating pin (*B*). Tilt the motor (*C*) for the angle desired on the bevel scale (*D*). Relock *A*. The motor unit automatically locates the popular 0-, 45-, and 90-degree bevel positions. Your compound angles and bevel cuts are measured for you with unequaled accuracy, and there is no limit to the bevel cuts.

To handle this machine, all you have to do is to remember that its flexible operation is based on three simple radial adjustments. The *arm* can be swung horizontally through 360 degrees around its column; the *yoke* can be revolved horizontally through 360 degrees under its roller carriage; and the *motor* can be tilted within the yoke to any angle desired. These three adjustments enable you to place the cutting tool easily in any position.

With so flexible a machine, you will soon be performing many operations which you had never thought possible. On the other hand, if you are not interested in a variety of operations—have just one operation to perform—the radial-arm machine will perform any one of its many operations as efficiently as any single-purpose tool. And if a change in your design or a change in your method is effected, the radial-arm machine can be changed quickly to perform with equal efficiency on another job.

In the succeeding chapters, you will see how easily this modern machine can be operated and what saving can be effected in your setup time.

Radial-arm Machine Sizes. Radial-arm machines are available in a range of sizes from ¾ to 10 horsepower, the smallest being the most popular one for home-shop use. This size machine cuts 2½ inches deep with a 9-inch blade, crosscuts 15 inches wide on 1-inch stock, and rips to the center of 48-inch-wide panels.

The radial-arm machine is equipped with a direct-drive motor. There are no belts, pulleys, gears, or other devices to worry about and to maintain. The cutting tool is mounted directly on the motor spindle, an operation done above the worktable so that there are no table inserts to fuss with. The motor operates at 3,450 rpm and is available in either 115-volt single-phase 60-cycle alternating-current or 220-, 440-, or 550-volt three-phase 60-cycle alternating-current models.

The direct-drive motor has grease-sealed-for-life bearings at each end of the motor shaft so that you never have to oil it. Motors of this type are protected against overloading by a manual-reset Klexon thermostat—it kicks out when the motor is overheated and loaded. To reset the motor, allow a few minutes, then "push in" the red button on the motor.

Safety Features. One of the outstanding virtues of the radial-arm machine is its safety features. (Other safety attachments are illustrated in Chapter 11.) For instance, a carefully engineered safety guard (see Figs. 2·3A and B) is used to cover the cutting tool so as to provide maximum safety to the operator. It is ad-

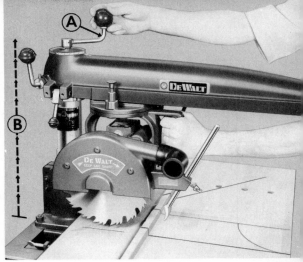

Fig. 1·2

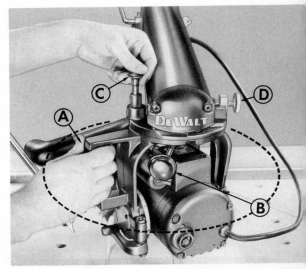

Fig. 1·3

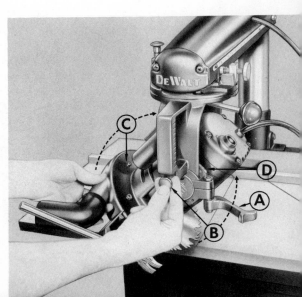

Fig. 1·4

justable and is provided with a kickback device for use in ripping operations, as well as with an adjustable dust spout that directs the flow of sawdust wherever desired. This guard is used for sawing, dadoing, shaping, and other operations, providing safety factors hitherto not possible with ordinary table saws.

Another important factor is an ignition-type motor-starting key (Fig. 1·5). Only this key will start the motor, and it fits a tumbler-type mechanism that is recessed

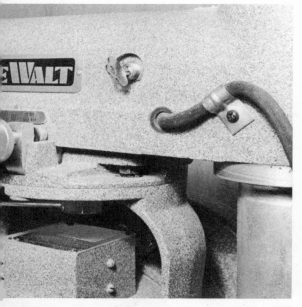

Fig. 1·5

in the side of the arm. This key is especially important in the home where there are children and, of course, prevents unauthorized use by others. This safety key switch is usually kept with other keys and gives the owner the assurance of safety so desirable in the home.

The fact that the blade is mounted above the worktable, instead of below it, is possibly the major safety feature of this machine. Since you can always see what you are doing, you can very quickly

do accurate cutting because you can easily follow the layout marks on the top of the material, and the mechanical arm guarantees a true cut regardless of the angle. For most operations the hand guides the saw blade through the work; this definitely lessens the chance of having the blade clip you. It, of course, eliminates overcutting and spoiling of the material.

Regardless of the operation, all setups are made above the worktable to simplify all jobs. The calibrated miter, rip, and bevel scales, as well as all control handles are above the worktable, clear of the work and easy to reach. There is never a need to stoop under the table and squint at the scales nor to turn any control handles underneath the table top.

Floor Space Required. The radial-arm machine is fundamentally a one-wall shop, and the over-all floor space required is approximately 3 square feet (about 75 per cent less operating floor space than is needed for any other machine). This design feature means that a workshop can be set up even in the smallest basement, utility room, garage, or attic. For instance, in the attic, the radial-arm machine can be placed back under the eaves, using space that would otherwise be wasted. Unlike a table saw, the radial arm does not require accessibility from all sides.

When locating the radial-arm machine, space should be allowed for handling material of the maximum lengths required. About 10 feet on either side will allow for most ripping and handling of long boards. And 2 feet of the operating area is all that is required at the front of the machine. Table extensions are preferable to support long work and should be solid or made of wood on metal rollers to help in conveying stock past the blade. Be sure to provide an ample light source, natural or artificial, to enable easy reading of

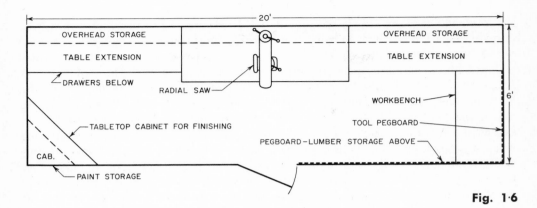

OVERHEAD STORAGE

TABLE EXTENSION

DRAWERS BELOW

RADIAL SAW

TABLETOP CABINET FOR FINISHING

CAB.

PAINT STORAGE

OVERHEAD STORAGE

TABLE EXTENSION

WORKBENCH

TOOL PEGBOARD

PEGBOARD—LUMBER STORAGE ABOVE

20'

6'

Fig. 1·6

angle and dimension dials and controls. A typical small workshop layout is shown in Fig. 1·6.

The ¾-horsepower machine which takes a 9-inch saw blade is practically portable. Weighing approximately 140 pounds, it is easily carried by two men, and when necessary it can be knocked down and handled by one. It will fit comfortably into the trunk of your car.

The radial-arm machine may be mounted on saw horses (temporary installation) or on a steel cabinet (Fig. 1·7) or built into a workbench (see Chapter 15). The machine is uncrated and assembled according to the manufacturer's instructions furnished with it.

Connecting the Machine to the Power Supply. To obtain the maximum efficiency from your radial-arm motor, the wire from the source of power to the machine should not be less than size 14 (B and S gauge). Be sure that the electric line is fused with a 15-ampere fuse. If an ordinary type of fuse blows during the initial fraction of a second when the machine is turned on, do not put in a new one of higher rating. Instead, replace it with a fuse of the same rating, but of the "slow-blow" or delay type. It contains a special fusible link that withstands a momentary overload without giving way.

Before plugging the cord into the wall or floor outlet, look at the name plate on your machine to see if it is marked 120 volts because this is the voltage in common use today in homes. If you ordered a radial-arm machine for use on a 240-volt line, be sure the name plate is marked 240 volts. Unless the voltage is delivered to within plus or minus 5 per cent of the motor name-plate rating, complete satisfaction cannot be guaranteed. In case the motor runs hot or short of power, call your local power company to check your voltage.

The radial-arm machine, as any other power tool, should always be grounded while in use. This precaution will protect the operator against possible electric

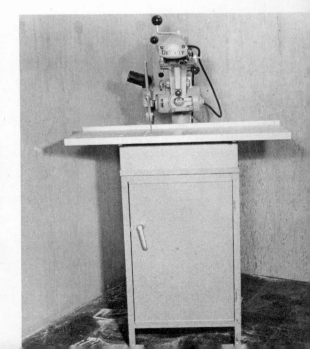

Fig. 1·7

shock should a short circuit or ground develop while the machine is being connected to the power outlet or during operation. The radial-arm machine offers new and assured grounding protection for your safety. In accordance with a ruling of the National Electric Code, it is equipped with a three-wire cord, one wire being a ground wire. For your complete safety while operating this saw, remember that the three-conductor attachment plug naturally requires a three-prong grounded outlet (5260 series). Just insert the three-prong plug and the machine is instantly grounded (Fig. 1·8*A*).

To permit use of this tool with a two-prong receptacle, an adapter is available. Match the wider prong of the adapter with the wider hole of the outlet. If you find that the adapter will not fit, file the wider prong to size. When using the adapter, the extending green wire should be connected to the outlet-plate retaining screw (Fig. 1·8*B*), provided that the outlet itself is grounded, or to any other known permanent ground, such as a water or an electric-conduct pipe. Caution: If an extension cord is used, be sure it is a three-wire cord and large enough (12 gauge) to prevent excessive voltage loss.

Fig. 1·8A   **Fig. 1·8B**

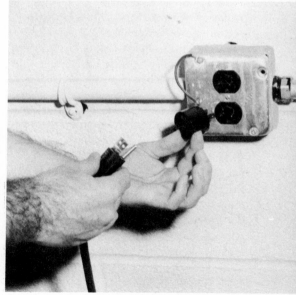

CHAPTER 2

Basic operation of the saw

HAVE YOU EVER stopped to think how many different kinds of saw cuts there are? Actually there are only six basic saw cuts in woodworking—crosscut, bevel crosscut, miter, bevel miter, rip, and bevel rip (Fig. 2·1). All other cuts, no matter how intricate, are combinations of these basic cuts (see Chapter 3). It is essential, therefore, to master the basic cuts in order to operate any power saw to its fullest capabilities.

With a radial-arm saw, the basic cuts are easy and safe. Because the blade is above the table top, you always work on the top side of the material, with your layout marks in clear view. The saw is never hidden beneath the material—you always know where it is. The saw also adjusts to the lumber for all cuts—no need to shift the wood when you change operations from cross to miter to rip, etc. With the material in a stationary position, your hands are always safely away from the blade.

CONTROLS

The versatility of the radial-arm saw is due, in part, to its controls. All the controls for depth of cut, miter angles, beveling, etc., are within plain sight and are easy to reach because they are all above the worktable. The controls are the keys to successful operation of the saw (Fig. 2·2). Learn to use them by adjusting the machine for all operations before actually starting to cut with it.

On the top surface of the table top (*M*), you will find several saw-blade kerfs $\frac{1}{16}$ inch deep which the saw blade (*H*) will follow or ride in when making most popular cuts. They are a straight crosscut, right 45-degree, straight 45-degree bevel, a concave cut in the center of the table for ripping, and a quarter-round circle in the front of the table for the saw blade to follow when swiveling 90 degrees to the in-rip position. The cuts are also made in the guide fence (*N*). For other cuts that can be made in the table, see page 25.

The elevating handle (*D*) raises or

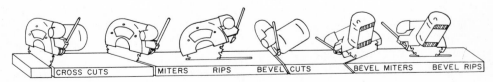

CROSS CUTS   MITERS   RIPS   BEVEL CUTS   BEVEL MITERS   BEVEL RIPS

Fig. 2·1

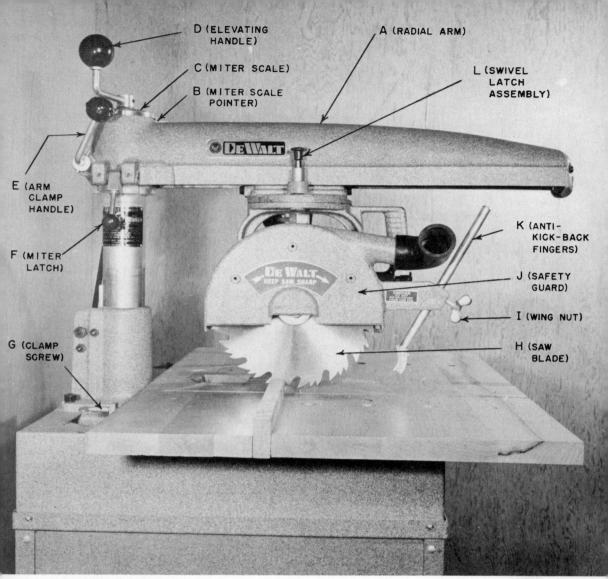

Fig. 2·2

lowers the arm, motor, and yoke. Each complete turn of the crank handle raises or lowers the machine $\frac{1}{8}$ inch. To raise the machine, follow the rotation arrow on top of the column. To lower the machine, turn the elevating handle in reverse of the rotation arrow.

The safety guard (J) is adjustable for cutting any thickness of material up to the capacity of the blade. To make the guard adjustments necessary for ripping, loosen the wing nut (P) which holds the guard to the motor, and rotate the guard down

to $\frac{1}{8}$ inch above the material that is to be ripped (Fig. 2·3A). Retighten the wing nut. Then on the opposite side of the guard, release the thumbscrew (I) which holds the anti-kickback fingers (K) and lower them to $\frac{1}{8}$ inch below the top of the material being ripped (Fig. 2·3B). Then retighten the thumbscrew. Adjust the dust spout (O) until it is turned toward the back of the machine so as to carry the dust away from you.

The radial arm (A) revolves a full 360 degrees on the column (EE). This move-

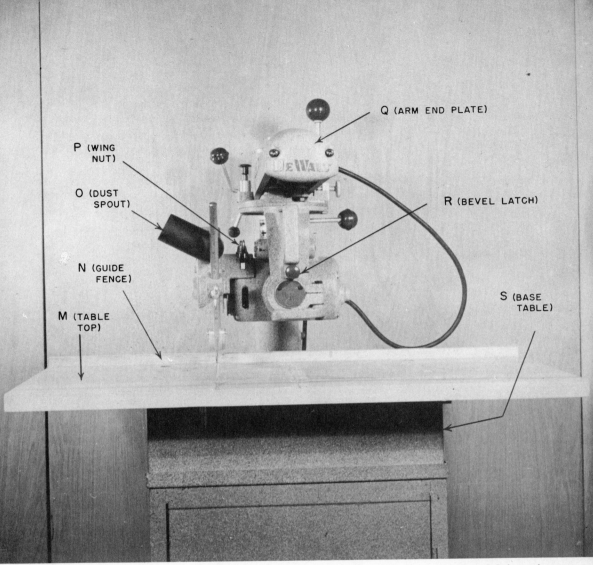

P (WING NUT)

O (DUST SPOUT)

N (GUIDE FENCE)

M (TABLE TOP)

Q (ARM END PLATE)

R (BEVEL LATCH)

S (BASE TABLE)

Fig. 2·2 (cont.)

ment permits you to set the saw for any angle cut desired.

To make this movement, release the arm clamp handle (*E*) by pulling it forward and lift the miter latch (*F*) from the slot in the column. Swing the arm left or right to the angle desired by following the miter scale (*C*) on top of the column, then lock the arm clamp handle.

For quick, positive location for straight cutoff or left and right 45 degrees, seat the miter latch into the proper slot on the column and lock the arm clamp handle.

The yoke (*X*) and motor (*T*) revolve a full 360 degrees on the roller carriage of the radial arm. This movement permits location of the saw in a positive locking position for (1) crosscutting, blade parallel with the arm; (2) in-ripping, swivel yoke and motor left 90 degrees from the crosscut position; and (3) out-ripping, swivel yoke and motor right 90 degrees from the crosscut position. To make these movements, release the clamp handle (*CC*) by pulling it forward and pulling up on the swivel latch (*L*). Swivel the yoke to one of the above three positions. The swivel latch accurately locates the position. Then tighten the clamp handle by pushing it back.

The rip-lock clamp (*BB*) locks the roller carriage to the radial arm for all operations where the material is moved to the cutting tool. When setting the saw for ripping, move the pointer (*AA*) to the desired width of the rip, by following the ripping scale (*Z*). Then turn the knurled head of the rip-lock clamp clockwise until tight

on the radial arm so that the roller carriage cannot move. The saw may then be set for either in- or out-ripping. Most rip cuts can be made from the in-rip position, whereas wide panel ripping is done in the out-rip position.

The motor mounted in the yoke will tilt to any angle or bevel position desired. To make the bevel adjustment, first elevate the column about twenty turns of the crank to provide clearance above the table. Then grip the safety guard (*J*) with

Fig. 2·2 (cont.)

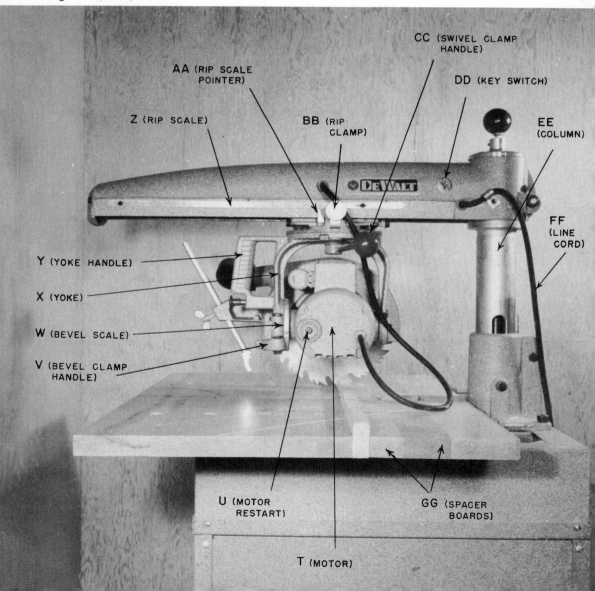

Fig. 2·3A   Fig. 2·3B

the left hand and release the bevel clamp handle (*V*) by pulling it forward. After pulling out the bevel latch (*R*), move the motor to the desired angle by following the calibrated bevel scale (*W*). Then lock the bevel-clamp handle by pushing it back. For quick positive location at 0, 45, and 90 degrees, the bevel latch will drop into these positions automatically.

TYPES OF BLADES

Combination Blade. Power saws usually come equipped with a combination blade which will crosscut, miter, and rip equally well. This blade is adaptable to most home-workshop needs to do general-purpose work. The combination blade is divided into segments and provides crosscut teeth and one raker tooth in each segment, with a deep gullet between. This arrangement of the teeth permits the blade to cut freely and smoothly both with and across the grain.

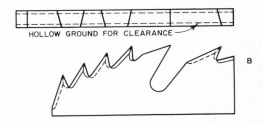

HOLLOW GROUND FOR CLEARANCE

In the flat-ground blade (two cutting teeth and one raker), the teeth must be set as in Fig. 2·4*A*.

Hollow-ground Blade. This blade generally has four cutting teeth and one raker, and the teeth have no set (Fig. 2·4*B*). The blade is beveled, or hollow-

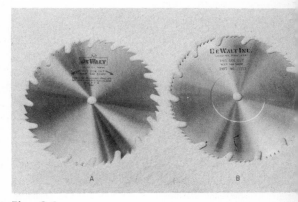

Fig. 2·4

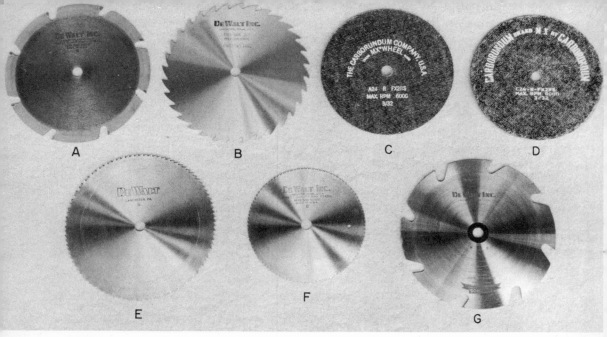

Fig. 2·5

ground, so that it is several gauges thinner near the hub than at the rim. Sometimes called a planer or miter blade, it is generally used by cabinetmakers when cutting stock to finish dimensions, as it cuts very smoothly both with and across the grain.

Carbide-tipped Blade. The eight-tooth carbide-tipped saw blade (Fig. 2·5A) rips and crosscuts like a combination blade, but it remains sharp for long periods of continued operation and outlasts ordinary blades many times over. It is ideal for cutting hardboard, plywood, asbestos board, and other similar materials. Carbide blades do not, however, produce so smooth a cut in the softer woods as the combination blade.

Ripping Blade. The ripping blade (Fig. 2·5B) is designed to do just one job—cutting with the grain of the wood. The blade will tend to tear the wood on crosscuts but cuts fast and clean on rip cuts. Since ripping usually puts a heavy load on the motor, this blade is recommended for general ripping jobs.

Cutoff Wheels and Special Blades. Cutoff wheels are flexible abrasive disks which mount on the saw arbor like a blade. The aluminum oxide wheel (Fig. 2·5C) is used for cutting steel and similar metals, while the silicon carbide wheel (Fig. 2·3D) works best for ceramics, porcelain, glass, plastics, etc. A special blade (Fig. 2·5E) is available for cutting nonferrous metal such as aluminum, copper, etc. It cuts solid, extruded, or tube with the greatest of ease. Figure 2·5F shows a fine-tooth plywood cutting blade. This blade does an excellent job on plywood and gummy, resinous woods.

"Safety" Blade. The "safety" blade shown in Fig. 2·5G has only eight teeth, but it is a combination blade, crosscutting and ripping equally well, and it produces a fairly smooth cut. It performs with maximum efficiency at minimum power consumption, too. Another outstanding feature is that it reduces kickback to a minimum.

HOW TO MOUNT THE SAW BLADE

Remove the arbor nut and arbor collars. Elevate the radial arm until the blade will slide on the shaft and clear the table top. Then place the ⅜-inch arbor collar on the arbor so that the recessed side of the collar will be against the saw blade. Place the saw blade on the arbor. The

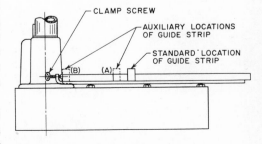

teeth of the saw blade must point in the direction of rotation when the saw blade is in the proper operating position. (Generally blades are marked "This side out," which means that the side marked should be on the same side as the arbor nut.) Then place the ¼-inch arbor collar, recessed side against the saw blade, on the arbor. Now place a wrench on the flat of the arbor shaft to hold it, and tighten the arbor nut with the arbor-nut wrench (Fig. 2·6). The arbor nut has a left-hand thread, which means that the nut must be turned and tightened counterclockwise.

Mount the safety guard over the saw blade and adjust it, on the motor stud, to the desired position for the cuts you are going to make and tighten the wing nut.

ALIGNING INSTRUCTIONS

Every radial-arm machine is thoroughly tested, inspected, and accurately aligned before leaving the factory. However, moving parts will wear, and the abrasive action of dust and dirt adds to this wear. Rough handling during transportation can also throw the machine out of alignment. Eventually adjustment and realignment are necessary in any machine to maintain accuracy—regardless of the care with which the machine is manufactured.

Checking the Guide Fence for Accuracy. For accurate work, the guide fence must be straight. This wood guide strip is inspected with a master straightedge at the factory before shipment and should arrive in perfect condition. If the machine has been exposed to the weather, it is possible that the wood table-top parts may be warped so that the guide fence is no longer straight.

It can be made straight by planing and sanding and can be checked with a straightedge or square before proceeding with other adjustments. Be sure that the

Fig. 2·6

clamp screws at the rear of the table are tightened. The main table board must be flat. If a straightedge shows this to be warped, it should be planed if necessary when you level the worktable top.

The guide fence, as shown in Fig. 2·7, is located in the most frequently used position on the worktable. This will take care of the normal cutting jobs. If you want maximum crosscut on 1-inch material or wider bevel-meter capacity, loosen the clamp screws at the rear of the table top and relocate the guide fence behind the 2-inch spacer board, location *A*. Be sure to tighten the clamp screws after this is done.

For maximum width in ripping, loosen the clamp screws and relocate the guide fence by placing it at the rear of the table top and against the column base, location *B*. Tighten the clamp screws to hold the guide fence rigidly in position.

CLAMP SCREW
AUXILIARY LOCATIONS OF GUIDE STRIP
STANDARD LOCATION OF GUIDE STRIP
(B) (A)

Fig. 2·7

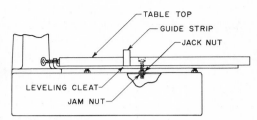

Fig. 2·8B

Fig. 2·8A

If the guide fence should become cut with many kerfs (and it does over a period of time), it can be replaced with a new one. Use a straight piece of pine or similar softwood the same size as the present fence. Plane, sand smooth, and check it with a straightedge or try square for straightness before putting it in place. For several operations, such as shaping, sanding, or jointing—detailed in later chapters—special guide fences will be required, but these are very easy to make.

Aligning the Work Top to the Arm Travel. The table top must align with the arm travel in every horizontal (parallel) position. The table top is mounted on adjustable steel cleats with adjustable jack nuts. To realign the top refer to Fig. 2·8*A* and *B*.

1. Insert a steel bar (about ½ by ½ by 12 inches) or a wrench between the saw-arbor collars in place of the saw blade.

2. Bring the motor to the forward position on the arm, swing the bar, and adjust the table top until the tip of the bar when oscillated barely scrapes the table top. Repeat at the back section of the table board, to the right and left, without changing the elevation.

3. Adjust the table top for the height in various positions until it is perfectly level. Loosen the jam nuts (*A*) under the table channel frame (top flange), and then you can raise or lower the jack nuts (*B*) as required. Be sure to retighten the jam nuts under the table flange after making the adjustments to hold the table board level.

Squaring the Saw Blade with the Table Top. The saw blade can be maintained square with the table top. Refer to Fig. 2·9.

1. Make sure that the table top is level at all points. Remove the safety guard.

2. Place a steel square (*C*) against the flat of the saw blade. The square should be placed in the saw gullets and not against the saw teeth. Make sure that the bevel latch is properly seated and the bevel clamp handle is locked.

Fig. 2·9

A. Nameplate	D. Miter Latch Adjusting
B. Allen Setscrew	E. Bevel Latch Assembly
Wrench	G. Socket Screws
C. Steel Square	H. Dial Plate

3. Remove the etched dial plate (*A*) from the motor yoke by taking out the Phillip's-head screws. You can now get at the two adjusting socket screws (*G*).

4. Release the two socket screws (*G*) approximately two turns with a socket wrench.

5. Firmly grasp the motor with both hands and tilt it until the saw blade is parallel to the upright steel square (*C*). After the saw blade is squared with the table top, be sure to tighten the socket screws (*G*) with a socket wrench (*B*). Replace the dial plate (*A*) and safety guard.

Many craftsmen nail a "wear" table of plywood or hardboard over the permanent front table as in Fig. 2·10. This table top takes the saw cuts, and keeps the permanent table from being cut up.

Squaring the Crosscut Travel with the Guide Fence. Place a wide board on the table top against the guide fence, and make a cut across with the saw. Check the material for accuracy with a steel square. If the saw blade does not cut square, this means that the arm is out of alignment with the guide fence. To adjust this condition refer to Fig. 2·11.

1. Loosen both the arm clamp handle (*E*) and the miter latch (*C*).

2. The adjusting screws (*D*) are locked in position by setscrews (*A*). Loosen the screws (*A*) with a ¼-inch Allen wrench.

3. Lay the steel square (*M*) against the guide fence. Move the saw forward along the steel square to determine which way the arm must be moved.

4. If the blade moves toward the steel

Fig. 2·10

square as you come forward, loosen the adjusting screw (*D*) in the rear (left) with a screwdriver and tighten the adjusting screw (*D*) in the front (right) to bring the arm parallel to the steel square. The arm will be parallel when the saw travels evenly with the steel square for its entire length.

5. If the saw blade moves away from the steel square as you come forward, make the opposite adjustments. Loosen the adjusting screw (*D*) in the front (right) with the screwdriver and tighten the adjusting screw (*D*) in the rear (left). When the saw travel is parallel to the square, lock the adjusting screws (*D*) in the front and rear by tightening both Allen setscrews (*A*) with a setscrew wrench (*B*). Engage

Fig. 2·11
A. Allen Setscrew
B. Allen Setscrew Wrench
C. Miter Latch
D. Miter Latch Adjusting Screws
E. Arm Clamp Handle
F. Arm Clamp Handle Stop
K. Elevating Action Handle

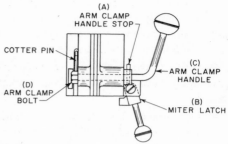

Fig. 2·13

Fig. 2·12

G. Base Pinch Bolt   J. Allen Setscrew
H. Hex Gam Nuts   Wrench
I. Wrench   L. Column Key Gib

the miter latch (*C*) and the arm clamp handle (*E*).

Adjusting the Base; Gripping, Tension, and Alignment. If at any time there is some motion at the end of the arm after the arm clamp handle is tightened, this indicates that there is play between the column and base or the gib needs tightening. Refer to Figs. 2·12 and 2·13.

1. Loosen the base pinch bolt (*G*), all hex jam nuts (*H*), and all setscrews (*I*).
2. Rotate the elevating crank handle (*K*) to raise or lower the column. Tighten the

base pinch bolt (*G*) so that the column still raises or lowers freely and without play.

3. The adjusting gib (*L*) must be secured against the column key (*2D*) to prevent side motion in the arm. Tighten the top setscrews (*I*) with a $\frac{5}{16}$-inch Allen wrench (*J*) until there is no play (side motion) in the column. Then lock all the hex jam nuts (*H*) securely with an open-end wrench.

Adjusting the Arm Clamp Handle. The arm clamp handle rigidly holds the arm in position for straight or miter cuts. When tightened in position, the arm clamp handle should be upright as shown in Fig. 2·14. If the arm clamp handle becomes worn so that it goes beyond the vertical position, relocate it.

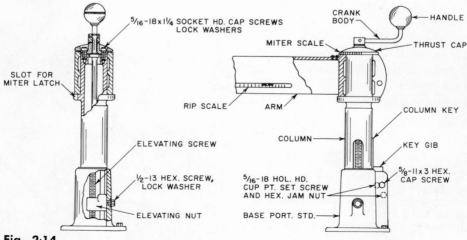

Fig. 2·14

1. Remove the clamp-handle stop (*A*) and lift the miter latch (*B*) upward against the side of the arm.

2. Unwind the arm clamp handle (*C*) by turning it clockwise (to the right). Make about three or four complete turns of this handle.

3. Push back the arm clamp bolt (*D*) from its hex socket so that the hex head can be turned.

4. Turn the hex clamp screw (*D*) about one-sixth turn counterclockwise to tighten the arm clamp handle.

5. Put the hex-screw head (*D*) back in the hex socket, retighten the arm clamp handle (*C*) in the upright position, and insert the arm-clamp-handle stop (*A*).

Adjusting the Roller Head Bearing to the Arm Track. The roller carriage is mounted on four ball bearings, two of which are on eccentric shafts whose movement is controlled by $\frac{5}{16}$-inch Allen socket screws. To adjust the ball bearings, refer to Fig. 2·15.

1. Remove the arm end plate from the arm and bring the saw carriage forward. Swivel the motor into the rip position to get at the adjustments.

2. Loosen the setscrews (*A*) with a $\frac{1}{4}$-inch Allen wrench in the front and the rear of the saw carriage since they lock the eccentric shaft (*F*).

3. Loosen the hex jam nuts (*B*) in the front and the rear of the saw carriage so that the eccentric shaft (*F*) can be turned in its socket.

4. Insert a $\frac{5}{16}$-inch Allen wrench (*C*) in

the eccentric shaft (*F*) and turn this shaft until the ball bearing it controls just touches the arm track. Do not tighten this bearing too much. Repeat on the ball bearing (*D*) in the rear of the saw carriage. The ball bearing (*D*) in the front and the rear of the saw carriage should now roll smoothly inside the arm. Tighten the hex jam nuts (*B*) and lock the setscrews (*A*) on both ends of the saw carriage.

Adjusting the Crosscut Travel Parallel to the Arm. To make sure the saw blade is cutting exactly parallel to the arm tracks, place a board approximately 6 inches wide on the table against the guide fence. Make a cut through the board, and stop just as the board is cut off with the back of the blade still in the board. If there is a slight ridge on the material where the blade is stopped, this will indicate the need of adjustment. Another method of checking is, when making the crosscut, to watch the back of the blade where the teeth come up through the board. If the blade is kicking up the wood fibers on the top surface of the board, this will indicate that the blade is not traveling parallel with the arm tracks. To adjust the crosscut travel, refer to Fig. 2·16.

1. If the saw blade is "heeling" on the left

Fig. 2·15
A. Allen Setscrew
B. Hex Gam Nut
C. Allen Socket
   Wrench
D. Ball Bearing
   (on eccentric shaft)
E. Ball Bearing
   (on permanent studs)
F. Eccentric Shaft
G. Wrench

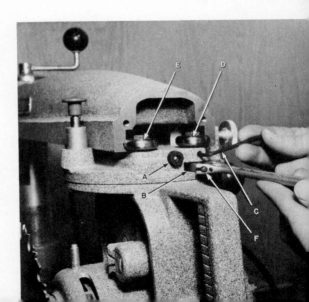

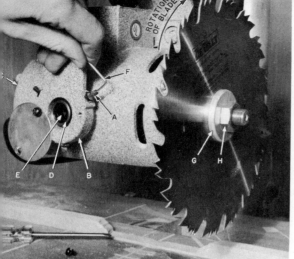

Fig. 2·16

A. Allen Setscrew
   (saw side)
B. Allen setscrew
   (bottom yoke trunnion)
C. Allen Setscrew
   (opposite saw side)
D. Rear Trunnion Stud
   Bushing
E. Rear Trunnion Stud
F. Allen Setscrew
   Wrench
G. Saw Arbor Collar
H. Saw Arbor Nut

side of the cut, loosen the setscrew (*C*) and tighten the screw (*A*), using a $\frac{5}{16}$-inch Allen wrench (*F*).

2. If the saw blade is "heeling" on the right side of the cut, loosen the setscrew (*A*) and tighten the setscrew (*C*) with a $\frac{5}{16}$-inch Allen wrench (*F*).

3. After adjustments 1 and 2 are made, the heeling may reappear when you place the saw blade in the bevel cutting position, in which case:

a. Loosen the setscrews (*A* and *C*), each about one-sixth turn, and tighten the setscrew (*B*) if the heeling is on the material on the bottom side of the saw cut.

b. Loosen the setscrew (*B*) about one-sixth turn and tighten the setscrews (*A* and *C*) evenly if the heeling appears on the upper side of the cut.

Adjusting the Bevel Clamp Handle. The purpose of the bevel clamp handle is to hold the motor rigidly in its yoke at any angle even though the bevel latch may be disengaged from the locating holes in the dial plate. The bevel latch locates 90-degree crosscut, 45-degree bevel crosscut, and 0-degree vertical positions only.

To adjust the bevel clamp handle, see Fig. 2·17.

1. Loosen the bevel clamp handle (*A*) and the hex jam nut (*F*).

2. Turn the cap screw (*E*) clockwise (to the right) until the bevel clamp handle rigidly clamps the motor in its yoke.

3. Be sure to tighten the hex jam nut (*F*) after the adjustment is made.

Adjusting the Yoke Clamp Handle. There should be no play between the roller carriage and the motor-yoke assembly. The yoke clamp handle in conjunction with the king bolt securely clamp

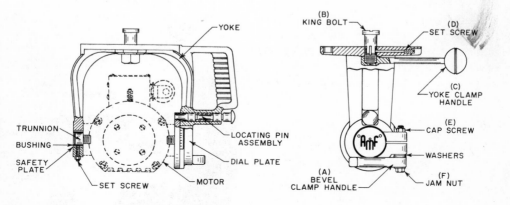

Fig. 2·17

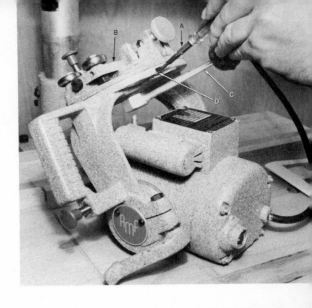

Fig. 2·18
A. Screwdriver   C. Yoke Clamp Handle
B. King Bolt   D. Dog Point Setscrew

the saw carriage to the yoke. To adjust the yoke clamp handle, see Fig. 2·18.

1. Remove the saw carriage and the motor yoke completely from the arm.

2. A dog-point setscrew (*D*) is located in the milled slot on the side of the king bolt (*B*). Its purpose is to keep the king bolt from turning when the yoke clamp handle is loosened or tightened. Remove the setscrew from the slot in the king bolt with a screwdriver (*A*).

3. Turn the king bolt (*B*) about one-sixth of a turn in a clockwise direction so that the dog setscrew may be located in the next slot in the king bolt. Tighten the dog setscrew in position to hold the king bolt.

4. This dog setscrew should be drawn up tight and then backed off slightly so that the king bolt can slide freely up and down as the yoke clamp handle is loosened or tightened.

Now that every moving part is in proper alignment, you are ready to start operating the machine. You should, however, observe certain basic rules for maximum safety and efficiency in operation.

RULES FOR SAFE OPERATION

The radial-arm saw is one of the safest power tools made. With any tool, however, certain precautions must be taken. Before operating the saw, read the following rules carefully and remember them always—for both your safety and that of the machine.

1. When mounting the saw blade, use two wrenches for tightening the arbor nut.

2. Always use the safety guard with the proper adjustment when operating.

3. Be sure all clamp and locking handles are tight before operating.

4. The saw and motor should always be returned to the rear of the table against the column after completing a cut.

5. The equipment should be shut off when relocating for any adjustment.

6. The saw blade or tools should be completely stopped before leaving the machine.

7. When cutting material, the stock should always lie flat on the table and be held firmly back against the guide fence.

8. Stock should not be removed from the table until the saw has been returned to the rear of the table.

9. For removing small pieces of scrap from the worktable, always use a stick. You should never get your hands in the path of the saw's travel.

10. The worktable should always be kept clean—no loose material should be left on it.

11. When ripping, the direction of rotation of the saw blade will be upward toward the operator. Always feed the material past the safety guard from the side opposite the anti-kickback fingers. (Observe the caution tag on the safety guard.) Never stand in back of or in direct line with the saw when ripping.

12. When making any kind of cut, keep in a balanced position. If crosscutting material from the left, put the left foot forward and place the left hand approximately 12 inches to the left of the saw-blade travel. Pull the yoke handle with the right hand. If cutting from the right side, put the right foot forward and hold the material with the right hand,

then pull the yoke handle with the left hand.

13. Always use the anti-kickback assembly when ripping or ploughing.

14. It is a good practice always to remove the key from the switch on the arm when changing tools or making adjustments.

15. Never use cracked or improper types of saw blades.

16. Never wear gloves or loose clothing which could come in contact with the saw. Remove your necktie.

17. Keep the saw blade sharp and properly filed.

18. Make sure the current available agrees with the current characteristics specified on the motor name plate. Consult the power company if necessary.

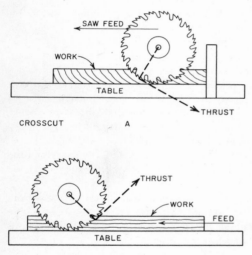

CROSSCUT   A

RIP   B

Fig. 2·19

19. The voltage should be within plus or minus 5 per cent of the motor-name reading; otherwise the motor will run hot and damage the stator winding.

20. If, when cutting, the motor speed decreases, it indicates that the motor is being overloaded. This may be due to low voltage, improperly filed saw blades, or the material may be fed too fast into the saw.

21. Do not force material into the saw or stall the motor. A stalled motor will heat up the starting winding and eventually burn it out.

22. About once a month you can lubricate moving parts to minimize normal wear due to friction. Apply good-grade machine oil to the elevating screw, miter latch, swivel latch, and bevel latch. The ball bearings in the motor are grease-packed and life-sealed. No further lubrication is necessary for the life of the bearing.

23. The tracks inside the arm should be wiped clean before starting to operate the machine. You can occasionally clean these tracks with lacquer thinner or carbon tetrachloride to remove grease and dirt. It is not necessary to oil or grease these tracks.

24. The machine should always be kept in good alignment and adjustment to prevent excessive vibration which will cause inaccurate cutting and cause the saw to grab or creep.

Basic saw cuts

The radial-arm saw is a pull-through cutoff type of saw and cuts in a straight line or at any angle. In the crosscutting action, the saw is moved in the same direction as its rotation (Fig. 2·19*A*). Ripping must never be done in the same direction as the saw rotation (Fig. 2·19*B*). For accurate and smooth cutting, a sharp blade must be used.

CROSSCUTTING

When straight crosscutting, the radial arm must be at right angles with the guide fence—indicated as 0 degrees on the miter scale. Locate the miter latch in the column slot at the 0-degree position, and then securely lock the arm with the arm clamp handle. Now the saw blade should follow the saw kerf in the table top. Use the elevating handle to drop the saw blade until the teeth are approximately $\frac{1}{16}$ inch below the top surface of the table in the saw kerf. This clearance is needed to cut through the board. Then return the saw all the way back against the column.

Place the material on the worktable against the guide fence. Adjust the guard parallel to the bottom of the motor, ad-

Fig. 2·20

Fig. 2·21

just the kickback fingers down to ⅛ inch above the material you will cut off. Turn on the power and give the motor sufficient time to attain top speed. Then pull the saw blade from behind the guide fence in one steady motion completely through the cut (Fig. 2·20). Never allow it to "walk" too rapidly through the work. Return the saw to the rear of the guide fence before removing the material from the table. Practice to get the "feel" of the cutting action—let the saw blade cut—don't force it!

To cut a board thicker than the capacity of the machine, set the blade just a little over half the thickness of the material. Pull the blade through in the same manner as for straight crosscutting, and then turn it over and complete the cut on the other side. When turning the material over, line its kerf with that on the table top to assure a square cut (Fig. 2·21). When the thickness of the material is greater than the capacity of the saw, cut to the limit on both sides first, and then cut the remaining stock with a hand crosscut saw.

Right- or Left-Hand Feed. Your first cut will pose the question of whether to use right-hand (Fig. 2·22A) or left-hand feed (Fig. 2·22B). You may have a tendency to use left-hand feed because it puts the holding (right) hand on the side

Fig. 2·22A

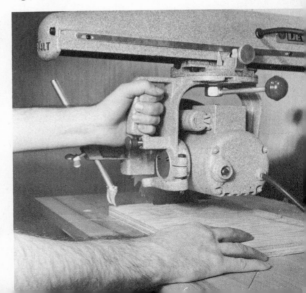

Fig. 2·22B

Fig. 2·23

away from the saw. However, right-hand feed generally is more practical and more comfortable, and you will quickly adopt this system.

The long part of the work should always be on the side of the holding hand. When using right-hand feed, for example, the long part of the material would be on the left since you would be holding it down with the left hand.

Crosscutting Wide Boards and Panels. To cut a board wider than the capacity of the machine, cut to the limit, then turn it over and complete the cut. Large pieces of plywood can be cut with ease by using the method shown in Fig. 2·23. The motor is placed in a horizontal rip position (page 28), and then the radial arm is swung to approximately a 30-degree left-hand miter (page 24). The motor is fully extended on the arm, allowing the blade to overhang the front edge of the work table. With the arm in this position, the blade overhang will extend beyond the plywood to be cut. Such an arrangement allows the panel to be pushed from right to left through the moving blade.

To support the large panel while cutting and to assure a square cut, a slotted two-by-four is placed on the floor to serve as a lower guide, while the front edge of the worktable. supports the top of the panel. The groove in the lower guide should be parallel and perpendicular with the front edge and can be cut as described on page 39. The lower guide can also be fastened to the front of the workbench for small panels.

Horizontal Crosscutting. This crosscut operation (Fig. 2·24) is used for cutting across the end of any size of stock. To locate the saw in the horizontal position, raise the radial arm by turning the elevating handle until the blade is approximately 3 inches above the table top. With the saw in the crosscut position, pull it to the front end of the arm. Holding the top of the safety guard in your left hand, release the bevel clamp handle by pulling it forward and pull out the bevel latch. Swing the motor and saw into the 90-degree horizontal position and lock the bevel clamp handle by pushing it back. (The bevel latch automatically locks itself in position.) The blade will now be parallel to the table top, and the motor will be in a vertical position. Then adjust the dust elbow on the guard, parallel to the table top. Push the motor and saw and guard back to the column.

Place the material to be cut against the guide fence and lower the saw blade to the point where the cut is to be made.

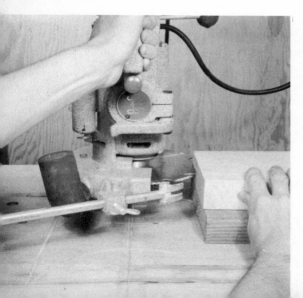

Fig. 2·24

The depth of the cut will be determined by the location of the material in respect to the saw blade.

Turn on the motor, and with the saw behind the guide fence, pull it through the material in the same manner as when crosscutting. If you wish to form a groove, push the saw back against the column and raise or lower the arm a full turn. Bring the saw forward again and then return it to the column. Repeat this procedure until the desired width of the groove is obtained.

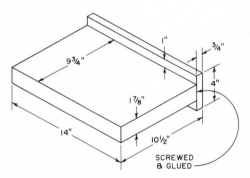

Fig. 2·25

When horizontal crosscutting thin stock, it will be necessary to build an auxiliary table and guide fence (as shown in Fig. 2·25) since the thickness of the safety guard will not allow the blade to be lowered more than 1¼ inches above the stationary table top. The auxiliary table is installed in place of the standard guide fence. To do this, release the two clamp screws, lift out the guide fence, slide in the auxiliary, and retighten the clamp screws. The material is now located against the auxiliary guide fence and cut as previously described.

BEVEL CROSSCUTTING

Bevel crosscutting, shown in Fig. 2·26, is similar to straight crosscutting, but the saw is tilted to the desired bevel angle. With the motor and saw back against the column, elevate the machine so that the blade will clear the table top when swiveling the motor in the yoke. Pull the motor and saw to the front end of the arm. To bevel your motor and saw, place your left hand on top of the safety guard to hold the motor from dropping and release the bevel clamp lock by pulling it forward. Pull out on the bevel locating pin and move the motor to the degree desired by following the bevel scale and pointer. Then lock the bevel clamp by pushing it back. Turn the elevating handle down until the saw-blade teeth touch the bottom of the concave kerf in the center of the table top. Push the motor and saw back to the column. If a common 45-degree bevel is desired, simply let the locating pin fit the 45-degree slot. Then lock the bevel clamp.

Place the material on the table top against the guide fence. Adjust the guard and keep back your fingers, the same as in crosscutting. You can make your bevel cutoff on the left side—hold the material with your left hand and pull the motor and saw with your right hand by using the grip handle on the yoke. If cutting on the right side, reverse the hand holds.

MITERING

Mitering is the same as crosscutting except that the radial arm is revolved on a

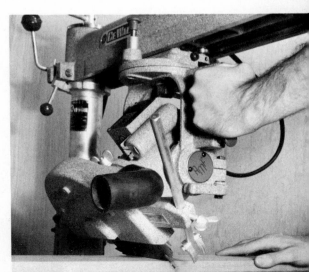

Fig. 2·26

horizontal plane to the angle of the miter.

Right-hand Miter. Make sure the motor and saw are back of the guide fence against the column. With your left hand, release the arm clamp handle and lift the swivel latch. With your right hand on the radial arm, swing it to the right to the angle desired by following the miter scales. Then lock the arm clamp handle. The popular 45-degree miter cut is set quickly with the miter latch seated in the 45-degree quickset slot in column. Simply lock the arm clamp handle. Now place the material flat on the table top and tight against the guide fence. Adjust the guard parallel to the bottom of the motor; adjust the kickback fingers down to $\frac{1}{8}$ inch above the material you will cut off. Hold the material with your left hand, and pull the saw through the material with your right hand (Fig. 2·27A). Return the saw to its original position at the rear of the guide fence before removing the material from the table top.

Left-hand Miter. Move the radial arm to the left to the desired angle in the manner described for a right-hand miter. To get the full capacity on a left-hand miter, move the guide fence to the rear of the table-top spacer boards. To make this adjustment, release the two clamp screws holding the boards and move the guide fence back. Then retighten the clamp screws. Now place the material to be cut flat on the table top and tight against the guide fence. Adjust the guard and kickback fingers, the same as for right-hand miter cut. With the right hand holding the material, pull the saw and motor through the material with your left hand (Fig. 2·27B). Then return the motor to its original position.

Left-hand miter cuts can also be made by swiveling the motor, yoke, and saw 180 degrees from the standard crosscutting position. Setting the saw in this position, it is not necessary to reposition the guide fence when making left-hand miter cuts. This setup is very important when making both left- and right-hand cuts on a molding where it is impossible to reverse the material.

You will note that when you swivel the saw 180 degrees the handle grip is at the rear of the yoke and bears against the column, causing the blade to extend beyond the front of the guide fence when in the 45-degree miter position. To prevent this, use a temporary fence in front of the regular guide fence. It should be $\frac{3}{4}$ inch thick by $1\frac{3}{4}$ inches wide and the same length as the guide already on the

Fig. 2·27A   **Fig. 2·27B**

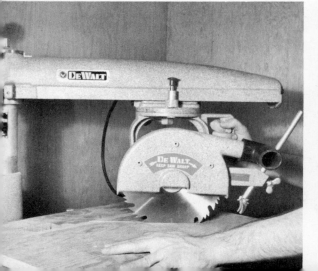 

Fig. 2·28   Fig. 2·29

table. To hold this fence in position, clamp or nail it to the original guide fence.

To swivel the motor, yoke, and saw blade to the left 180 degrees, elevate the column by turning the crank handle a couple of turns; then pull the yoke forward and lift up the swivel latch. Swivel the yoke to the left 180 degrees and drop the swivel latch. Retighten the yoke-swivel clamp handle by pulling it forward. With your left hand, release the arm clamp handle by pulling it forward; then lift up the miter latch. With your right hand on the end of the radial arm, swing it to the left 45-degree miter position and drop the miter latch into the slot in the column. Tighten the arm clamp handle by pushing it back.

With the machine set to the 45-degree left-hand miter position, pull the motor and saw to the front end of the arm. Turn the machine on and, with the saw blade running, turn the elevating handle down until the saw blade cuts a kerf $\frac{1}{16}$ inch deep in the table top. Then push the motor and saw back through the guide fence to cut a kerf through it. Turn the current off. Since the blade is cutting toward you, tilt the safety guard forward so as to clear the material you are cutting by approximately $\frac{1}{16}$ inch. With your right hand, hold down the material tightly

against the guide fence. Since the yoke hand grip is at the rear, grip the yoke itself with your left hand and pull the saw through the material (Fig. 2·28). Return the motor and saw to the rear of the guide fence before removing the material from the table top.

BEVEL MITERING

A bevel miter (sometimes called a compound or double miter) is a combination of a miter and a bevel (Fig. 2·29). First set the motor and saw to the angle desired by following the bevel scales and then lock the bevel latch and clamp handle. Then release the arm latch and clamp handle and swing the radial arm into the desired miter position, following the same routine as for miter cuts. To make the cut, follow the normal operating routine described under crosscut beveling.

Left-hand bevel-miter cuts are often used when making shadow-box picture frames where it is impossible to turn the material because of the irregularity of the molding on the frame. To make the left-hand bevel-miter cut, release the arm clamp handle and latch and swing the arm left to the same degree as it was set in the right-hand miter. Then lock the arm clamp handle and latch. Pull the motor and saw to the front end of the radial arm. Release the swivel clamp handle by pulling it forward and pull the swivel latch up. Swivel the yoke and motor to the left 180 degrees; drop the swivel latch and tighten the swivel clamp handle. Return the motor and saw to the rear of the table.

Lay the material on the table top and back against the guide fence and adjust the safety guard down to the material as close as possible. With the saw in this position, the rotation of the saw blade and the cutting action will be up through the material and toward the operator. Hold the material on the table with your right hand and pull the motor and saw through the material with your left hand.

RIPPING

Straight ripping is done by having the saw blade parallel with the guide fence and feeding the material into the saw blade. You can rip from either the left or right side of the machine. The feeding of the material to the saw depends on the rotation of the saw blade. When ripping from the right side of the table (in-rip), the motor and saw must be swiveled to the left 90 degrees from the crosscut position. If ripping from the left side of the machine (out-rip), swivel the motor and saw to the right 90 degrees from the crosscut position.

In-ripping. To set your saw to the in-rip position, pull the motor and saw to the front end of the radial arm. Release the yoke-swivel clamp handle by pulling it forward and lift up the location pin. Swivel the yoke clockwise 90 degrees from the crosscut position. (The swivel location pin will snap into position automatically.) Now tighten the swivel clamp handle.

The rip scale or rule on the right side of the arm is set with the guide fence in its standard position, which is between the stationary top and the spacer boards. With the saw blade against the guide fence, the pointer on the roller head should read zero on the *top* side of the ruler marked "in-rip" (Fig. 2·30A). This rule and pointer can be off as much as $\frac{1}{16}$ inch because of difference in the types of saw blades. Some saw blades have set teeth, while others may be hollow ground with no set in the teeth. To adjust the rule, release the two Phillip's-head screws and adjust the scale to the proper setting. Now set your saw to the desired width of the rip by following the pointer and rule. Then tighten the rip-lock clamp screw to hold the saw in position.

Before ripping, adjust the safety guard and anti-kickback to the proper position, as is described here and as illustrated in

Fig. 2·30A

Fig. 2·30B

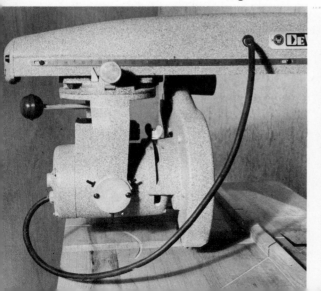

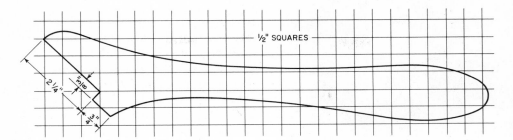

½" SQUARES

Fig. 2·31A

Fig. 2·3A and B. Lay the material on the table top close to the guard. Release the wing nut holding the guard to the motor and rotate the guard down to approximately ⅛ inch above the top surface of the board you are ripping. Retighten the wing nut. On the opposite end of the safety guard is the anti-kickback assembly. Release the thumbscrew holding it and adjust the rod down until the fingers are ⅛ inch below the top surface of the board you are ripping. Retighten the thumbscrew. On the top side of the guard is the dust spout. Adjust it until the spout is turned toward the back of the machine so as to carry the dust away from you.

With the saw set to in-rip position, you must feed the material into the saw from the right side of the machine. With your left hand approximately 6 inches back of the safety guard, hold the material down and back against the guide strip. Now with your right hand, move the material into the saw by standing on the right front side of the machine and let the material slide through your left hand (Fig. 2·30B). When your right hand meets your left hand, continue the balance of the rip by using a pusher board, approximately 18 inches long (Fig. 2·31A). Hold the pusher board back against the guide fence and against the end of the board you are ripping and continue on through until the board you are ripping clears the saw blade on the opposite side by 2 inches

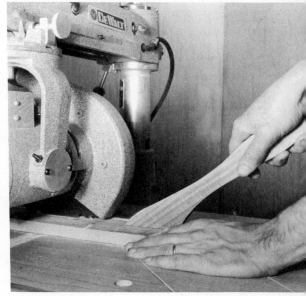

Fig. 2·31B

(Fig. 2·31B). Now pull the pusher board straight back.

Out-ripping. When ripping wide materials such as panel boards, you should swivel the saw 90 degrees counterclockwise from the crosscut position to out-rip position. With the saw set to out-rip position, follow the *lower* edge of the rip rule on the radial arm (Fig. 2·32A). This rule can be used to a capacity of 17½ inches with the guide fence in its standard position. If ripping wider material, it is necessary to move the guide fence to the rear of the table boards. Make the safety guard and anti-kickback adjustments as previously described for in-ripping. When

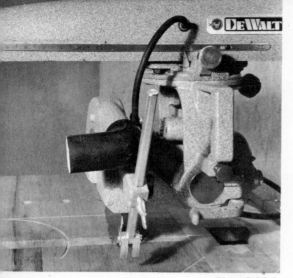

Fig. 2·32A

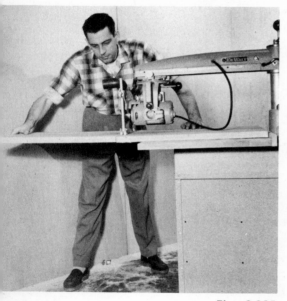

Fig. 2·32B

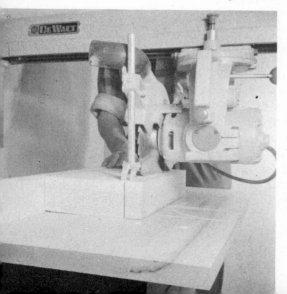

Fig. 2·33

the saw is set for out-ripping, the material must be fed into the saw from the left side of the machine (Fig. 2·32B).

Resawing. If extremely thick wood or hardwood is being ripped into thinner boards, it is often necessary to cut part way through the board, invert the board, and complete the cut. This operation is generally called "resawing."

When resawing, the saw should be placed in the in-rip position. The blade should be set just a little over half the width of the board when the board is *less* in width than twice the capacity of the saw. To illustrate this, let us assume that it is necessary to resaw a board 4 inches wide by ¾ inches thick into two boards 4 by ⅜ inches. Making an allowance of ⅛ inch for the kerf or the wastage material by the blade, and taking into consideration that the capacity of the particular saw blade is 2½ inches, about 1½ inches is left for the second cut (Fig. 2·33). However, when the width of the board to be resawed is greater than twice the capacity of the machine, make the cuts as deep as possible from each edge. Then finish the ripping by hand. When resawing 4-inch stock and larger, use a guide fence approximately 3½ inches high.

An important point to bear in mind always when resawing is to keep the same surface of the board against the guide fence for both cuts—reverse the board end for end, never side for side. Be sure to follow all the safety rules for straight ripping when resawing.

Horizontal Ripping. This operation is similar to horizontal crosscutting except that the cut is made on the side of the stock rather than on the end. To place the saw blade in the horizontal rip position, first set the saw in the in-rip location and then turn it to 90 degrees as indicated on the bevel scale described in horizontal crosscutting.

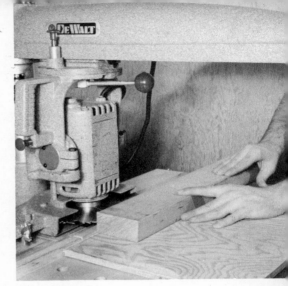

Place the material to be cut against the guide fence, either standard or auxiliary depending on the thickness, and locate the height and depth of the cut. As shown in Fig. 2·34, a piece of ¾-inch plywood can be used as an auxiliary table, and it is pushed along with the stock when the cut is made. The rip clamp is tightened and the material is pushed past the blade in the same manner as in straight ripping. If a groove is desired, the arm may be raised or lowered a full turn at a time and the operation repeated until the proper width is obtained.

Fig. 2·34

BEVEL RIPPING

Bevel ripping is simply ripping with the saw motor tilted for angle cuts (Fig. 2·35). With the saw swiveled to the rip position (either in- or out-rip), elevate the column by rotating the handle and then release the bevel clamp handle and latch. Turn the motor within the yoke to the desired angle. If the popular 45-degree position is wanted, the bevel latch will quickly locate it. If any other angle is desired, set it and securely clamp the motor in place with the bevel clamp handle. Adjust the guard on the in-feed end so that it is within ⅛ inch of the material, but do not adjust the anti-kickback device. Use a pusher board as previously described to prevent kickback of the material. Push the material through as previously described.

Fig. 2·35

As you will see in succeeding chapters, one of the most useful jigs you can make is a V block. It can easily be made by bevel-ripping. After placing the blade in the 45-degree position, lower the blade to the desired depth of the V. Locate the blade in the desired position on the rip scale and lock the rip clamp. Start the motor and pass the stock past the blade as previously described. Then reverse the stock and pass it through the saw again (Fig. 2·36).

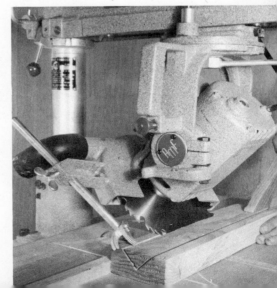

Fig. 2·36

CHAPTER 3

Special cutting operations of the saw

AS WE FOUND in Chapter 2, there are six basic saw cuts. However, by combining these six cuts, we are able to perform such special operations as tapering, chamfering, kerfing, cove cutting, or making saw-cut moldings. While this work may seem more complicated, it is easy and safe to do on a radial-arm saw.

KERFING

It is often necessary to bend wood. When the problem of curved surfaces arises, you have a choice of three methods: (1) bending the wood by steaming it (this calls for special equipment), (2) building the curve up by sawing thick segments of the circle on a saber saw (which means that a great deal of expensive wood would be wasted), or (3) cutting a series of saw kerfs to within ⅛ inch of the outside surface to make the material more flexible for bending. The latter is the most practical method (Fig. 3·1).

The distance between these saw kerfs determines the flexibility of the stock and the radius to which it can be bent. In order to form a more rigid curve, the saw kerfs should be as close together as possible. To determine the proper spacing, the first step is to decide on the radius of

the curve or circle to be formed. After the radius has been determined, measure this same distance (the radius) from the end of the stock as shown in Fig. 3·2 and make a saw kerf at this point. The kerf

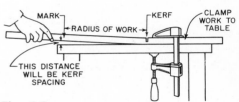

Fig. 3·2

can be made in the crosscut position, with the blade lowered to ⅛ inch of the bottom of the stock.

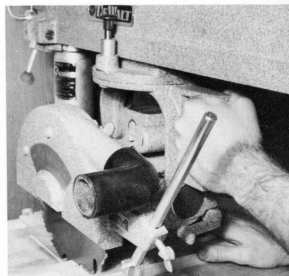

Fig. 3·1

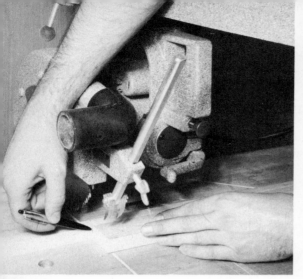

Fig. 3·3   Fig. 3·4

Now clamp the stock to the table top with a C clamp. Raise the end of the stock until the saw kerf is closed, as shown at *A*. The distance the stock is raised to close the kerf determines the distance between saw kerfs in order to form the curve.

Since most bending operations require many saw kerfs, mark this distance with a pencil on the guide fence. This is a great timesaver (Fig. 3·3). The first kerf is made in the standard crosscut position, with the end of the work butted against the mark. The remaining cuts are located by placing each new kerf over the guide-fence mark and making the new cut.

When the kerfing is complete, the stock is slowly bent until it matches the required curve (Fig. 3·4). Wetting the wood with warm water will help the bending process, while a tie strip tacked in place will hold the shape until the part is attached to the assembly. Even compound curves may be formed in this manner by kerfing both sides of the work. When kerfing is exposed, veneers may be glued in place to hide the cuts.

When bending wood for exterior work,

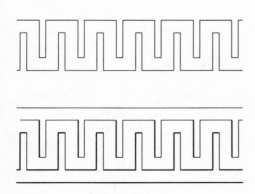

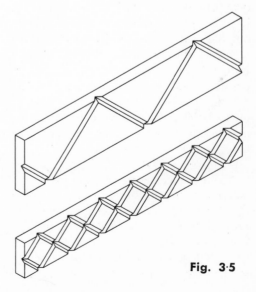

Fig. 3·5

the kerfs should be coated with glue before the bend is made. After making the bend, wood plastic and putty may be used to fill the crevices. When finished properly, only a close examination will show the method used to make the bend.

SAWCUT MOLDINGS

Several attractive moldings can be made with cuts similar to those used for kerfing. The zigzag shape shown in Fig. 3·5 is commonly called a dentil molding, although this term has a broad application and can include many different shapes.

A spacer mark on the guide fence, as for kerf bending, should be used; the distance from the mark of the blade determines the spacing of the saw cuts. The saw is set in the crosscut position, and the blade is lowered to the depth desired. Repeat cuts are made by alternately turning the work face up and face down, as shown in Fig. 3·6A. The molding is then made by ripping narrow strips from the work, as shown in Fig. 3·6B. A ripping operation on work as narrow and delicate as this demands care and accuracy. Use a pusher strip to push the molding past the blade.

Molding should be cut with a hollow-ground or planer blade to assure clean cutting. After the dentil molding is cut, it can be used as an overlay, or the molding can be applied to a heavier backing piece of contrasting color.

TAPER RIPPING

Taper ripping is generally used to construct tapered furniture legs. One of the several jigs shown here may be used. But before using a jig, all edges to be tapered should be squared if uniform sides are desired.

One such jig is shown in Fig. 3·7. When hinging the ends, keep the two pieces clamped together. The crosspiece or brace which secures the setting can be made of metal or hardwood. When the jig is complete, mark a line across both pieces 12 inches in from the hinged end. Set the jig by measuring between these two marks to determine the taper per foot. The formula used for a so-called two-sided taper (actually, all four sides are tapered) is

Taper per foot =

$$\frac{W \text{ (top width)} - w \text{ (bottom width)}}{L \text{ (length of taper)}} \times 6$$

For example, if you are making a coffee-table leg 18 inches long, 5 inches wide at the top, and $3\frac{1}{2}$ inches wide at the bottom, you would require a $\frac{1}{2}$-inch taper per foot.

Fig. 3·6A

Fig. 3·6B

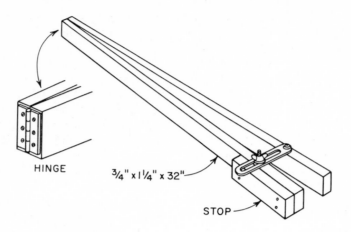

HINGE   ¾" x 1¼" x 32"   STOP

Fig. 3·7

Taper per foot =

$$\frac{5 - 3.5}{18} \times \frac{6}{1} = \frac{1.5}{3} = 0.5 \text{ or } \frac{1}{2} \text{ inch}$$

By opening the jig ½ inch at the 1-foot mark, you have the proper setting.

For a so-called one-side taper (two sides are tapered) use the following formula:

Taper per foot =

$$\frac{W \text{ (top width)} - w \text{ (bottom width)}}{L \text{ (length of taper)}} \times 12$$

Using these dimensions, you would find the one-side taper as follows:

Taper per foot =

$$\frac{5 - 3.5}{18} \times \frac{12}{1} = \frac{3}{3} = 1 \text{ inch}$$

To use the jig, place the flat side against the fence and place the material to be tapered in the stop at the end of the jig. With the saw in the rip position, push the jig past the blade as if it were a normal ripping operation (Fig. 3·8). Continue the ripping operation on all four sides in the same manner.

When the project calls for a two-side taper, double the jig setting for the second pass. Be sure that the first tapered side of the work is placed against the jig when making the second pass.

Square legs with a taper on each face are made by setting the location of the saw blade to equal the combined width of the jig and the work. Make one pass; then make the second pass on the adjacent face. Open the jig to twice the original setting and adjust the blade so that the wide end of the work just touches it. Make the third pass on the next adjacent

Fig. 3·8

face and then make the fourth and final pass.

The step jig shown in Fig. 3·9A is good for production work because it eliminates setting the variable jig for different tapers. The steps gauge the taper and are dimensioned for the various tapers needed. One corner of the work is placed in the correct step while the other end rides against the arm of the jig. The material is placed in the first notch of the jig, and the combined jig and work are pushed into the saw in a rip position (Fig. 3·9B). An adjacent side of the work is cut in the same manner. The two remaining sides are cut with the work in the second notch.

Tapering with a radial-arm machine can be done without the use of a specialized jig. This also includes taper ripping long stock which cannot be handled in the jig. Simply by clamping a piece of narrow stock to the lower edge of the material to be ripped, the front edge of the table top becomes a second "guide fence" for this operation. You can taper rip at any predetermined angle with this method. Just decide the degree of taper desired; then clamp on the lower guide board accordingly.

As shown in Fig. 3·10, the saw is placed in the out-rip position (that is, swiveled to the right rather than the left) for this tapered-rip operation. This allows the blade to be positioned directly above the front edge of the worktable. Thus, the completed rip cut corresponds exactly to the angle at which the guide board is clamped to the stock.

This latter taper-cutting technique can also be used for ripping raw edges of lumber or irregular shapes. A straight-edge is clamped to the work and is pushed past the saw blade, with the straightedge riding against the front edge of the saw table (Fig. 3·11).

Regardless of the method used, a

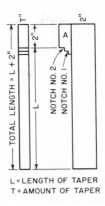
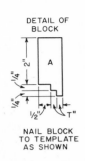

L = LENGTH OF TAPER
T = AMOUNT OF TAPER

DETAIL OF BLOCK

NAIL BLOCK TO TEMPLATE AS SHOWN

Fig. 3·9A

Fig. 3·9B

Fig. 3·10

planer blade is the saw to use for taper ripping since it cuts more smoothly. However, if another saw is used, the taper cuts can be smoothed by taking a light jointer cut (see page 72) on each of the four surfaces. Be sure to use the proper rip feed: in-rip from right to left, out-rip from left to right. The safety guard and anti-kickback fingers, in taper ripping, are adjusted in the same manner as for straight ripping.

Fig. 3·11

WEDGE CUTTING

Any number of similarly shaped wedges or glue blocks can be cut by using a template similar to the one shown in Fig. 3·12. Cut the shape of the wedge or glue block into the edge of 1-inch template stock.

Set the saw in the in-rip position and adjust the blade so that it just passes the template when it is against the guide fence. Back off the template and fit the stock into the notch in the template. Then move the stock and template past the saw in the normal ripping manner. When cutting a series of wedges, reverse the stock from end to end for each new wedge.

Short wedges can also be cut in the normal cutoff manner, with the arm in the proper miter position.

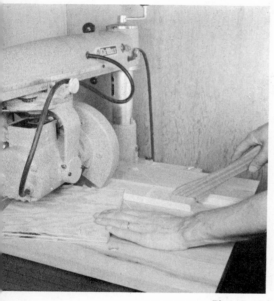

Fig. 3·12

CHAMFER CUTTING

This operation (Fig. 3·13) is simply making bevel cuts along the top edges of stock. Set the saw in the rip-bevel position at an angle of 20 to 45 degrees. Position the blade so that it overhangs the stock by the desired width of the cut and lock it in place with the rip clamp. Push the stock along the guide fence and through the blade path. Then reverse the material and cut along the other top edge in the same manner.

Cross-chamfer is achieved by placing the blade in the crosscut-bevel position at the desired angle. Position the blade so

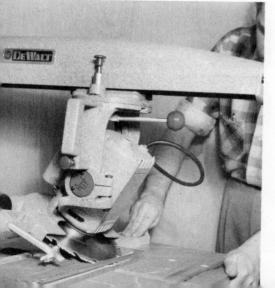

Fig. 3·13

that it overhangs the stock by the desired width (as for rip-chamfer). Then pull the motor and saw through in the prescribed crosscut method.

The octagon shape required for spindle lathe work can be cut in the same manner as described for chamfer cutting.

RAISED-PANEL CUTTING

This operation (Fig. 3·14) can add immeasurably to the beauty of a finished-door project. Actually, raised-panel cutting is simple rip-bevel sawing. For this operation, an 8-inch diameter saw should be used in place of the standard 9-inch blade since the latter may strike the column base and ruin it. Place the saw in the in-rip position and turn it to the 90-degree bevel position. Then raise it 5 to 10 degrees (indicated as 85 to 90 degrees on the bevel scale). Position the blade so that it overhangs the guide fence (either on the stationary or auxiliary table, depending on the thickness of the material) by the desired width for the cut. To do this, move the saw the desired amount from the column and lock it in position with the rip clamp. When starting the motor, make sure that the saw blade moves freely. Then push the stock along the guide fence and through the blade path. The resulting smooth finish is comparable to the most expensive millwork. A piece

of hardboard under the work makes it slide easily.

GROOVING

This operation (Fig. 3·15) is the same as the horizontal saw cuts described on pages 28 and 29. Place the saw in the crosscut or rip position, depending on the type of groove desired, and turn it to the 90-degree bevel position. Locate the position of the blade (height and depth), place the material against the fence and past the blade, or pull the saw through the material. If the blade strikes the guide fence, the stock should be placed on an auxiliary table. Then raise or lower the blade a full turn at a time and repeat the operation until you obtain the proper groove width.

RABBETING

Rabbeting is merely cutting a groove along the edge of a board by taking two saw cuts at right angles to each other so as to remove a corner down the length of the stock. It is used for picture, mirror, and window frames and for some furniture joints.

Lay out the rabbet on the end of the board and mark it off. To make the first cut, place the material on edge against the fence. With the saw in the in-rip position, lower the blade to the depth of the

Fig. 3·14   **Fig. 3·15**

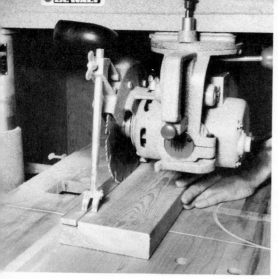

Fig. 3·16

Fig. 3·17A (above)   Fig. 3·17B (below)

rabbet. (For best results, set this cut a little short of the mark.) Push the work past the blade with a pusher block. (This cut can also be made by placing the material flat on the table top and against the fence and then making the cut with the saw in the horizontal rip position.) The second cut, with the material laid flat against the fence, is set a little deeper, cleaning the corner (Fig. 3·16).

Under such circumstances, a strip of wood will be cut loose and probably shoot back at the operator with considerable force unless the piece is held by a pusher board. If this cut is made in the out-rip position, of course, the piece will simply fall off—no kickback whatsoever to worry about.

The bevel rabbet is cut in the same manner except that the first cut is a bevel rip (Fig. 3·17A) followed by a rip cut (Fig. 3·17B). An auxiliary table is generally used for this cut.

To make an end rabbet, lay the material flat against the fence and make the first cut along the end with the saw in the horizontal position (Fig. 3·18). Make the second cut to the depth of the rabbet with the saw in the standard crosscut position.

A rabbet can also be cut in the same manner as a groove. With the saw in the

Fig. 3·18

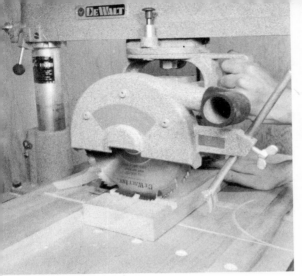

Fig. 3·19   Fig. 3·20

horizontal position, set the depth of the rabbet and start cutting at the top edge of the board. Then lower the blade a full turn at a time until the desired rabbet is obtained.

Rabbets can be cut with only one pass by using the dado head (page 52).

DADO CUTTING

A dado is a groove cut across the grain (Fig. 3·19). With the saw in the crosscut position, lower the blade to the desired depth of the dado. Start at one end of the dado and pull the saw through the material. After returning the saw to the column, shift the material over ⅛ inch and bring the saw forward again. Continue this operation until the desired width of the dado is obtained.

The dadoing technique can also be used for cutting end laps and rabbets (Fig. 3·20). By placing the saw in the in-rip position, a similar technique will produce grooving and rabbet cuts. Lower the blade to the desired depth and locate it at one end of the cut. Push the material past the blade as when ripping. Then move the motor ⅛ inch toward the other end of the cut and push the material past the blade as before. Continue this operation until the desired width is obtained (Fig. 3·21A and B).

Dadoes can also be cut with one pass by using the dado head (page 48).

Fig. 3·21A

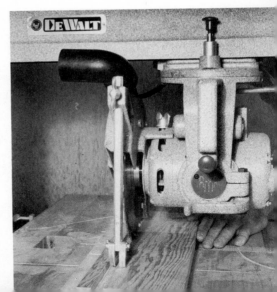

Fig. 3·21B

CONTOUR CUTTING

One of the most novel techniques in radial-arm saw operation is the contour feed for cutting coves. On the standard circular saw this is a fairly difficult task, but on the radial-arm saw it is simple. Place the material flat on the table top against the guide fence. Set the saw at a bevel 45-degree position and swivel the motor 45 degrees to the left. Locate the motor so that the lowest point of the blade is on the center line of the material and tighten the rip clamp. Back the material off from the saw and lower the blade so that it is ⅛ inch below the top surface of the stock. Turn on the machine and push the material past the saw blade as when ripping (Fig. 3·22). Continue this procedure, lowering the blade one full turn (⅛ inch) at a time, until the desired depth of the cut is obtained. The final cut should be a light one for a smooth finish.

The saw cut can be made in different angle positions for different effects. For instance, you may set the bevel at 45 degrees and the motor swivel at 30 degrees, or the bevel at 30 degrees and the motor swivel at 45 degrees. Experiment with scrap wood until you get the effect you desire.

A half-circle effect, suitable for mod-

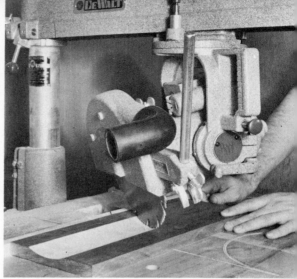

Fig. 3·23

ern picture frames, is cut by establishing the depth of cut at the edge of the material and pushing the material past the blade in the same manner as just described (Fig. 3·23).

SAUCER CUTTING

This cut makes intricate decorative patterns easily. Place the stock flush with the edge of table front and clamp it to the table top. Locate the saw arm so that the lowest portion of the blade is on center line of the stock, and tighten the rip clamp. Lower the blade until it touches the material, swing the motor to the 90-degree bevel position, and then lower the motor by turning the elevating handle one full turn. With your left hand on the anti-kickback rod, pull out the bevel latch with your right hand. Then swing the motor in an arc past the stock (Fig. 3·24). Lower the saw blade one full turn of the elevating handle and continue the cutting process until the desired depth is reached.

COMPOUND-ANGLE CUTTING

Compound-angle cutting on the radial-arm saw is a fairly simple operation. Actually a compound angle is a combination of a miter and a bevel cut. Any frame or open structure with sloping sides requires a compound-angle cut (Fig. 3·25). A

Fig. 3·22

peaked figure (with any number of sides) such as a doll- or bird-house roof or a fence-post top and such house-construction jobs as cutting jack rafters, hip rafters, etc., also require a compound-angle cut.

To join two pieces of wood to form a 90-degree miter corner, you would set the radial arm at a 45-degree miter position. Strange as it may seem, when a compound-angle or shadow-box joint is made, the bevel that forms the miter must be cut at some angle, but it is never at 45 degrees. If, for example, a shadow box is to be made having the sides slanting at 25 degrees as shown in Fig. 3·25, the angle at which the miter must be cut is 40 degrees and not 45 degrees although, when the pieces are assembled, the two 40-degree angles form a corner of 90 degrees. The reason for this can be found in the fact that, when the pieces are assembled, they are revolved to a plane different from the plane at which they were cut. These are facts that are difficult to understand unless you are thoroughly familiar with advanced geometry.

You need not know any geometry in order to make a cut for a shadow-box joint on the radial-arm saw, if the chart shown on page 42 is used. The only thing you have to know is the slant at which you want to make the sides and whether you are making a box with four, six, or eight sides.

The use of the chart is quite simple and can best be explained by an example. If a four-sided shadow-box frame such as is shown in Fig. 3·25 is to be made, with the sides slanting at an angle of 25 degrees, the information is applied to the chart in the following manner.

Since the frame has four sides, the quadrant on the chart marked "square box" is used. The angle of the stand, which is 25 degrees, is located on this quadrant. The vertical line that intersects or crosses the quadrant at the 25-degree mark is followed to the bottom of the chart. The vertical line is marked 39¾ at the lower end. This 39¾ means that the radial arm must be set at the 39¾-degree miter position (either right or left).

In order to cut the second angle at the same time, the motor must set in a bevel position at the angle shown at the left of the chart. To determine this angle, the original 25 degrees is followed across the chart, either right or left, to the vertical-degree markings. This vertical line shows

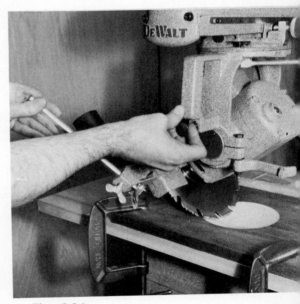

Fig. 3·24

the angle of the bevel setting to be 23¼ degrees. After the radial arm is set at the 39¾-degree miter position and the saw tilted to 23¼ degrees in the bevel position, place the stock against the guide fence and pull the saw through it. Duplicate this cut (both right and left miter) for each end, positioning the stock as needed.

If a six-sided frame is to be made, the quadrant on the chart marked "six-sided box" should be used to determine the angles at which the arm and motor should be set. In the case of the 25-degree side

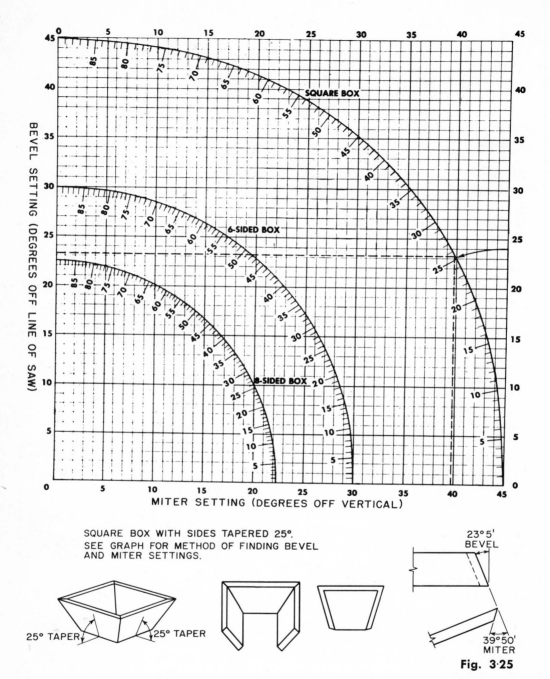

SQUARE BOX WITH SIDES TAPERED 25°.
SEE GRAPH FOR METHOD OF FINDING BEVEL
AND MITER SETTINGS.

25° TAPER | 25° TAPER

23°5'
BEVEL

39°50'
MITER

Fig. 3·25

slant, the radial arm would be set in the 27-degree miter position and the motor would be tilted to the 13½-degree bevel setting. In the case of an "eight-sided box," the arm should be located at the 20-degree miter position and the saw blade tilted to a bevel of 9¾ degrees.

Chair and table legs are sometimes splayed outward, and this construction calls for a compound cut at the top and bottom. Work of this type is usually at less than a 10-degree tilt, and for these small angles direct setting to the work tilt gives a satisfactory joint. For a 10-degree

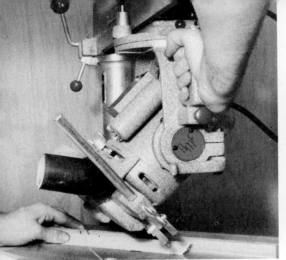

Fig. 3·26   Fig. 3·28

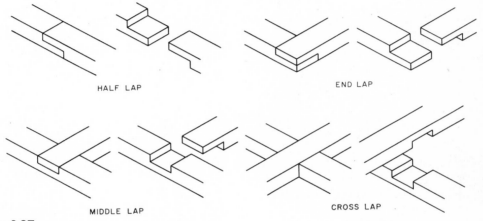

HALF LAP   END LAP

MIDDLE LAP   CROSS LAP

Fig. 3·27

tilt, the saw is set at the 10-degree bevel position and the arm swung to the 10-degree miter position; for a 5-degree tilt as seen from the front and a 10-degree tilt as seen from the end, the bevel is tilted for one of the angles and the radial arm is swung for the other.

Diamond shapes involve another form of compound-angle cutting. After bevel ripping the stock into V strips, set the motor at the 45-degree right-hand miter position and the 45-degree bevel position (Fig. 3·26). Such cuttings make beautiful decorative patterns.

LAP-JOINT CUTTING

There are several types of lapped or halved joints (Fig. 3·27). To make the end lap, place the motor in the vertical position (the horizontal crosscut sawing position) and install the auxiliary table shown in Fig. 2·25 in place of the standard guide fence. Both pieces of stock that are to form the joint can be cut at once—laid side by side on the auxiliary table. Make the first cut with the blade passing through the center of the stock, following the technique described for horizontal crosscutting. Then elevate the blade $\frac{1}{8}$ inch (the width of the blade) by turning the elevating handle one full turn with each successive cut until all excess stock has been removed (Fig. 3·28).

The other types of lap joints shown in Fig. 3·27 are combinations of end lap joints and dado cuts. Production work

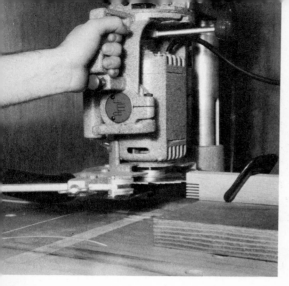

makes use of the dado head in order to reduce the number of passes needed (page 54).

LOCK-JOINT CUTTING

This joint, when properly made and reinforced with glue or dowels, can be one of the strongest joints available. It is accomplished with the machine positioned exactly as when making the lap joint. Instead of removing half the stock, however, each alternate ⅛ inch is left standing (Fig. 3·29). Use a standard ⅛-inch-thick blade to make this joint and judge your cuts by remembering that each complete turn of the elevating handle represents exactly ⅛ inch. The opposite ends are cut opposite so that the two pieces will mesh together.

Fig. 3·29

TENON AND MORTISE CUTTING

The tenon is made in the same manner as the lap joint except that the stock left standing is in the middle rather than on one side of the material (Fig. 3·30*A*). The full tenon, when combined with a tight-fitting mortise and properly glued or doweled, gives a very strong joint which is widely used in all phases of cabinetmaking and general woodworking.

The mortise is the other half of the joint into which the tenon fits. Making the mortise consists simply of cutting a groove to the same width as a previously made tenon (Fig. 3·30*B*).

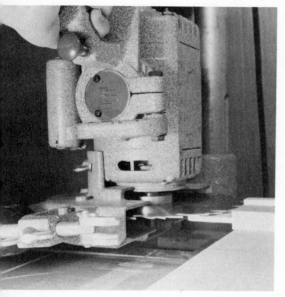

Fig. 3·30A

BEVEL-SPLINE JOINT

The bevel-spline joint (Fig. 3·31*A*) is made by bevel crosscutting the ends of the stock with the motor locked in the 45-degree bevel position. To make the slot for the spline, reverse the stock on the table and, with the motor still in the bevel position (but elevated to the proper height, approximately ⅜ inch, so that the blade will not completely cut through), pull the saw across the previously made

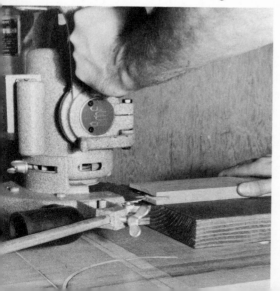

Fig. 3·30B

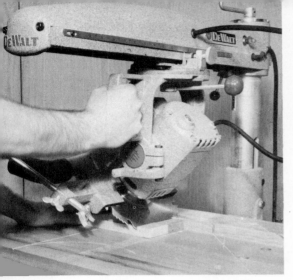

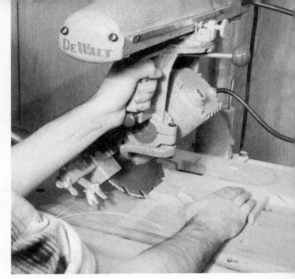

Fig. 3·31A **Fig. 3·31B**

bevel crosscut, leaving the shallow slot (Fig. 3·31B). Make the spline itself from any ⅛-inch rippings you may have—simply cut to the size desired to fit the spline joint.

CUTOFF-WHEEL OPERATION

Cutoff wheels can be used for cutting light metals, ceramics, porcelain, tile, brick, and similar materials. The wheels commonly used are 8 inches in diameter by ³⁄₃₂ inch thick, with a bonded abrasive (page 12). Although these wheels possess remarkable strength, they will chip or break if improperly handled. The feed should be steady and of sufficient pressure to prevent glazing of the wheel. How-

ever, the work should not be forced too greatly, since this will shorten the life of the wheel considerably. Because cutoff wheels are mounted on the motor arbor as a saw blade, the safety guard should be used.

When cutting masonry materials, it is advisable to score ⅛ inch deep, then break clean with a mason's hammer or a brick chisel (Fig. 3·32).

To cut thin-wall tubing, it is wise to hold it in a V block. The block is clamped to the guide fence as shown in Fig. 3·33. The tubing can project beyond the block or the block may have a saw kerf to permit the passage of the wheel.

Fig. 3·32 **Fig. 3·33**

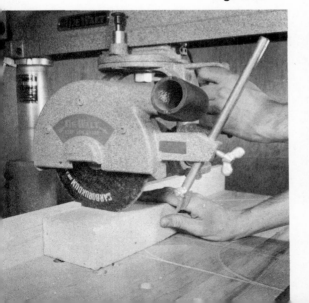

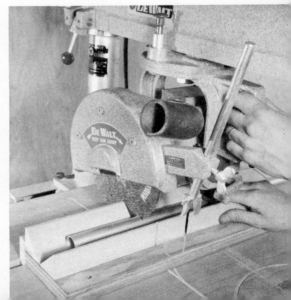

To cut aluminum and other nonferrous metals, a special blade is available (page 12). With this blade, these metals are cut in the same manner as wood (Fig. 3·34)

CUTTING OFF THE TABLE

All cuts thus far discussed have been made on the standard woodwork surface or on an auxiliary table. The maximum elevation of the radial arm, in this position, is 7 inches—this is sufficient for most operations. In instances where this is not sufficient, it is possible, because the radial arm rotates a full 360 degrees around the column, for the machine to be operated with the cutting mechanism positioned directly behind the worktable (180 degrees to normal crosscut position). In this station, the up-and-down travel of the arm allows considerably more latitude because it is not limited by the motor or cutting tool coming into contact with the worktable. Used thus, of course, it is necessary to devise a temporary table or work support such as shown in Fig. 3·35. Also, make certain that the steel table frame is firmly anchored in front, so that when the arm with the motor carriage, etc., is swung to the rear the excess weight does not overbalance the entire machine.

Most operations described in this book —sawing, dadoing, shaping, jointing, saber sawing, boring, routing, and sanding—can be done in this position.

Fig. 3·34   **Fig. 3·35**

CHAPTER 4

Dado-head operations

MOST LIKELY the first accessory you will want for your radial-arm machine is a dado head. This home-workshop essential contains a series of saw blades (Fig. 4·1) that can cut grooves, rabbets, mortises, tenons, dadoes, etc., in thicknesses from $\frac{1}{8}$ to $1\frac{3}{16}$ inch in a single pass. In other words, the dado head cuts down the time consumed in making most wood joints.

There are basically two types of dado heads: the flat ground and the hollow ground. While the latter is more expensive, it produces a much smoother cut and should be used in high-quality work. Either type consists of two outside saws, each about $\frac{1}{8}$ inch thick, whose teeth are not given any set, and inside saws, or "chippers" as they are called—one $\frac{1}{4}$ inch, two $\frac{1}{8}$ inch (some heads include two additional $\frac{1}{8}$-inch chippers instead of the $\frac{1}{4}$-inch one), and one $\frac{1}{16}$ inch thick (thickness at the hub). The cutting portions of the inside cutters or chippers are widened to overlap the adjacent cutter or saw. When assembling a cutter head, arrange the two outside cutters so that the larger raker teeth on one are opposite the small cutting teeth on the other. This produces a smoother cutting and easier running head. Be sure also that the swaged teeth of the inside cutters are placed in the gullets of the outside cutters, not against the teeth, so that the head cuts clean and chips have clearance to come out. And stagger the inside cutters so that their teeth do not come together (Fig. 4·2A). For example, if three cutters are used, they should be set 120 degrees apart.

MOUNTING THE DADO HEAD

The dado head is installed on the motor shaft in the same manner as the saw blade (page 12). In other words, for dado cuts up to $\frac{1}{2}$ inch, place the $\frac{3}{8}$-inch arbor collar on the shaft first, with its recessed side against the saw; the dado-head as-

Fig. 4·1

sembly next; then the ¼-inch arbor collar, with its recessed side against the dado head; and finally tighten the arbor nut with two wrenches (Fig. 4·2*B*). For cuts over ½ inch, omit the ¼-inch arbor collar. If using the full dado head, first put on the ¼-inch arbor collar, the 1¾16-inch dado, and then the arbor nut. Mount the safety guard over the dado head, adjust for the cut on the motor stud, and tighten the wing nut.

In a dado head there is quite a mass of metal revolving at a fairly high speed in the flywheel manner, and if it is not running true it will set up a noticeable vibration. This can be avoided, of course, by staggering the teeth properly and tightening the dado to the full extent.

Never use the chipper blades without the two outside saws. For example, to cut a dado ½ inch wide, use the two outside saws, each ⅛ inch in width, plus a single ¼-inch or two ⅛-inch chippers. Actually any width dado head can be used (the size being limited only by the length of the motor arbor). However, most dado-head sets have enough blades to make cuts only up to 1¾16 inch wide.

When the width of the finished cut is to be more than 1¾16 inch, set up the dado head to a little more than half the required width of the cut and make two successive cuts. Each cut must overlap a bit at the center. If the width of the dado is to be more than twice the capacity of the cutter head, set it for a little over one-third of the width and make three overlapping cuts. Figure 4·2*C* shows how the outside saw and the inside chipper overlap, and how a paper washer can be used as needed to control the exact width of the groove. These washers, 3 to 4 inches in diameter, can be cut from paper and are placed between blades and chippers. If you wish to increase the width slightly, cardboard (up to 1/16 inch thick) can be substituted for the paper.

The design of the cutting teeth of the dado head permits cutting with the grain, across the grain, or at an angle.

OPERATING THE DADO HEAD

The dado head is operated in the same manner as the saw. The settings for the various cuts are the same. The safety precautions are also the same.

Plain Dado. A plain or cross dado is a groove cut across the grain. It can be done in the way described for crosscutting. With the motor in the crosscut position, elevate or lower the radial arm until the depth of the groove is obtained. Then pull the motor past the stock, which has been placed tight against the guide fence (Fig. 4·3).

To locate the dado, mark a line across the stock to indicate one side of it. Hold the second member over it and mark the width of the dado. Draw a line across either edge and mark the depth of the dado, usually half the thickness of the

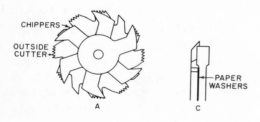

CHIPPERS
OUTSIDE CUTTER
PAPER WASHERS
A
C

Fig. 4·2A and C

Fig. 4·2B

stock. You can predetermine the depth
of the cut by lowering the dado to the
top of the stock, barely touching it, then
lowering the arm by means of the elevating handle—one full turn equaling ⅛
inch.

Angle Dado. This cut has many uses in
cabinetmaking, construction work, and
general woodworking. Among other applications, the angle-dado cut is used to
recess treads in stepladders, in joining
the sill to the upright members of a window frame, and to recess the narrow
strips in shutters, louvers, etc. This cut is
made in the same manner as the cross
dado, except that the radial arm is moved
to the right or left to the desired degree
of angle as indicated on the miter scale
(Fig. 4·4). Raise or lower the arm the
desired depth of the cut by means of the
elevating handle (each full turn equals
⅛ inch).

Parallel Dadoes. These are a series of
dado cuts exactly parallel to one another.
With the radial-arm machine, these cuts
are easy to make because the material
remains stationary, the cutting head doing
the moving. As a result, any two cuts
made with the radial arm in the same
position (whether crosscut or any degree
of miter) are always exactly parallel to
one another. Mark your guide fence (see
page 24) and make successive cuts the
exact distance apart.

Parallel dado cuts at right and left
miter can be done as shown in Fig. 4·5.
Cut the right-hand angle dadoes first and
then swivel the motor 180 degrees. Swing
the arm left to the same angle as the right-
hand cut (see page 24—cutting left-hand
miter). If you mark the guide fence
properly, you can be assured that successive cuts will be the exact distance
apart.

Blind Dado. A blind dado or gain is
cut only partly across the board. With the
stock against the guide fence, mark off

Fig. 4·3

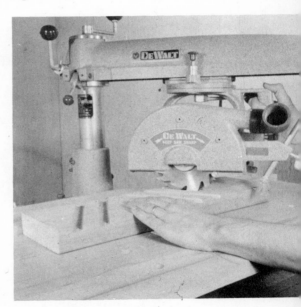
Fig. 4·4

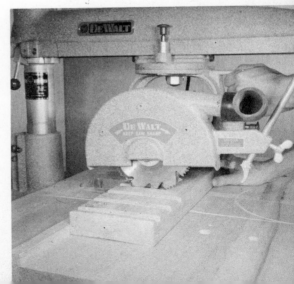
Fig. 4·5

Fig. 4·6A

Fig. 4·6B

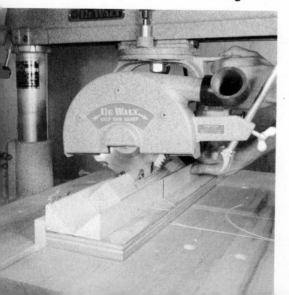

Fig. 4·7

where you wish the dado to stop. Then place a stop clamp on the machine as shown in Fig. 4·6A. With the dado head in the crosscut position and the arm set at the proper height, pull the yoke forward until it hits the stop, and then back off the motor (Fig. 4·6B). If a square cut at the blind end of the dado is desired, it can be made with a wood chisel.

Corner Dado. To make a corner-dado cut, place the stock at 45 degrees in a V block and clamp the block against the guide fence. Raise or lower the arm until the proper depth is obtained. Pull the motor through the stock (Fig. 4·7) in the standard crosscut procedure. The stock can project beyond the block, or the block may be partially cut away to permit the passage of the dado head.

Ploughing. The ploughing operation with a dado head corresponds to the rip cut with a saw blade and is done in the same way. Set the radial arm at 0 degrees (crosscut position); swivel the yoke 90 degrees from crosscut position; move the carriage out on the arm to the desired width and lock; raise or lower the column to the desired depth for the groove. (Remember that each turn of the elevating handle represents exactly ⅛ inch.) For a ¼-inch groove, lower the column two turns from a position where the blades just touch the top surface of the stock. Adjust the safety guard so that the infeed part clears the stock, lock the wing nut, and then lower the anti-kickback fingers ⅛ inch below the surface of the board. Push the material against the guide fence past the blade from right to left in the same manner as when ripping (Fig. 4·8).

Center or blind ploughing is done by raising the column until the stock to be cut will slide beneath the dado head. Then lower the moving head into the lumber to the desired depth (Fig. 4·9A). Push the stock as when ripping or ploughing

Fig. 4·8   Fig. 4·9B

until the groove is as long as you want it (Fig. 4·9B). Then raise the arm until the dado head is clear and the lumber can be pulled from beneath the cutting member.

Bevel Ploughing. This operation leaves a smooth, accurate V groove in the stock. This cut has many applications, both functional and decorative, in cabinetmaking and general woodworking. It also can be used to make V-block jigs. Bevel ploughing is done with the radial arm and yoke positioned as for straight ploughing. In this operation, however, the motor is tilted to a 45-degree position. To tilt the motor, release the bevel clamp and the bevel latch, drop the motor, and then

reset these controls. The bevel latch locates the 45-degree angle automatically. (Other angles can be used and are located on the scale and locked with the bevel clamp.) With the material against the fence, move the motor out on the arm to the desired width and lock the rip clamp. Then raise or lower the arm to the desired depth for the V and push the stock past the dado head in the usual rip method (Fig. 4·10).

Fluting. This operation consists of making a series of V grooves parallel to one another. Fluting is done with the motor in the bevel-plough position. With many conventional-type woodworking machines, it is a real problem to get the

Fig. 4·9A   Fig. 4·10

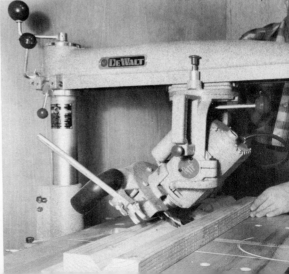

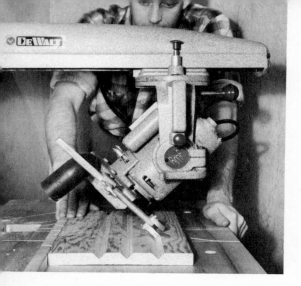

Fig. 4·11

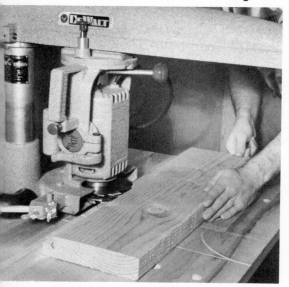

Fig. 4·12

grooves an equal distance apart and exactly parallel. This problem is eliminated with a radial-arm machine because the accurate rip scale allows you to position the motor exactly, and the rigid, square guide fence ensures that the cuts will be parallel. The elevating handle controls the depth of the cut, and the material is pushed past the cutter as in all other ploughing operations (Fig. 4·11). The finished cuts can be used to simulate pillars or columns in cupboards or fireplace mantels.

Rabbeting. Grooving a notch from the side and top of the lumber is simple and effective with the radial-arm machine. Elevate the arm until you have sufficient space beneath the motor to allow the cutting member to swing to a vertical setting. Then release the bevel clamp and the bevel latch to put the dado head in the vertical position (horizontal sawing position, page 28). To set the width of the rabbet, use the rip scale located on the radial arm. Then lower the arm to the desired depth for the groove and pass the material past the cutters from the right side of the table (Fig. 4·12). If thin stock is to be rabbeted, use the auxiliary table top shown in Fig. 2·25 and set it in place of the standard guide fence.

To lay out a rabbet joint, hold one edge of the second member over the end or side of the first and mark the width of the rabbet. Then draw a line down the sides or end and measure one-half to two-thirds the thickness of the first member as the depth of the rabbet. If the cutter "burns" the stock, it indicates a minor misalignment. Simply release the arm, and swing it approximately 5 degrees to the right-hand interposition. This will relieve the drag and will result in a clean cut.

The bevel rabbet is made in a manner similar to the straight rabbet except that the motor is placed at some angle less

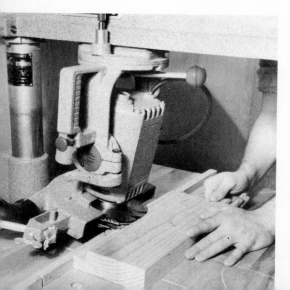

Fig. 4·13

than 90 degrees (vertical position), depending upon the degree of the bevel desired (Fig. 4·13). This cut is widely used throughout construction, cabinetmaking, and general-millwork operations.

Grooving. Although the term "groove" is used to denote many types of dado cuts, it is properly applied to the dado operation made on the side as opposed to the top or end surface of stock. The operation is exactly the same as for rabbeting except that the arm is lowered so that the cutting head is below the top surface of the lumber. Thus the finished cut is bounded on two sides by remaining stock, instead of only one as in the rabbet cut (in Fig. 4·14, note the use of the ¼-inch hardboard as an auxiliary table to clear the guide fence). Using the dado head gives you an extra-wide groove cut, eliminating a number of passes that are necessary when grooving with a saw blade.

Blind mortising or blind grooving is similar to grooving except that the cut is not carried completely through the ends of the stock. In many cases, where the ends of the lumber will be exposed, it is desirable not to show the side groove. In such cases, the stock is "heeled" or pivoted into the cutting head some inches back from the end (see Fig. 4·15).

Mortising and Tenoning. For both operations, the motor is placed in the vertical position (as for horizontal crosscutting). A spacing collar is inserted into the dado head at the proper place so that the stock forming the tenon is left standing. On the auxiliary table, place the material against the fence and mark the stock for the tongue or groove depth desired. The dado head should be located at the proper height, and the motor can be brought forward to the tenon (Fig. 4·16).

Mortising is actually a reverse cut of the one used for tenons. Making the mor-

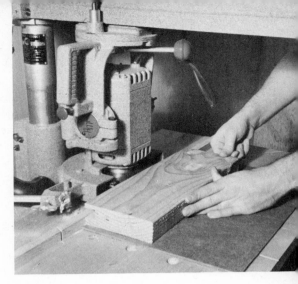

Fig. 4·14

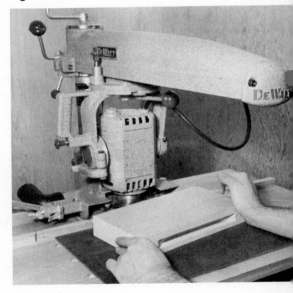

Fig. 4·15

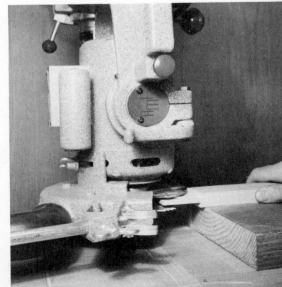

Fig. 4·16

tise consists simply of cutting a groove to the same width as a previously made single tenon. Be sure the length of the tenon and mortise is the same.

Cutting Lap Joints. The lap joint is found in simple furniture legs, tables, frames, and chairs, as well as in many other pieces. The basic one is the cross-lap or middle-half-lap joint. Adaptations of this are the edge-lap, middle- or tee-lap, end-lap, and half-lap joints. The cross-lap joint is one in which two pieces cross, with the surfaces flush. They may cross at 90 degrees or any other necessary angle. On modern furniture legs, for example, they frequently cross at 45 degrees.

To lay out a *cross-lap* joint, mark a line across one surface of one member to indicate one side of the dado. Place the second member over it and mark the width. Invert the pieces and mark the width on the second member. Draw lines down the edges of both pieces and mark the depth of the dado, which should be one-half the thickness of the piece.

The *edge-lap* joint is identical except that the members cross on edge. The *middle-* or *tee-lap* joint is made with one member exactly like the cross-lap joint and the second member cut as a rabbet.

The *end-lap* joint, which is used in frame construction, is made by laying out and cutting both pieces as rabbets. The *half-lap* joint is cut in the same way except that the pieces are joined end to end.

The *end-lap* and *half-lap* joints are actually two tenons with the stock removed from only one side. With the motor in the vertical position, lay the stock, side by side, against the guide fence on the auxiliary table. Raise or lower the radial arm until the lower blade is in the middle of the stock and then pull the cutter through as in the ordinary crosscutting procedure.

Cross-lap and *edge-lap* joints are cut similar to a cross dado, except that the lap joints are usually wider. Make the layout and cut in the manner described for cross dadoes (Fig. 4·17).

In the *middle-lap* joint, one member is cut like a tenon and the second like a dado. Follow the instructions for making each of these two kinds of cuts (Fig. 4·18).

Radius Cutting. This is a dado operation used to produce a concave cut along the face of a piece of lumber. It is accomplished by elevating the column (the radial arm and yoke remain in the normal crosscut position) and dropping the motor

Fig. 4·17   **Fig. 4·18**

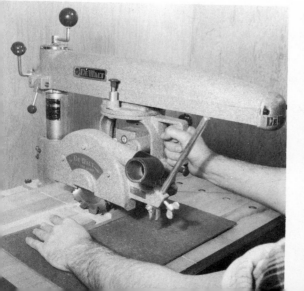

to the 45-degree bevel position. The motor is moved in or out on the radial arm to the correct position in relation to the stock to be cut and is locked in place. The lumber is then pushed under the cutting head as when ripping or ploughing (Fig. 4·19). The first cut should be about ⅛ inch and the dado head should be lowered one full turn at a time until the desired concave is obtained. This operation is similar to contour cutting with a saw blade (page 40).

Scalloping. For window valances, scallop cutting is ideal. Place the dado head in the horizontal ripping position. Locate the motor on the radial arm so that the dado head overhangs the guide fence as shown in Fig. 4·20, and lock it in place after determining the width of the cut desired. Then lower the column to position the blade to the desired depth of the cut. Start the machine and feed the stock into the dado by heeling or pivoting it on the right side of the guide fence as shown. The design may be varied by changing the position of the overhang of the dado head.

Tongue and Groove. By cutting a tongue and groove, you can make your own flooring, wood panels, etc. The tongue and groove is really a combination of tenon and grooving, previously described. With the saw in the horizontal rip position, cut the tongue by using the dado inserts with collars to the exact dimension needed (Fig. 4·21A). Push the stock past the blade to complete the tongue. Cut all the tongues on the panels required first; then turn the stock over and cut the groove as shown on page 56 (Fig. 4·21B). The groove must match the tongue for a good fit.

Tongue-and-groove cuts can also be made with a molding head on the shaper (page 67).

Panel Sinking. This decorative door pattern is a combination of cross dado

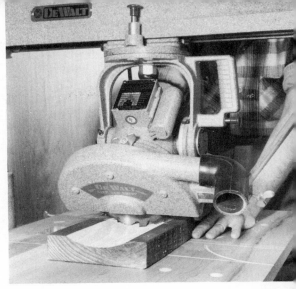

Fig. 4·19

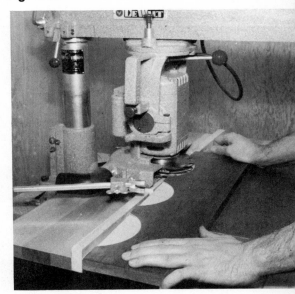

Fig. 4·20

Fig. 4·21A

Fig. 4·21B

Fig. 4·22A

Fig. 4·22B

Fig. 4·23A   **Fig. 4·23B**

and ploughing. Mark the layout of the design and locate the motor above the beginning of the first cross-dado cut. Turn the machine on and lower the blade until it is ⅛ inch below the surface of the panel. Then pull the yoke to the end of the marked design (Fig. 4·22A) and elevate the motor. Repeat the cut at the other end.

Now swing the motor to the in-rip position and lower the arm into the beginning of the cross-dado cut. Then push the material past the dado until it reaches the other cross-dado cut (Fig. 4·22B). Elevate the motor and cut the other side of the design in the same manner. Use a wood chisel to square the corners.

Cutting and Dadoing. It is possible, by combining a saw blade and the dado head, to get both a cutoff and dadoing operation at the same time. Install the saw blade first on the arbor, followed by the dado head. Then, with the saw in the crosscut position, pull the yoke through the material (Fig. 4·23A). Result—cutoff and dado in the same action. Use a 9-inch saw blade and an 8-inch-diameter dado head, as a rule, for deep cuts.

It is also possible to rip and plough at the same time. Mount the saw blade and dado head on the arbor and put the motor in the rip position. Lower the column to the desired depth and push the stock past the blade and dado head (Fig. 4·23B). Result—both cuts in a single operation.

CHAPTER 5

Shaper-jointer operation

THE SHAPER attachments for a radial-arm machine are used for straight and irregular shaping, matched shaping, tongue-and-groove cutting, planing, sizing, and jointing, chamfer cutting, and making drop-hinged leaf joints. It is easy to perform these operations and to turn out this superior work quickly and accurately. The tilting-arbor shaper of the radial-arm machine offers many advantages over the conventional shaper. For instance, standard makes of shapers are maneuverable in only two directions—the cutting head can be raised and lowered, the guide fence can be moved forward and back. But unlike the radial-arm shaper, there is no provision for tilting the arbor or cutter head. This unique flexibility adds approximately 50 per cent more shapes to each cutter. Also, you can shape in the center of wide stock, which is impossible with the limited spindle capacity of the ordinary shapers.

Be sure the table is level (page 14). It is a good idea to use a ⅛-inch hardboard top clamped or nailed over the wood table top to minimize friction and to allow the stock to be cut with ease (see page 15 for details).

SHAPER ACCESSORIES

Nearly all common moldings can be cut on the radial-arm machine with a special cutterhead. Molding heads with a ⅝-inch bore come in two- and three-knife styles, either one of which will produce smooth, clean work.

There are also two types of cutters available for shaper work. One is the loose type mounted on a safety head as shown in Fig. 5·1A (two styles are illustrated), and the other is the solid cutter (Fig. 5·1B). The latter is milled from a solid bar of hardened and properly tempered tool steel, ground to the required shape. The loose-type knives are held in the head by means of fillister-head socket screws. Since the spindle moves clockwise and is not reversible, all cutters must point in the same direction.

There are many cutting-knife shapes

Fig. 5·1

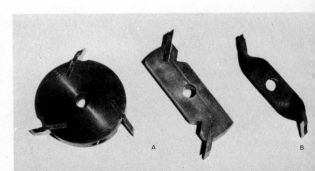

A   B

available. You can start your collection of knives with a few basic types, then add new ones as you need them. There are combination blades that permit different cuts, depending on which part of the contour you use. With these, you can shape table edges, make your own moldings, and do many other decorative jobs.

Standard cutters are each·designed to do a specific job and usually require use of the full contour of the blade. These can cut shaped edges for glue joints, door lips, tongue-and-groove joints, drop-leaf tables, and quarter-round molding. Figure 5·2 illustrates profiles of some of the common types of cutters or knives.

The head is mounted on the arbor of the saw in the same way as a saw blade or dado cutter. To mount the molding head, remove the safety guard, arbor nut, cutting device, and arbor collars from the motor shaft. For the solid type of cutter, replace the ¼ -inch arbor collar (recessed portion on the outside), the cutter, and the arbor nut. The safety guard is used when the molding head is in the horizontal and chamfering positions.

To mount the solid-cutter type, place the arbor collars (⅜-inch-thick collar first), the molding head, and the arbor nut. The safety guard is used with the molding head in the horizontal and chamfering position. With this type, be sure that the knives are in place and tightened securely.

Right after use, clean the knives of gum and sawdust and coat them with oil to prevent rust. Store them so that the cutting edges will be protected from nicks. The head itself should also be cleaned, especially the slots in which the knives sit. Never leave knives locked in the molding head.

Shaper-Jointer Fence. A shaper-jointer fence is available for the radial-arm machine and should be used for straight shaping. This fence replaces the standard guide fence (metal portion on the right side) and fits directly into the standard guide slot. As shown in Fig. 5·3 the infeed side of the fence is adjustable for any capacity up to a full ½ inch, while

Fig. 5·3

Fig. 5·2

A. Miter Lock Joint	M. Cove and Bead
B. Drop-Leaf Table	N. Nosing Cutter
C. Cupboard Door Lip	O. Nosing Cutter
D. Fluting Cutter	P. Bead and Cove
E. Bead and Cove	Q. Surfacing Knives
F. O. G. Molding	R. Tongue and Groove
G. Nosing Cutter	S. Straight Jointer
H. Quarter Round	T. Fluting Cutter
I. Panel Raising	U. Quarter Round
J. Glue Joint	V. Nosing Cutter
K. Cupboard Door Lip	W. Cone and Bead
L. Quarter Round	X. Cupboard Door Lip (7° rake)

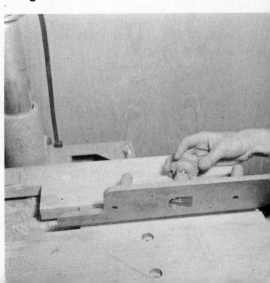

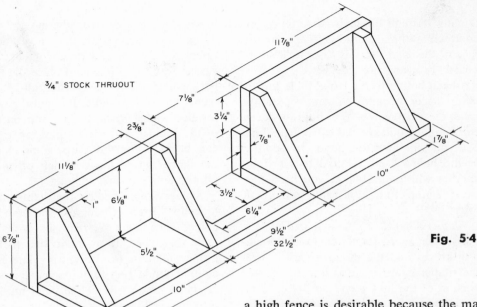

3/4" STOCK THRUOUT

Fig. 5·4

the outfeed side remains in a fixed position. This, of course, is of prime importance in the jointing operation when a portion of the surface of the lumber is being removed. Because the infeed side of the fence can be recessed by the exact amount of stock being removed by the jointer, there is always full support of the lumber both before and after contact with the cutting knives. The result is a smooth, clean surface, free from "ripples" and "dimples."

Since the fence is designed for insertion in the guide slot of the radial-arm machine, either the infeed or outfeed side can be independently moved closer to the center of the table or farther out toward the ends. This flexibility of positioning allows the user to place the center ends of the fence right up to within ⅛ inch of the cutting diameter of the shaping or jointing head, no matter what that diameter may be.

For certain types of straight shaping,

a high fence is desirable because the material being shaped should never be higher than the fence. Figure 5·4 shows the construction of an easily made jig to replace the standard guide fence and rear table boards. The jig is clamped into place by tightening the thumbscrews at the rear of the table in the usual manner. Note that a square hole has been cut into the horizontal board to allow the motor shaft and arbor nut to project down through the surface of the table.

The close-up photograph (Fig. 5·5) shows the action of the molding head ex-

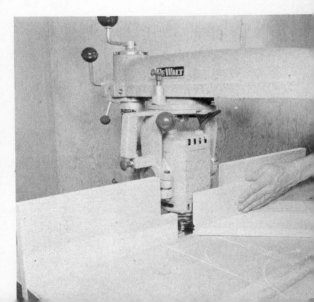

Fig. 5·5

tending through the high guide fence and completing the decorative shape on the face of the stock. In this case, a "hold-in" board (construction details, page 65) has been bolted to the wood table top for more accurate and efficient operation. Like the high guide, this hold-in device can be made quickly and easily from lumber you will have on hand. In addition to the board itself (slotted to allow for varying widths of stock), you need only two C clamps to hold it firmly to the table top.

Shaper Guard. As shown in Fig. 5·6, the shaper guard totally encloses the cutting knives and the motor spindle. After the shaper guard is fitted into the slotted portion of the motor end bell (Fig. 5·7), the hole in the guard flange is placed over the stud on the motor in exactly the same manner as when installing the saw guard. To allow the circular wall to be raised to a height permitting the user to check the precision of the cut, two thumbscrews, located on either side of the center wing nut, permit the protecting portion of the guard to be freely raised and lowered on the small circular columns. When raised on the columns, and locked in position by retightening the thumbscrews, the guard permits full access to the cutting knives. Thus you can look and reach

beneath the guard—with the motor "off," of course—to position the knives accurately for the desired depth of cut. The easiest way to do this is to place the lumber against the knives. After all adjustments have been made, the guard can be lowered right down to the top surface of the lumber and the shaping operation can begin. (For the purpose of clarity, the shaper guard has been left off in the photographs in this chapter.)

Shaper Ring. To allow the shaping head to follow irregular curves, the standard guide fence must be removed from the table top. Then, to maintain the stock in proper relation to the cutting knives, a circular guide ring of the same diameter as the cutting circle of the head must be provided. Although you can buy a steel shaper ring for this purpose, you may find it more convenient and less expensive to make a variety of these rings for your own use.

Figure 5·8*A* shows the simple construction of the shaping ring. To determine the diameter, measure the shortest distance between the cutting surfaces of the opposing shaper knives. This will ensure that the stock will enter the knives to an exact and uniform dimension. The inner circle of wood is removed from the ring to allow the motor shaft to project

Fig. 5·6   **Fig. 5·7**

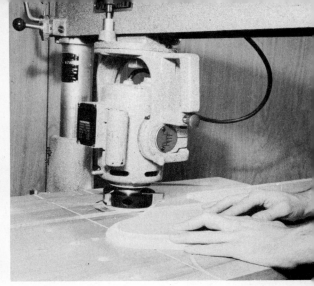

Fig. 5·8A   **Fig. 5·8B**

below the surface. Details for cutting and sanding the ring are illustrated in Chapters 7 and 9. The shaper ring is then nailed to a small piece of 1-inch scrap lumber which replaces the standard guide when the machine is to be used for this operation (Fig. 5·8B).

SAFETY RULES

Before starting to work on the shaper, memorize the safety rules listed below.

1. Remove your necktie and roll up your sleeves.

2. Use the fence and the safety shaper guard whenever possible.

3. Remove all tools and materials from the table top before turning on the power.

4. Check the entire setup and see that the arbor rotates freely before starting the motor.

5. Feed the work against the rotation of the knives (from the right side of the table).

6. Never "back up" any work, because it may be thrown out of your hands. It is better to start the operation all over again.

7. Do not attempt to shape too small pieces that cannot be held safely.

8. Do not take your eyes off the work for one moment.

9. Keep the work between the cutter and your hands in such a position that a slip does not throw the hands against the cutter.

10. Cross-grained woods, or wood shaped against the grain, sometimes split or sliver on the short grain. When this occurs, the work slips rapidly past the cutters. The hands must be

in position to clear the cutters when this occurs.

11. Unlike a saw blade, which removes a small amount of material, a molding cutter takes a big bite. Never force the work through the blade or try to cut too deeply.

12. Keep the cutters sharp at all times (page 134).

Shaper operations

Shaper operations may be divided into four main classifications, according to the methods used in holding or guiding the material against the cutters:

1. Holding the stock against the guide fences. This method is used for cutting stock with straight edges or faces.

2. Holding and guiding stock against the shaper ring. This method is used principally for cutting stock with curved edges or faces and irregular shapes.

3. Cutting stock by following patterns. This method is used in production work when many pieces of the same shape have to be made.

4. Holding stock on special jigs. This method is generally used for stock that cannot readily be held except on special jigs.

STRAIGHT SHAPING

For most jobs on straight edges, the jointer fence is ideal. Install the fence on

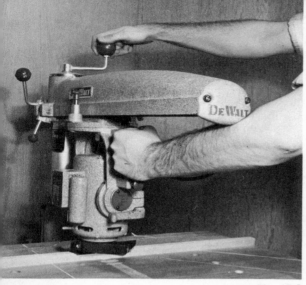

Fig. 5·9

Fig. 5·10

the table and hold a straightedge as a guide to make sure that both halves of the fence are aligned. If an entire edge must be shaped, the front half or infeed side of the fence will have to be set back an amount equal to the depth of the cut so that the molded edge will ride on the other half after it is completed.

The standard guide fence may be used for shaping, too. Place the motor in the vertical position, locate the motor on the carriage arm until the knives overhang the stationary guide by the desired amount, and lock the motor in place. Then turn on the motor and lower the cutter slowly, by using the elevating handle, through to the guide fence until the desired height of the cutterhead is reached (Fig. 5·9). The standard fence can also be replaced with two pieces of wood separated at the center to clear the cutters. For certain work, the high shaper fence is desirable. For underside work, a sheet of plywood on the table elevates the piece high enough to permit the cut. Tack a strip to the edge of the plywood so that part of it replaces the guide fence and part extends above the table and is used as the fence (Fig. 5·10).

In making any molded edge, the pattern is usually made on the end of the work. The proper cutter is then mounted on the motor shaft, after which the arbor is raised or lowered to the proper height. This is done by adjusting the elevating handle.

The work should always be fed from

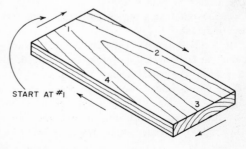

START AT #1

Fig. 5·11B and A

the right side into and against the cutters rotating counterclockwise. When cutting all edges of a piece, the first cut should be made across the end grain. (Follow the steps shown in Fig. 5·11A—start at point 1.) Each edge should be taken in turn so that the final cut is with the grain (Fig. 5·11B). When cutting across the grain, use a pusher board or backing board of the same thickness as the stock to push the board past the cutters to eliminate splintering of the edge and for the safety of the operator (Fig. 5·12). To take a molding cut across the end grain and underside of a piece of work with the radial machine, block up the work, clamp a stopblock to the fence or table, and advance the motor, feeding forward (Fig. 5·13).

Turn on the machine and stand to the back and slightly to the left. Never stand directly back of the cutter. Hold the work firmly against the fence and table with the left hand and feed the work slowly into the revolving cutter, with your right hand applying the forward pressure. Never allow your fingers to come anywhere near the cutter. (This possibility is greatly reduced if you use the shaper guard.) When cutting narrow stock, be sure to use a feather board and a pusher.

To make the feather board illustrated in Fig. 5·14A, cut a bevel approximately 30 degrees across the end of a piece of scrap stock; then make a series of saw kerfs with the grain, about 6 inches long and about ⅜ inch apart (Fig. 5·14B).

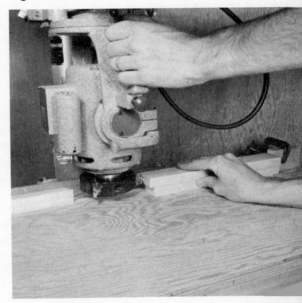

Fig. 5·12

Fig. 5·13

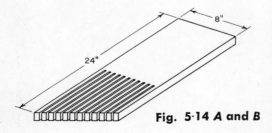

8"

24"

Fig. 5·14 A and B

Never force the work past the cutters or try to cut too deeply. Be sure to keep the piece on the table continually, because the slightest lifting will cause the cutter to gouge into the work. On very deep cuts, make several passes, adjusting the height of the knife after each one, to attain the full depth of cut required. The final pass should be a fine cut to give smoothness. If the machine stalls, vibrates, makes it hard to hold the work steady, or throws out chunks of wood instead of fine shavings, you are trying to cut too heavily. Make trial cuts in scrap wood before cutting actual parts. This is especially important when you are using matching pairs of cutters, such as for panel inserts, window sash, or tongue-and-groove joints. The mating cutters must line up perfectly or the joints will be spoiled. If the fit is tricky and you are in doubt, it is best to make the cuts on slightly thicker stock, join them, and then trim off the excess wood. Always feed with the grain when possible, to minimize splintering.

It is also a good idea to cut the full profile shape of each knife as soon as you buy it and to keep it for reference. Then you can easily tell, without practice cuts, what knife, or what part of the knife, you need.

Strip Molding. Much molding-head work is in the form of strip molding. Short runs of narrow strip molding are usually carried out by shaping the edges of wide boards and then ripping off the strips to the required width or thickness, as the case may be. On longer runs the use of precut strips is faster. Using a hold-in (feather board) and hold-down as in Fig. 5·15, strips can be pushed into the cutter one after the other in rapid succession. Stock to be precut should be carefully selected for straightness of grain and freedom from knots.

Joinery Work. In addition to molding, the molding head does a remarkable variety of joinery work. *Straight knife and surfacing cutters* do all the jobs of dadoing, rabbeting, grooving, and panel raising (Fig. 5·16) common to the saw blade and dado head. The *drawer-joint cutter* (Fig. 5·17) is one of several one-purpose cutters. It is symmetrical and cuts both parts of the front-to-side joint. The front of the drawer is cut first, and the depth of the cut is equal to the sidestock thickness; you can cut to within $\frac{1}{8}$ inch of the front surface. The side of the drawer is cut with the work flat on the table. Test this on scrap stock and you will see how the joint fits.

The *symmetrical glue-joint cutter* is a

Fig. 5·15   **Fig. 5·16**

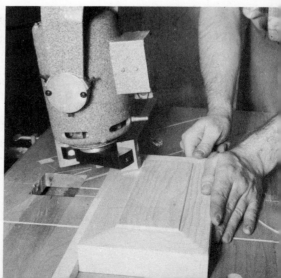

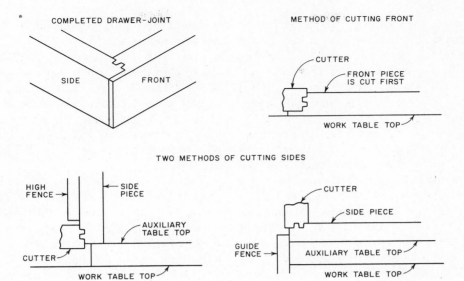

COMPLETED DRAWER-JOINT

SIDE FRONT

METHOD OF CUTTING FRONT

CUTTER

FRONT PIECE
IS CUT FIRST

WORK TABLE TOP

TWO METHODS OF CUTTING SIDES

HIGH
FENCE

SIDE
PIECE

AUXILIARY
TABLE TOP

CUTTER

WORK TABLE TOP

CUTTER

SIDE PIECE

GUIDE
FENCE

AUXILIARY TABLE TOP

WORK TABLE TOP

Fig. 5·17

one-purpose knife used only for making glue joints. The work must be exactly centered on the cutter, Fig. 5·18*A*. Properly centered, any two pieces will fit together when one of the pieces is reversed end to end. When the work has a definite face side, the reversal is done while cutting, molding one piece with the face side next to the fence and the joining piece with the face side away from the fence.

The *tongue-and-groove* joint is run with two cutters, one making the groove and the other the tongue. Both cutters are the same length so that, when the depth setting is made for one, the same setting is used for the other (Fig. 5·18*B*). All work is done in the same position, that is, with the face side to the fence. Tongue-

and-groove cutters can also be used for drawer and corner joints.

A *rule joint* is used on tables with folding leaves. It is rather hard to make by hand, but on a shaper it is made easily and quickly. A table usually has two leaves, which are hinged to the central part that is fastened to the rails of the table. When laying out the rule joint, first set a marking gauge to half the thickness of the knuckle of the hinge and gauge the ends of the boards as shown in Fig. 5·18*C*. The centers of both the concave and convex cuts lie in the gauge lines. The radius is the distance from the gauge lines to the upper surface, less ¾ inch for the square edge. Select a cutter that will fit the convex curve and cut both

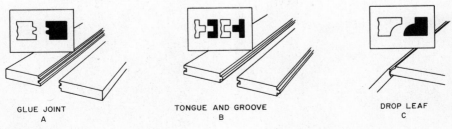

GLUE JOINT
A

TONGUE AND GROOVE
B

DROP LEAF
C

Fig. 5·18

edges of the fixed top. The cutter for the concave cuts in the leaves should be the reverse of the first cutter, but with a radius $\frac{1}{32}$ inch larger so that there will be clearance for the two moving wood parts. (One-pass cutters are also available.)

Turn the top and leaves upside down and place them flat on a bench. The kinds of hinges used are called "backflaps" and have one leaf longer than the other (page 158). As screw holes are countersunk on the reverse side of the hinge, the knuckles must be set into the wood. If it is difficult to obtain the right kind of hinges, ordinary hasp hinges may be used.

The *door-lip cutter* is a special-purpose knife which rabbets and rounds the edge in one pass (Fig. 5·19). Or you can do the same thing in two steps. In the second method, the rabbet is run first with a straight cutter; then a guide is clamped to the shaper fence and adjusted to a height that will permit the lip of the stock to slide under it. The cutting heads shown in Fig. 5·2 can make combination cuts to give many effects.

Top-side Cutting. As shown in Fig. 5·20, it is possible to cut moldings on the top side with the radial-arm machine. This method is ideal for applying decorative patterns on wood paneling. Place the

motor in the outrip position, locate it on the arm at the spot where the cut is to appear, lock the rip clamp, and lower the column to the desired depth of molding cut. Then feed the material into and against the cutter from the left side of the table. The safety guard should be used over the shaper head. Reeding and fluting combinations can be made in this manner, too.

Top-side cutting can also be done in the standard crosscut manner. The depth of the molding is limited in this position by the projection of the blades and the motor clearance above the workpiece. For angle cuts, swing the radial arm to the angle of the mitered end of the workpiece.

Chamfer Cutting. As shown in Fig. 5·21, it is possible to cut chamfers with any shaper head and straightedge knives. This is accomplished by placing the motor in the out-rip position and setting it in a bevel position. Any degree of angle can be placed on the edge of the stock simply by changing the bevel angle of the motor. Place the material so that the side to be chamfered is opposite the fence, place the motor at the proper location on the radial arm, and lower the column to the proper depth of cut. Feed the material slowly past the knives from the left side

Fig. 5·19   Fig. 5·20

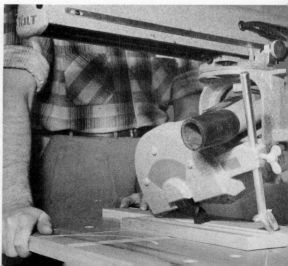

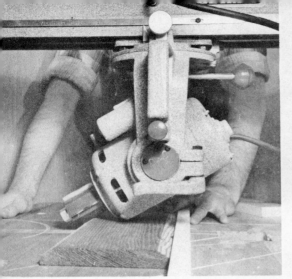

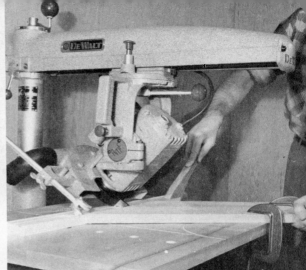

| Fig. 5·21 | Fig. 5·22 |

in the same manner as when ripping. Be careful of whirling blades. Use pusher sticks wherever possible. Octagon shapes required for some lathe work can be cut in the same way.

Any molding pattern desired can be cut on an angle or bevel in this manner on the radial-arm machine (Fig. 5·22).

IRREGULAR SHAPING

Irregular shaping is the shaping of the irregular edges of oval-shaped tables, curved legs, chair and table stretchers, and decorative moldings on curved edges.

To set up for irregular shaping, drop the motor to the vertical position (with the cutting tool horizontal). To allow the shaping head to follow irregular curves, remove the standard guide fence from the table top. Then, to maintain the stock in proper relation to the cutting knives, use a circular guide ring (page 62) the same diameter as the cutting circle of the head. The shaper ring, placed on the arbor outside the shaper head or used in place of the guide fence, allows the stock to be turned freely beneath the cutting knives.

In setting up the shaper, the positioning of the motor is determined by (1) the amount and position of the cutting surface to be utilized on each shaper and (2) the decision of the operator to shape the work with an undercut or an overcut.

When you have decided on the direction of rotation, place the cutter and spacer collar in position and adjust the column for height. The depth of the cut is limited by the diameter of the spacer collar. The collar must be free of the resinous and charred substance that tends to accumulate on its surface; if it is not clean, it will make an uneven molding. Remember that the work will rest against the edge of the guide fence before it enters the cut.

Some judgment is necessary in selecting the place to start a cut. It is not always possible or advisable to begin at the end of the stock. Frequently it is necessary to select a point along the side in order to favor cross grain or to prevent the molding from splitting out the end grain.

When the place of entry has been determined, hold the stock firmly on the table, clear of the cutter, with the edge resting against the right side of the fence. The corner of the fence is used as the fulcrum or starting point. Advance the work along so that the edge, at the point of entry, is tangent to the cutting circle of the cutters (Fig. 5·23). As soon as the stock rests firmly against the collar, swing it clear of the edge and run with no other bearing than the collar. Do not try to rest the stock against the collar and the edge

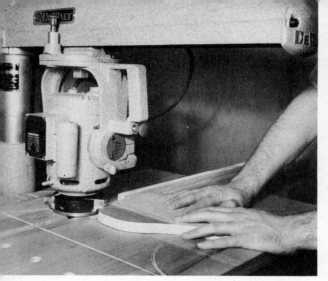
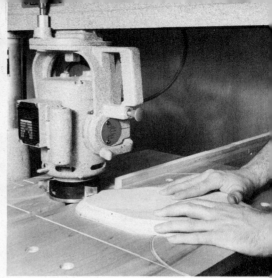

after the cut has been started, because it is difficult to hold the stock to the collar in this position. Once away from the collar, the work tends to be thrown back as the cutters bite in.

When at the point for turning the corner (Fig. 5·24), swing the stock until the point rides on the left front of the collar, with the unshaped edge tangent to the collar. During this shift, keep the stock moving steadily forward in firm contact with the collar. This is the secret of successful freehand shaping.

In shaping the small curves at the top, turn the point and swing the stock until the curve is directly in front of the arbor. Then advance the stock slowly, straight into the cutter, with the pressure bearing on the left-hand side. The side is tangent to the collar on this side.

When you reach the bottom of the curve, shift the pressure to the right-hand side of the collar and pull the stock straight out. Shape the remaining corners and curves in a similar manner until you reach the starting point. When cutting against the grain, feed the work very slowly.

The interior edges of curved frames are shaped in the same way. The edge of the guide fence, located where it is convenient for swinging the inner side of the work against the cutter, is used.

PATTERN SHAPING

Patterns are used as guides when several pieces of the same shape have to be made or when the whole edge of a table top has to be shaped or rounded. The pattern must be of the exact shape of the article wanted.

Make the pattern of plywood, hardboard, or a piece of hardwood. Cut it to conform to the outline of the work, sand all edges perfectly smooth, and rub a little paraffin wax into them.

Place the work face down on the table top. Place the pattern on the work and drive several small wire nails or brads through it and about $\frac{1}{16}$ inch into the work to prevent the pattern from slipping. Adjust the collar and cutter for the desired depth of cut. The shaper collar rests against the finished edge of the pattern, and the cutter can cut into the work only as far as the pattern will permit.

The pattern is guided against the collar, and the work may be placed on its underside (Fig. 5·25). The front edge of the guide fence is used as a starting point as described previously for irregular shaping.

Fig. 5·25

For undercutting molding work, a filler should be used between the pattern proper and the work to lift the piece for shaping

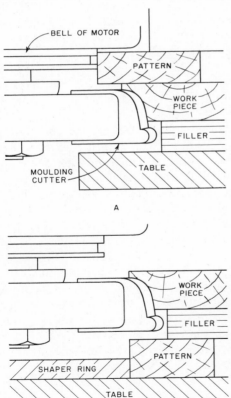

Fig. 5·26

the underside or the entire edge (Fig. 5·26A). The pattern and the workpiece must line up. The filler is bradded to both the workpiece and the pattern.

The bell of the motor also can be used as a collar. Since the diameter at the neck of the motor is less than that of the molding-head assembly, the pattern must be made correspondingly oversize. This stationary guide scores little and will not burn the edge. A plywood filler (Fig. 5·26B), clamped to the table top, lifts the work enough above the table to permit shaping underneath, and cutter guarding is almost perfect.

JIG SHAPING

Some shaping jobs can be done with a simple jig. To shape the edge of round stock, cut out a large V in a piece of plywood. There should be a clearance hole at the bottom of the V to house the cutter. Place the guide fence at the back of the stationary table. Then clamp this plywood jig in the proper location on the stationary table top. The jig can be adjusted forward or back until the desired edge can be cut. The stock can then be rotated as it is held against the V block (Fig. 5·27).

The circle jig shown in Fig. 7·10A, page 91, can be used in circular shaping. Locate the jig on the table, clamp it to

Fig. 5·27

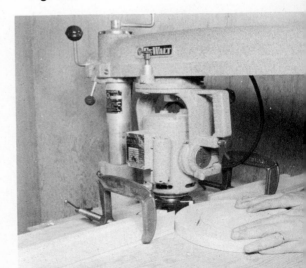

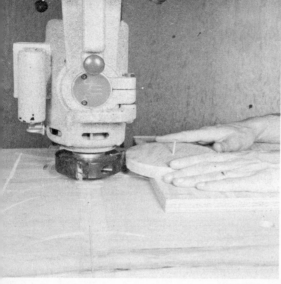

Fig. 5·28

Fig. 5·29

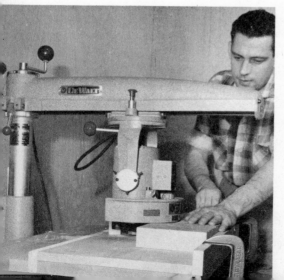

Fig. 5·30

the top, and fasten the stock on the pivot point. Rotate the disk against the motion of the cutter (Fig. 5·28). With this jig a roughly sawed disk is molded to dimension and a true circle directly.

JOINTING

For *edge jointing* (or face jointing up to 2 inches) place the four-wing jointer on the arbor shaft and install the jointer fence. To install the jointer, remove everything from the arbor shaft. Then slide on the jointer and tighten the special adapter nut which comes with the jointer blade. Use the wrenches to tighten. Now place the motor in the vertical position and locate it on the radial arm so that the lead portions of the jointer blades line up with the rear or outfeed fence. Lower the motor to the desired cut by means of the elevating handle.

The 2-inch straightedge jointing or surfacing shaper knives can also be used in the same way as the four-wing jointer.

The front or infeed fence must be about $\frac{1}{32}$ inch back of the cutter head for light cuts and $\frac{1}{8}$ inch back for rough cuts. Turn the handle in back of the infeed fence to bring it in or out. Always use the shaper guard whenever possible.

Place the material flat on the table and tight against the infeed fence. Then feed the material past the jointer blade, keeping it against the infeed fence (Fig. 5·29). When about one-half to two-thirds of the board has passed the cutter head, move your left hand to the board over the outfeed fence. As most of the board passes over the cutter, move your right hand to the board over the outfeed fence to finish the cut. Feed the material slowly past the blade and take two thin cuts rather than one big one.

In *face jointing*, always use a push stick to push the board through. Push the material past the cutter in the same manner as for edge jointing. Always cut with the grain when jointing.

Sizing and jointing in the same operation require an easily made jig (Fig. 5·30) which has the guide fence located at the front of the table rather than at the rear. The exact width of the finished stock is determined by measuring the distance between the front guide and the cutters. Lock the carriage at the desired position on the arm. Feed the stock into the cutters from the right side of the table (Fig. 5·31). The result is perfect width and perfect edge with only one cut. To joint the flat surfaces, remove the jig and place the stock against the guide fence. Lower the jointer blade until it hits the top surface and keep lowering it until it takes off the desired amount (Fig. 5·32). Push it past the blade in the rip manner and keep passing it over the surface until the surface is smooth and even.

Rabbeting operations are accomplished with the jointer head by raising the motor to the desired height (Fig. 5·33). Feed the work through as you would for normal edge cutting except that the two fence portions should be aligned.

Rotary Surfacer. This attachment—actually a rotary jointer—will quickly and efficiently cut warped boards down to uniform thickness and convert them into usable stock ready for sanding or finishing.

To install the rotary surfacer, remove all items from the motor shaft. Then screw on the rotary surfacer directly to the motor shaft (Fig. 5·34). Drop the motor to the vertical position (the surfacer will be in a horizontal position), locate the motor on the arm where the surfacing is to be done, lock the rip clamp, and lower the column until the surfacer knives project slightly below the top surface of the material.

Place the stock flat on the table against

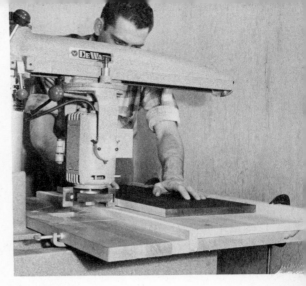

Fig. 5·31

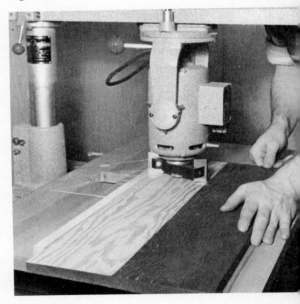

Fig. 5·32

Fig. 5·33

Fig. 5·34   Fig. 5·37

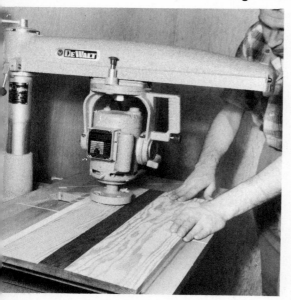

Fig. 5·35

Fig. 5·36

the fence and feed the work into the rotary planer from right to left, following the grain (Fig. 5·35). For wide pieces, make successive cuts at the same depth setting; move the motor on the arm. Keep the work flat on the table to prevent gouging. When the top side is planed flat, turn the piece over and plane it parallel with the first side.

Plane off arcs or irregular-edged surfaces by guiding the piece against the same type of curved jig you would use for shaping. Plane bevel edges by setting the motor at the desired angle.

To cut rabbets and tenons, line up the work at a right angle to the guide fence and take several light cuts (rather than a single deep cut) with the rotary planer (Fig. 5·36). Stepped shoulders can be cut in much the same manner by taking a series of cuts at each position. Panel raising can also be done with a rotary planer (Fig. 5·37).

CHAPTER **6**

Boring
and routing

THE FLEXIBILITY of the radial-arm machine brings you unlimited boring capacity. Equipped with the boring-bit attachments, it overcomes certain limitations of the conventional drill press. For example, you are not restricted in the length or width of material you can bore because of the size of the throat opening or the length of the downstroke of the press. The boring action of the radial-arm machine is horizontal rather than vertical. Thus, material several feet in length can be end-bored with perfect precision and accuracy. And the depth of the hole to be bored is limited only by the length of the bit itself, not by the stroke of the press.

MOUNTING THE BORING BIT

To mount the boring bit, remove the safety guard, the arbor nut, the cutting device, and the arbor collars from the motor shaft. Replace the two arbor collars (the ⅜-inch-thick collar first) and then screw on and tighten the special motor-shaft adapter (Fig. 6·1). The desired size of bit can now be placed in the adapter, and the adapter setscrew should be tightened.

Wood-boring bits for the radial-arm machine are available in the following sizes: ¼, ⁵⁄₁₆, ⅜, ½, ⅝, ¾, ⅞, and 1 inch. Since a left-hand feed and point are required with this machine, conventional bits cannot be used.

SAFETY RULES

Safety practices for the boring operation of the radial-arm machine are the same as for all other accessories. In addition, observe the following:

1. Keep your fingers away from the revolving tool.
2. Never remove chips with your fingers.
3. The boring bit must be secure in the adapter.
4. Keep the cutting bits sharp.

Fig. 6·1

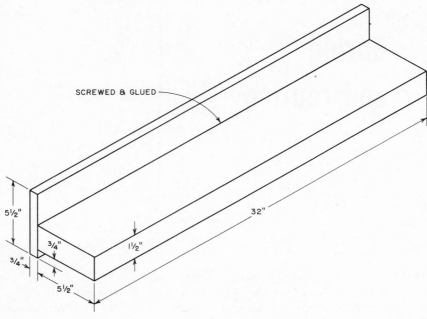

SCREWED & GLUED

5½"

¾"

¾"

5½"

1½"

32"

Fig. 6·2A

WOOD-BORING OPERATIONS

For various boring operations, a simple jig (Fig. 6·2A) is needed to raise the material above the surface of the table top and to provide a higher guide fence. Place a wedge between the jig and column to add support when boring (Fig. 6·2B).

Laying Out the Work. Accurate layout is a basic requirement of hole boring. The simplest method of marking the lo-cation of a hole is to draw lines which intersect at the center of the hole. For such work, a combination square is ideal, since it can be used to draw lines parallel with the edge of the work and as an edge-marking gauge. Dividers are handy when it is necessary to transfer a measurement from one piece to another or to mark off a line in a number of equal spaces. If a pencil is used for marking, select a hard one (3H or harder) and keep it sharp so that the lines will be well defined.

Face Boring. Locate the center of the hole and mark it with a center punch or scratch. Insert the proper bit in the adapter and tighten the setscrew. Bring the motor forward to the front of the arm and swing it to the in-rip position (the bit will face toward the column of the machine). Set the material on edge atop the boring jig against the guide fence. Raise or lower the arm so that the bit touches the stock at the desired spot. Turn on the machine and slowly push the yoke assembly backward on the arm until the bit

Fig. 6·2B

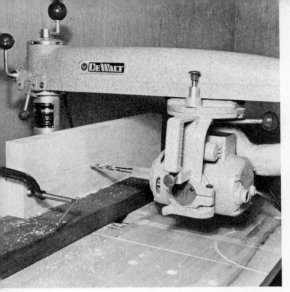

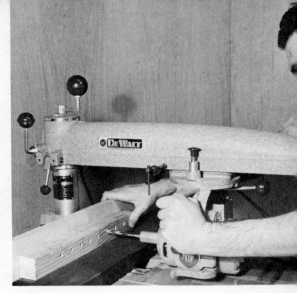

Fig. 6·3   **Fig. 6·4**

has entered the stock to the desired depth (Fig. 6·3). Hold the stock firmly and apply even pressure to the yoke. If the stock is hardwood or the hole is deep, rack out the bit once or twice to remove the chips before finishing the hole.

For boring more than one hole of the same depth, place a stop clamp on the arm (Fig. 6·4) to limit the travel of the head.

If you plan to bore all the way through the board, place a piece of scrap wood behind the hole location. Always bore through the hole and into the scrap wood. If no backup board is used, the wood will split out as the bit goes through the stock.

Edge Boring. Place the material flat on the jig and against the fence. With the motor in the in-rip position, raise or lower the arm until the desired location is obtained. Then push the yoke assembly back on the arm until the hole has been bored to the correct depth (Fig. 6·5). Push with slow, even pressure. Back out the bit once or twice to remove the chips. A stop clamp on the arm will assure you of equal depth for multiple holes.

End Boring. Place the material flat on the boring jig (Fig. 6·6*A*) and against the fence. Place the motor in the standard crosscut position, place the motor on the radial arm so that the bit touches the stock at the desired spot, and lock with

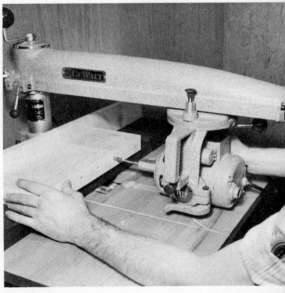

Fig. 6·5

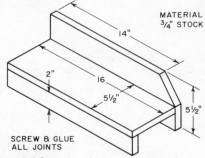

MATERIAL
3/4" STOCK

14"

2"   16

5½"

5½"

SCREW & GLUE
ALL JOINTS

Fig. 6·6A

Fig. 6·6B

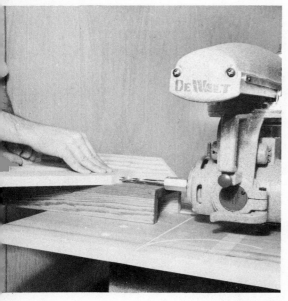

Fig. 6·8

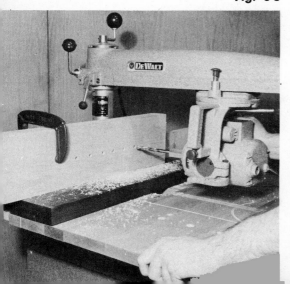

Fig. 6·9

the rip clamp. Then push the stock into the bit until the hole is of the desired depth (Fig. 6·6*B*). On deep holes, back off from the bit once or twice to remove the chips.

Miter Boring. Miter joints are often strengthened with dowels. Using the same jig and with the motor placed exactly as for end boring, just push the stock into the bit at any desired angle. Use a "pusher" board (Fig 6·7) with a mitered end to direct the stock into the bit at the proper angle (Fig. 6·8). Note that since the bit remains stationary it is possible to bore holes in the same position on the ends of more than one piece of stock. When moving for a second hole, the accurate rip scale on the right of the arm makes precise placing of the bit an easy job.

Parallel Boring. This is merely making a series of holes in the manner described for face boring. Because the stock remains positioned at exactly the same level on the boring jig and the bit enters at exactly the same height (riding on machined tracks inside the arm), there can never be any question as to whether the holes will be parallel to one another (Fig. 6·9). Parallel boring can be done in the vertical

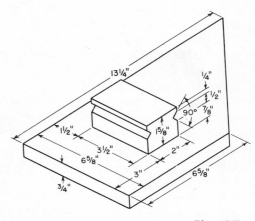

Fig. 6·7

Fig. 6·10

Fig. 6·11

direction, too. Space the holes evenly by lowering or raising the arm with the elevating handle the same number of turns (Fig. 6·10).

To bore equal-depth holes at an end of board, the use of a stop block simplifies the work, as shown in Fig. 6·11. Clamp the block in position so that it hits the bell of the motor when the desired depth is reached.

Boring in Round Stock. Round work can be pushed tight against the fence and jig table or a V block and held as shown in Fig. 6·12*A*. The hole is then cut as described for face boring. To bore holes around a circle, either on a disk or some other shape, pivot the work on the center of the circle, using a bolt through the piece or a nail filed to a point and driven into an auxiliary table (Fig. 6·12*B*).

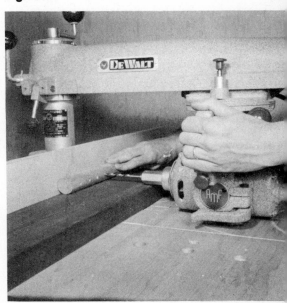

Fig. 6·12A

Angular Boring. The stock is positioned on the jig exactly as for face boring. The radial arm, however, is moved either to the right or left so that the bit will enter the stock at any desired angle when pushed back on the arm (Fig. 6·13). The calibrated miter scale atop the column allows you to determine within a fraction of a degree the angle at which the bit will enter.

Boring Mortises. Very good mortises with round ends can be bored on the

Fig. 6·12B

Fig. 6·13

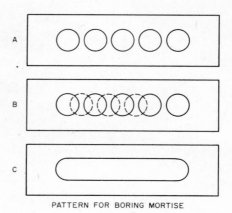

A

B

C

PATTERN FOR BORING MORTISE

Fig. 6·14

radial-arm machine in the same manner as edge boring. First determine the depth of the mortise and set the clamp as illustrated in Fig. 6·4. Bore the first hole at the point where the left end of the mortise is to be cut. Bore the holes fairly close together (Fig. 6·14); then drill other holes between, as shown by the dotted lines. Push the work into the drill to clean out the mortise. The tenon for a round-end mortise can be cut as described on page 44 and rounded off on the disk sander.

ROUTING

The radial-arm boring machine can quickly be converted into a router by substituting a router bit for the boring bit.

There are two general classifications of router work—straight or irregular. Straight work is done against a fence; irregular work can be cut freehand or with a pattern. In either case, the work feed must be against the rotation of the cutter. This means that the material being cut is fed from left to right. The depth of all routing should be $\frac{1}{8}$ inch or less per pass; if a deeper cut is desired, make it with the necessary number of repeat cuts.

Straight routing is done with a guide fence. The standard guide fence is re-

Fig. 6·15

Fig. 6·16

placed with two pieces of wood separated at the center to allow the router to rotate. If you have a shaper-jointer fence (Fig. 6·15), it will serve the same purpose. In either case, the fence is installed in place of the standard guide fence.

With the motor in the 90-degree bevel position (the shaft in a vertical location), place it on the arm for the width of the cut and lock the ripclamp. Then lower the arm by means of the elevating handle to the depth of the cut. Turn on the machine and, keeping the work firmly pressed against the fence, move it slowly past the cutting tool (Fig. 6·16).

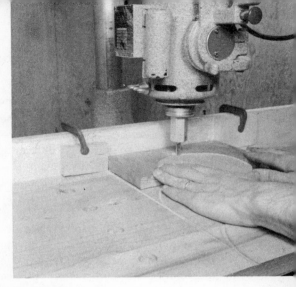

Fig. 6·17

Rabbeting can be done as just described. But remember, never attempt to take more than a ⅛-inch cut at a time. If a greater depth is desired, lower the arm one turn of the handle at a time. For rabbets wider than the bit, move the motor forward on the arm so that cuts just overlap each other. Clamp the motor in position and push the stock past the router bit. Continue this movement away from the fence until the required width of the rabbet is obtained.

Methods of routing grooves in curved or round work are shown in Figs. 6·17 and 6·18. In each case a guide block is clamped to the table and the motor is positioned to make the cut where it is needed. If the work is saber-sawed carefully, the waste stock can be utilized as the guide for the work. Be sure to hold the work firmly as you move it around the guide.

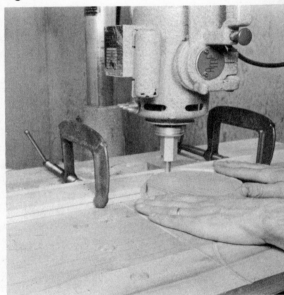

Fig. 6·18

Dadoes can be cut with the router bit, too. In this operation the work remains stationary and the bit is moved through it. With the stock against the fence and the router bit behind it, pull the yoke slowly forward on the arm in the same position as when you are crosscutting (Fig. 6·19). Several passes may be necessary to get the desired width and depth of the dado.

Fig. 6·19

Edge Routing. Edge grooving is accomplished by placing the material on the boring jig and setting the motor in the position for edge boring. The difference between edge boring and routing is that in the latter the material is moved past the bit instead of remaining stationary (Fig. 6·20).

The round-end mortise, previously described as being formed with the boring bits, can be cut by the edge-routing method to take a round-end tenon. Use the fence as a guide, with a stop clamped to it to control the length of the slot. Deep cuts should be made in several passes, moving the bit closer to the column after each pass until the full depth of the cut has been obtained.

Freehand Routing. Signs and decorations are sometimes made freehand with the router. Carefully lay out the areas to be removed. Place the motor in the 90-degree bevel position and lower the radial arm so that the depth of the bit will make the proper cut. Locate the motor on the arm at a convenient location so that the work can be swung around the bit and lock it in position with the rip clamp. Turn on the machine and move the work along past the router, following the outline (Fig. 6·21). Always work from left to right and place a piece of hardboard under the stock for easy movement.

MAKING DOVETAIL JOINTS

The most desirable joint for most drawer construction is the dovetail. This is extremely difficult to make by hand but is very simple with a router and dovetail jig.

To make the dovetail jig (Fig. 6·22), dado cut the frame support *D* ¼ inch deep to receive part *E*. Use four wood screws and glue to hold these members together. Dado cut the base *A* ¼ inch deep to receive the frame-support assembly. Fasten guide *B* to base *A* with four wood screws. Then mount the frame support (*D* and *E*) in the dado grooves in base *A* and glue and nail in place. Raiser *R* may now be nailed in place in front of *D*. Mount hinge *K* to base *A* with three wood screws. Attach pressure clamp *G* to hinge *K* with a countersunk bolt 1½ inches long, a washer, and wing nut. Drill holes in *E* to line up with the upper slots in *G* in the position shown. Nail cleats *C* to base *A*. With a pair of scissors cut out the template (this can be traced from Fig. 6·23 onto thin cardboard). Using this as a pattern, carefully trace the exact outline for the dovetail slot on pressure clamp *F*. Mount hinge *H* to pressure clamp *F* with three wood screws and to the base *A* with a 3-inch bolt, washer, and wing nut. Drill a hole in *D* to line up with

Fig. 6·20   **Fig. 6·21**

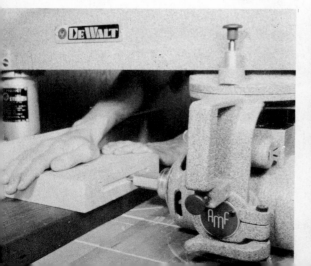

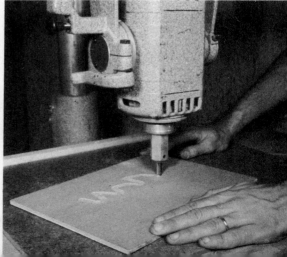

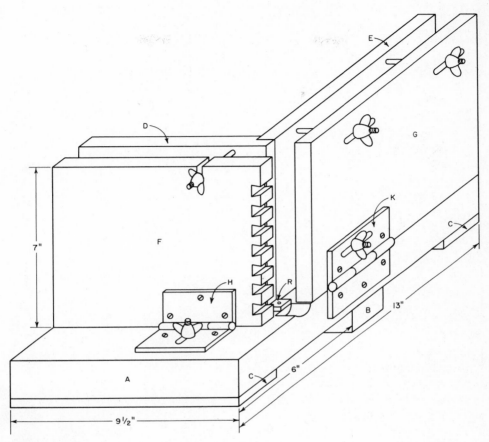

Fig. 6·22

the upper slot in *F* for a 3-inch bolt, washer, and wing nut.

If you prefer, a simple jig may be made by eliminating the pressure clamps, hinges, and wing nuts and substituting pairs of C clamps or wooden clamps to hold the drawer front and side in position.

Using the Jig. After the jig has been assembled, position it on the table top as shown in Fig. 6·24. With the motor in the rip position and the dovetail router screwed into the arbor, slide the jig assembly right or left until the router extends for a cut exactly ⅜ inch deep into *F* according to the template lines you have traced. Place a piece of ¾-inch stock 5¾ inches wide by 10 inches long

behind clamp *F*. These pieces of stock represent the equivalent of a drawer front and side. Raiser *R* will lift the drawer side ¼ inch for proper offset when the matching pieces have been simultaneously dovetailed. Tighten the wing nuts to hold both pieces securely.

Lower the arm with the elevating handle until the router is directly in front of and ready to cut the bottom of the dovetail slot. Start the motor and push it slowly forward, moving it back and forth to clear chips. Proceed until the shoulder of the router has passed through clamp *F*, through the ½-inch stock, and into the ¾-inch stock and comes to rest against the front edge of clamp *G*. With

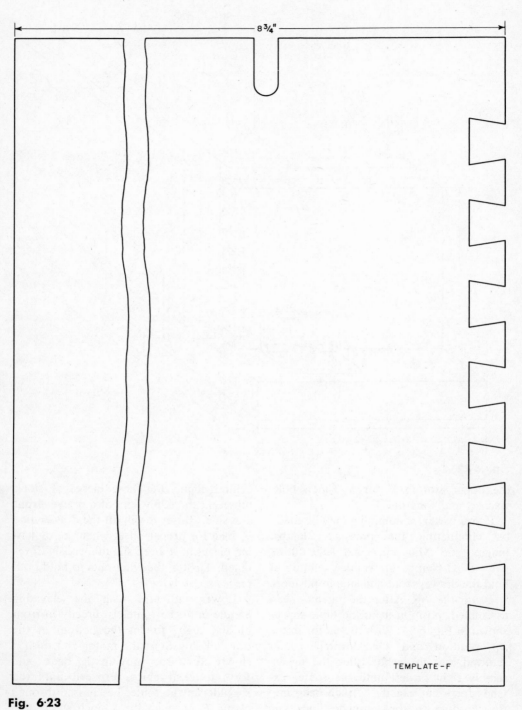

8 3/4"

TEMPLATE - F

Fig. 6·23

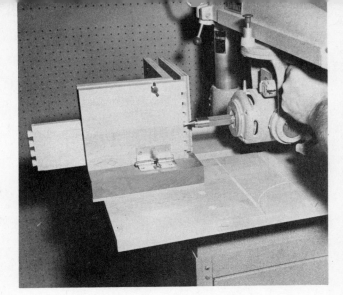

Fig. 6·24

the first dovetail slot completed, move the router to the next position and repeat the operation. Continue until all seven slots have been made.

To undercut the back of the drawer side (the final operation), remove the drawer front from behind *G* and turn the elevating handle to raise the router slightly above the top edge of the drawer side. With the edge of the router extending over the stock about $\frac{1}{16}$ inch, set the rip clamp firmly. Now turn the elevating handle slowly downward so that the lip of the router will remove the required undercut from the back edge of the drawer side. Remove the side from behind *F*. The side and front should now fit together.

The dovetail jig described will cut matching drawer sides and fronts in stock of the following widths: $1\frac{3}{8}$, $2\frac{1}{4}$, $3\frac{1}{8}$, 4, $4\frac{7}{8}$, and $5\frac{3}{4}$ inches. For other widths or when the drawer front has a *CC* lip, use the stock for the drawer side $\frac{1}{2}$ inch wider than needed and trim off to fit after the dovetail cuts are made.

CHAPTER 7

Operation of the saber saw

NO TOOL ADDS so much to the versatility of the radial-arm machine as a saber saw. It will cut all types of intricate scrollwork and irregular curves—either square or beveled—in wood, plastic, or light metal. It can also be used for power filing, sanding, and similar operations.

The saber saw shown in Fig. 7·1A will cut material up to 2 inches in thickness. The table top of the radial-arm machine allows you to do intricate scrollwork on large panels with full support of the stock, for there is more than 27 inches of clearance between the blade and the column.

The saber-saw unit mounts directly on the radial-arm motor brackets and takes just about one minute to install (Fig. 7·1B). The Scotch-yoke mechanism encased in the unit converts the rotating motion of the shaft into the reciprocating motion necessary to drive the saber saw. Oil-impregnated bearings eliminate lubrication worries.

MOUNTING INSTRUCTIONS

The installation of the saber saw is a simple operation. But before you make the setup for the first time, you must bore a small hole (about ½ inch in diameter) through the wood table top to allow the saber-saw blade to project down through the table. This hole can be placed anywhere on the wood top so long as it does not come directly above any of the channel braces in the steel table frame. From experience, a location about three inches to the inside of the second hold-down screw (counting from the rear) is ideal. This position allows maximum use of the table-top working surface.

To mount the saber-saw unit, follow these steps:

1. Remove the safety guard and the circular-saw blade (or other cutting tool) from the motor.

2. Place the pulley, provided with the

Fig. 7·1A

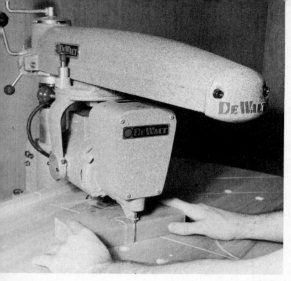

Fig. 7·1B

unit, on the motor shaft (groove toward the motor), then replace and tighten the arbor nut. Check to be sure that the belt is on the pulley in the saber-saw unit. If not, remove the back of the unit by removing the four Phillip's-head screws, slide the belt on the pulley, and replace the back.

3. Hold the saber saw in your right hand and slightly tilt the bottom in toward the motor. Place the belt in the groove on the motor pulley.

4. Hook the bottom lip of the saber saw into the groove in the lower front end of the motor bell (Fig. 7·2). Then slide the top bracket of the unit into place in the safety-guard stud atop the motor. Replace and tighten the wing nut on the guard stud.

5. Align the saber-saw blade with the hole in the wood table top by swinging the radial arm to the left and swiveling the motor yoke to the right. Then lock all controls—arm clamp, yoke clamp, and rip lock.

6. Lower the radial arm by means of the elevating handle until the saber-saw guide barely touches the top surface of the material to be cut.

When saber sawing, the guide fence, in most operations, should be removed from its normal position and placed at the extreme rear of the table.

SABER-SAW BLADES

To operate the saber saw with maximum efficiency, become familiar with the various blades available. For most uses, four blades will do the job. The table below lists various materials and suggests the size of saber-saw blades for cutting them.

Always use the blade with the coarsest teeth that will cut the material cleanly and that will cut the sharpest curve in any pattern you are working on. As you progress with your saber sawing, your experience with various materials and blades will help you in choosing a blade for the particular operation on hand.

Mounting the Blade. To mount a saber-saw blade, turn the machine on and off until you stop the chuck at the bottom of its stroke. Loosen the Allen-head setscrew on the side of the chuck with a

Material	Thickness, inches	Blade size, teeth per inch
Softwood	Up to ½	15 or 20
Softwood	Over ½	7 or 10
Hardwood	Up to ½	15 or 20
Hardwood	Over ½	10 or 15
Nonferrous metal	Up to ⅛	20
Nonferrous metal	Over ⅛	15 or 20
Plastic, ivory, bone, etc.		10, 15, or 20

Fig. 7·2

wrench and insert the blade approximately ⅜ inch into the chuck against the insert, with the teeth pointing downward (Fig. 7·3). Then tighten the chuck setscrews and you are ready to start cutting.

OPERATING THE SABER SAW

Since the prime purpose of the saber saw is to cut curves and patterns, lay out and plan your work before cutting. Except for simple designs that can be sketched directly on the material, it is necessary to make a full-size pattern of work and transfer it to the stock being cut. Be sure you have a clean outline to follow.

For average work, always stand directly in front of the blade with both hands resting comfortably on the table. Guide the work with both hands, applying forward pressure with the thumbs (Fig. 7·4). Make sure the guide finger on the unit always rests lightly on the work.

Where the work is of such length that it will strike the column before the cut is completed, cutting from the side or using an extension table is necessary.

Side cutting requires the motor to be swiveled until the blade of the saber unit is parallel with the guide fence.

The extension table shown in Fig. 7·5 is made of ¾-inch plywood and is clamped to the stationary table top. A ½-inch-diameter hole should be drilled directly under the saw blade when the motor is completely extended on the arm; this allows a capacity of over 27 inches between the blade and the column.

Technique of Cutting. To keep blade breakage at a minimum and to produce perfectly cut work, keep these two things in mind:

1. Do not crowd the blade; that is, do not apply too much pressure as you feed the wood into the blade in an effort to speed up the cutting. Maintain steady, even pressure.

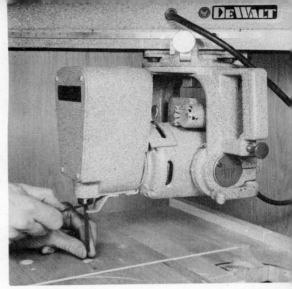

Fig. 7·3

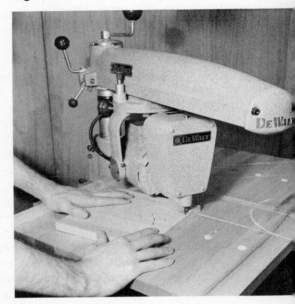

Fig. 7·4

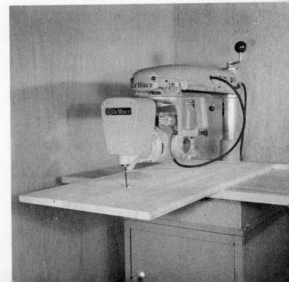

Fig. 7·5

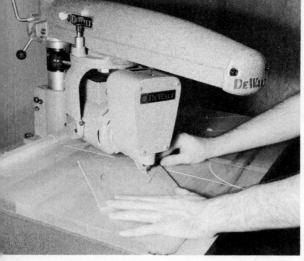

Fig. 7·6

2. When cutting curves, swing the stock so that the blade is at a tangent to the curve at all times. Side pressure need never be applied in order to keep the saw blade cutting on the line or parallel to it.

Frequently, if a dull blade is used to cut thick hardwood, the blade will have a tendency to follow the grain and pull away from a line, no matter how you feed the stock. The remedy is to replace the blade with a sharp one. On most hardwoods and for all metals, a little soap or wax applied to the blade will help the cutting and will keep the blade sharp.

Cutting External Curves. Install the correct blade and lower the radial arm until the guide fingers rest lightly on top of the material (each complete turn of the elevating handle raises or lowers the arm exactly $\frac{1}{8}$ inch). Place the work on the table with your forefinger over it on either side and the other fingers on the table. Turn on the motor and begin to cut. Apply forward pressure with the thumbs. Start in the waste stock and come

up to the layout line at a slight angle, applying as much pressure as necessary to keep the cutting going without vibration (Fig. 7·6).

A smooth cut is obtained only when the work is carefully guided. Do not twist the blade, as it is easily broken. When cutting sharp curves, apply almost no forward pressure and turn the work slowly. Extremely sharp curves can be cut by first making many relief cuts to within $\frac{1}{32}$ inch of the layout line (Fig. 7·7A). The stock will then fall away as the curve is cut. Sharp curves can also be cut by first making several relief cuts (Fig. 7·7B) or by making tangent cuts (Fig. 7·7C).

When it is necessary to cut to the end of a long, thin opening, cut to the corner, back out the blade a short way, and "nibble out" the corner until the work can be turned.

Although a corner may be sharp, the material being cut should never be swung suddenly at a sharp angle; this will result in blade breakage. The cutting of sharp corners can be accomplished by cutting into the waste portion of the material in order to change the direction of the cut.

To cut a square opening from the edge, make straight cuts to the top of the opening on one side, arc across the waste, and back out the blade. Then start at the other side and cut an arc across the waste stock to the top of the other side (Fig. 7·8). Complete the cut by nibbling out the top.

Cutting Internal Openings. With a small boring bit, drill a hole in the waste

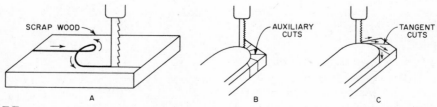

SCRAP WOOD

A

AUXILIARY CUTS

B

TANGENT CUTS

C

Fig. 7·7

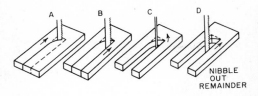

Fig. 7·8

NIBBLE
OUT
REMAINDER

Fig. 7·9

stock large enough for the blade. Sometimes it is wise to make the hole part of the design. For example, if a rectangular opening with rounded corners is needed, bore four holes of the desired radius, one at each corner.

Elevate the radial arm by means of the elevating handle until the end of the saber-saw blade is high enough off the table to allow the stock to pass beneath it. Place the hole you have drilled in the stock directly beneath the blade; lower the arm until the fingers of the guide rest on top of your material. Then turn on the motor and begin to cut (Fig. 7·9A). The cutting technique for internal openings is the same as for external work. The machine should be stopped while freed sections are removed (Fig. 7·9B).

Cutting Circles and Arcs. A circular piece can usually be cut freehand in the same manner as other curves, although it is somewhat more difficult. If many circular pieces are to be cut, make a simple wood jig as shown in Fig. 7·10A. The auxiliary table is made of ¾-inch plywood, and the groove or dado is cut at right angles to the teeth of the blade and parallel with the guide fence. A hardwood or aluminum strip slips into the groove and is flush with the top of the auxiliary table. A sharp pin, brad, or screw is placed at the end of the sliding bar to act as the center point of the arc or circle. It is a good idea also to put a small flathead screw next to the bar so that when

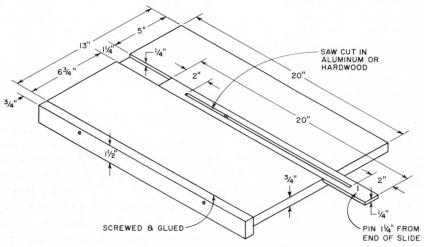

Fig. 7·10A

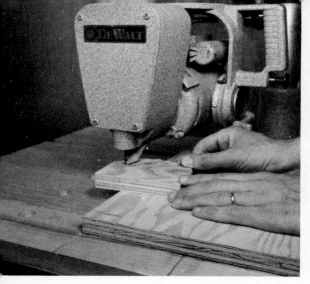

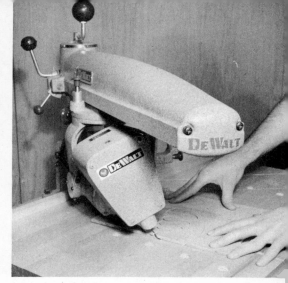

Fig. 7·10B   **Fig. 7·11**

it is tightened down the bar will not move.

The auxiliary table is placed on the right side of the table tight against the guide fence and is clamped to the stationary table top in the front. Place the material on the center point and lower the saber blade until the guide fingers rest lightly on top of the stock. (Remember: The blade must be at right angles to the sliding bar and in line with the front.) Now adjust the pin equal to the radius of the desired circle. Switch on the machine and turn the material slowly as the circle is cut (Fig. 7·10B).

Patterns. With the exception of circles, arcs, or straight lines, most designs to be cut on the saber saw require the use of patterns. Patterns are usually laid out on paper and then are transferred to the stock. If the paper is to be used only once, it can be glued or cemented to the stock. Use rubber cement, mucilage, or shellac.

With rubber cement, apply a thin coat to the back of the pattern and allow it to dry a minute or two. Start by placing the edge of the paper on the stock; then, as you lay the pattern down, smooth it out with your hands. Do not attempt to lay the entire pattern on the stock in one movement.

If mucilage is used, spread the liquid

on the wood only. Apply one coat, allow a short time for it to dry, then apply a second coat before placing the pattern on the stock. Lay the pattern on as described for rubber cement.

If shellac is used, the stock only should be given a coat. When the shellac becomes tacky, which takes only a few minutes, roll the pattern on the stock in the same manner as you would with rubber cement.

When a paper pattern is to be used several times, the outline can be transferred to the stock with carbon paper. Place a sheet of carbon paper on the stock with the prepared side down, and place the pattern over the carbon paper. Hold the pattern in position with several thumbtacks placed outside the areas that are to be used. With pencil or stylus, go over the pattern outline with sufficient pressure to transfer the design through the carbon paper onto the stock. In the absence of carbon paper, the same result can be obtained by coating the back of the pattern with graphite from a soft pencil, then proceeding as outlined above.

If a design is to be used a number of times or if you want to keep the design for future use, it is advisable to prepare a wood pattern. Glue the paper pattern to a piece of ⅛-inch hardwood or ¼-inch

Fig. 7·12

plywood, then cut the outline on the saber saw. The edges should be finished smooth. A pattern of this type becomes a permanent piece of your shop's equipment and can be used indefinitely.

Multiple Cutting. Multiple cutting is done by arranging the pieces in a pile, then applying the pattern to the face of the top piece. The total thickness of such pieces, when piled one on the other, should not exceed 2 inches (the capacity of the saw). The pieces should be held together with several brads or nails driven through the pile. The brads should be outside the areas that are to be used or in the waste wood. Thus, the nails or brads, when removed, will not leave holes in the finished work.

Beveling. A bevel or chamfer can be cut by loosening the wing nut on the stud atop the motor housing and twisting the entire attachment to any desired degree of bevel. You can do the most intricate inside- or outside-beveled scroll work (Fig. 7·11) in the same manner as the external and internal cuts previously de-

scribed. The jig described on page 91 can be used to cut beveled circles.

Cutting Grooves in a Dowel Rod. A dowel rod with slight grooves holds better for gluing because the glue can penetrate along the entire length. Swivel the motor so that the blade is parallel to the guide fence. Tilt the saber unit at an angle of 15 to 20 degrees and place a V block tight against the guide fence. Now place the dowel rod in the V and push it into the saw to the desired depth (Fig. 7·12). By rotating the dowel past the blade, the saw will automatically cut a spiral groove along the rod.

Cutting Plastics and Metals. In general, plastics and light metal can be cut on the saber saw with the same technique as used on wood. Check the proper size of blade for this type of operation on page 88. Thin sheet metal should be shellacked to a wood base to prevent burring on the underside. Take it easy when cutting these materials. Never force them against the blade or cut them when they start to heat up.

Sanding and Filing. The saber-saw attachment can be used for sanding and filing. To convert it to such uses, remove the saber blade, the blade guide (held by two Phillip's-head screws), and chuck insert (the semicircular piece of metal in the chuck). Files and sanding attachments are available at your local power-tool dealer and are set in the chuck. Machine files of this type have their teeth pointing downward to draw the work against the table. Ordinary hand files should not be used for this work.

CHAPTER 8

Lathe in action

WOOD TURNING is a fascinating art—and no wonder, for no other machine work is so responsive to the whim of the craftsman. Under the chisel, the whirling wood is molded like clay on the potter's wheel, and only imagination limits the forms than can be evolved. Table legs, lamp bases, bowls, and candlesticks shaped in countless designs are but a few of the items to be made with a lathe.

The 12-inch lathe shown in Fig. 8·1 is designed as a radial-arm-saw accessory. It is complete and ready to use, taking its driving power from the saw's motor. The lathe also can be operated as a separate unit with any motor $\frac{1}{3}$ horsepower or larger.

LATHE PARTS

Wood lathes are designated according to the maximum diameter of the work that can be swung over the bed—a lathe capable of swinging a 12-inch-diameter disk of wood is called a 12-inch lathe. The lathe in Fig. 8·1 will take work 37 inches long between centers.

The principal parts of a lathe are the headstock, tailstock, and tool rest.

The headstock contains the driving mechanism, the step pulley for changing speeds, and the spindle. The spindle of the headstock lines up exactly with the tailstock spindle. The two main attachments are the spur center, which fits the headstock spindle and is commonly known as the "live center," and the cup center, which fits the tailstock spindle and is known as the "dead center." The work is mounted between these two centers, the spurs of the live center serving as the driving member. The faceplate is fastened to the headstock spindle in certain types of turnings in place of the spurs.

The tailstock assembly can be clamped to the bed at any position. A hand wheel can be turned to move the tailstock spin-

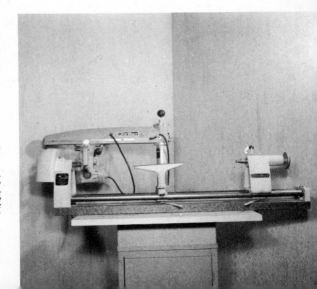

Fig. 8·1

dle in or out 3¼ inches. This spindle is hollow, with a No. 2 Morse taper. The cup center fits into this end.

The tool rest and holder clamp to the bed and can be adjusted to various diameters of work.

TURNING TOOLS

The standard tools used in wood turning are shown in Fig. 8·2. The gouge (A) is used for straight turning and for cutting concave and convex surfaces. A bevel is ground on the convex side at an angle of about 30 degrees.

Skews (B) are used for finished turning, smoothing straight surfaces, cutting shoulders, trimming ends, and cutting V's and beads. They get the name from the fact that the cutting edge is askew, usually at an angle of about 60 degrees. The tool is ground from both sides. The upper end is called the toe and the lower end the heel. Usually two sizes, 1 inch (large) and ½ inch (small), are needed.

The parting tool (C) is slightly wider at the center and narrower at either edge. The point is ground from both sides. It is used for trimming ends and for making and turning to various diameters. When in use, it is held on edge and forced into the work.

The round nose (D) is similar to an ordinary chisel except that it is ground with a semicircular end. The bevel is on

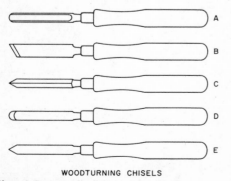

WOODTURNING CHISELS

Fig. 8·2

one side and at an angle of about 45 degrees. It is used for many scraping operations such as cutting coves or large recesses. It is also used on all faceplate work.

The spear or diamond point (E) is ground to a sharp point with a bevel on one side at an angle of about 45 degrees. It is used for scraping operations such as forming sharp V's or corners.

MEASURING TOOLS

For most lathe work, you need a good 1- or 2-foot rule, inside and outside calipers for checking diameters of work, and a divider for laying out circles, especially on faceplate work. Spring-type calipers are best, since they are often applied directly to the revolving stock and must be depended on to hold a set dimension when in this position.

SETTING UP THE LATHE

Because of the unique flexibility built into the radial-arm machine, it is a simple operation to convert it into a wood-turning lathe by following this procedure:

1. Remove the safety guard and the cutting tool from the motor shaft.

2. Swivel the motor to the out-rip position and swing the radial arm to the left 90 degrees and lock securely.

3. Set the lathe on the table top of the radial-arm machine with the base of the lathe tight against the fence. The headstock should be at the left.

4. Set hold-down clamps with the long part of the L's beneath the machine's table top and the short part resting against the bottom of the lathe base. Locate the two carriage bolts in the holes on the base of the lathe, push them through the clamps, and place the wing nuts on the bolts. Then draw the nuts tight against the bottom of the clamps.

5. Place the belt pulley on the motor

shaft, hub side out, and tighten the setscrew in the hub. Place the arbor nut on the shaft and tighten.

6. Position the motor directly behind the headstock and align the headstock pulley with the one on the motor shaft. This may require raising or lowering the motor by means of the elevating handle. When aligned, tighten the rip clamp and carriage arm and attach the drive belt.

SAFETY RULES

While the lathe is one of the safest tools to operate on your safe radial-arm machine, accidents can happen. Before attempting to do any work on a lathe, it is advisable to become familiar with certain precautions for your own safety.

1. Make sure that the wood you are going to turn is free of knots, checks, and other defects. Do not turn stock that is badly cracked. It might come apart when run at high speed. If turning glued stock between centers, it is advisable to cut it a little longer than needed and insert a screw in both ends.

2. Fasten the work securely between the centers or to the faceplates and tighten the two clamps on the tailstock and tool post, because work thrown from the lathe strikes with tremendous force.

3. After tightening all the clamps, revolve the stock by hand to make sure that it clears all points.

4. Remember to put soap or oil on the end running on the dead center, because the friction at this spot will usually burn the wood and its exact center may be lost. It may also become loose and possibly fly out of the lathe.

5. Place the tool rest as close to the work as possible and do not change its position while the lathe is running because you might injure your hand.

6. Never allow any other person to stand near the lathe when it is in operation.

7. Hold all tools firmly and use only sharp ones. Dull tools are always very dangerous to use.

8. Do not turn stock that is too far out of center, as it causes excessive vibration and may be thrown from the lathe.

9. Plane off any sharp edges of large-diameter stock, because it will run smoother and prevent large splinters from flying off the stock.

10. Do not screw a faceplate part way on to the live spindle and then turn on the power, since it will generally cause the faceplate to jam very hard against the live spindle, and it will be difficult to remove it.

11. Do not run the lathe at a high speed, especially not until the stock has been rounded off. In general, stock up to 3 inches in diameter may run at full speed, or about 3,150 rpm; from 3 to 6 inches in diameter, at 2,100 rpm; and more than 6 inches in diameter, at 1,260 to 1,575 rpm. The slower operating speeds are by far the safest to use.

12. It is especially important that your sleeves be tight, your necktie off, and that you wear no loose clothing when working the lathe.

SPINDLE TURNING ON THE LATHE

Spindle turning or turning between centers means the turning of all work held between the live and dead centers. This is the principal type of wood turning, as typified by table and chair legs, lamp stems, etc. The turning of a spindle can be done with either a scraping or cutting technique.

The scraping method is the simplest and easiest for the beginner to learn. All the tools are used as scraping tools, and the wood is removed by wearing away the fibers. It does not produce as smooth a surface, but with sanding it is very satisfactory. For the operator who makes only an occasional piece on the wood lathe, this method can be recommended. All faceplate work is done by the scraping method.

With the cutting or paring method, the wood fibers are sheared off. This requires considerably more practice. If you plan to do a good deal of wood turning, it will pay to learn this method. Of the basic operations described in this chapter, the scraping method will be discussed first.

Select a piece of wood of the desired kind. Cut a piece slightly larger than the diameter to be turned and about 1 inch longer than needed. If the stock measures more than 3 inches square, cut it into an octagon shape on the radial-arm saw or jointer.

Locating Center Points. If the center points on the ends of the stock are not properly located, a considerable amount of vibration will result, and it will be impossible to make an accurate turning.

To locate the exact center point on the end of square stock, draw diagonal lines across the end (Fig. 8·3A). On round material determine the center point quickly with a pair of calipers or dividers (Fig. 8·3B). If the stock is lopsided, the center can be found by laying it on a bench and scribing the ends with a pair of dividers as shown in Fig. 8·3C.

Mounting the Stock. To make mountings more easily, make two diagonal saw cuts across the end that is to be at the headstock of the lathe. If the wood is extremely hard, saw a kerf about ⅛ inch deep across each corner and drill a small center hole, 1/16 inch in diameter and ⅛ inch deep, in either end for insertion of the centers. In soft woods, mark the center with a prick punch or scratch awl.

Remove the spur center from the headstock spindle by loosening the Allen-head screws. With a soft-faced mallet drive the spur of the headstock into the saw cut at the center point (Fig. 8·4A). Never drive the piece of wood against the headstock of the lathe by hammering on the far end. This will damage the bearing on the lathe and in time will knock the headstock

out of correct alignment. Replace the spur center on the headstock spindle and tighten the setscrews.

Lubricate the dead center of the tailstock with oil, or if the stain is objectionable, fill the cup with soap, paraffin, or other solid lubricant so that the stock will not be burned by the friction on the dead center (Fig. 8·4B).

Move the tailstock of the lathe so that its point of dead center is approximately ½ inch from the end of the stock. Secure the tailstock in place by tightening the adjusting wrench. Then, continue by turning the handwheel of the tailstock so that when the dead center enters the stock it will be set in so firmly that the work cannot be turned by hand. Turn the handwheel in the opposite direction to loosen it just enough so that the work can now be turned by hand. Tighten the dead-center clamp at the top of the tailstock to hold the stock firmly in position.

Adjusting the Tool Rest. The proper location of the tool rest is the last preliminary operation before starting the actual turning. The tool rest should be adjusted so that its top is ⅛ to ¼ inch above the center. The top of the tool rest should be parallel to the stock and about ⅛ inch away from the farthest projecting edge of the material being turned. Turn the stock by hand to be sure that it has the proper amount of clearance. Check that all clamps and adjusting wrenches are tight and all necessary adjustments made before turning on the motor switch on the radial arm.

Lathe Speeds. Generally speaking, the larger the work, the slower the speed.

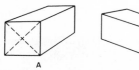

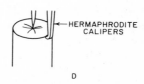

HERMAPHRODITE CALIPERS

A   B   C   D

Fig. 8·3

Turning large work at excessive speed is very dangerous and should never be attempted. Suitable speeds for various size turnings have been established with regard to both safety and procedure, and these should be followed. The four-step pulleys on the radial-arm lathe provide four speeds, which are adequate for all your turning jobs. Position 1 (the largest diameter) gives a speed of 1,260 rpm, position 2 gives 1,575 rpm, position 3 gives 2,100 rpm, and position 4 (the smallest diameter on the lathe pulley) gives 3,150 rpm.

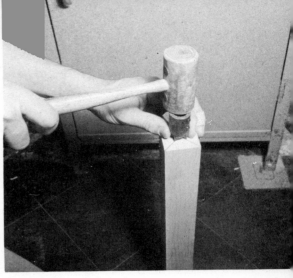

Fig. 8·4A

Diameter	Speed, rpm		
of work, inches	Roughing cut	General cutting	Finishing
Under 3	1,575	2,100	3,150
3–6	1,260	1,575	2,100
6–8	1,260	1,575	1,575
Over 8	1,260	1,260	1,260

Shaping Square Stock to a Cylinder. The first step in the process of shaping a rectangular piece of stock into cylindrical form on the lathe is called roughing. This process consists of cutting off the square edges of the material until the piece is approximately cylindrical.

Take a position in front of the lathe with the left side turned a little nearer to the lathe than the right. Take an easy position that permits you to sway from side to side. Start the lathe, but not at its highest speed, and proceed to round off the piece with a 1-inch gouge. If you are right-handed, hold the gouge in your left hand, using whichever of the following methods is most suited to you:

1. Grasp the gouge about an inch from the cutting end, with the thumb on the inside and the other fingers around the outside or convex side. The index finger, then, will act as a stop against the tool rest (Fig. 8·5A).

or

2. Place the hand over the concave side of the gouge, with the thumb under-

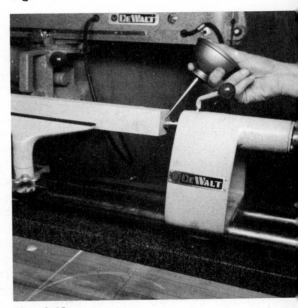

Fig. 8·4B

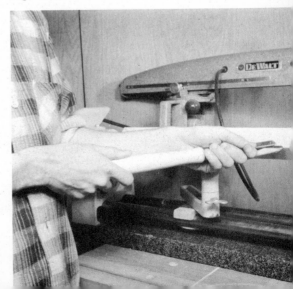

Fig. 8·5A

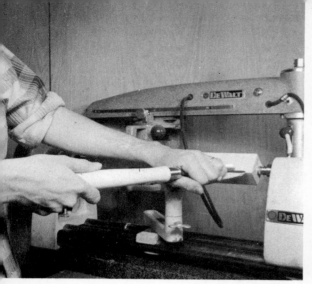
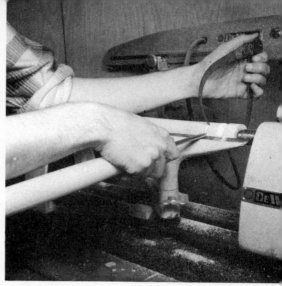

Fig. 8·5B   **Fig. 8·6**

neath. The wrist must be bent to act as a stop against the tool rest (Fig. 8·5B).

Hold the handle of the turning tool firmly in the right hand. Place the convex side of the gouge against the tool rest about 2 inches from the dead center. (Never start a cut at the end of the stock; the cutting tool is apt to catch and be forcibly thrown from your hand). The index finger or your wrist should be held firmly against the rest and the cutting tool against the top. Twist the turning tool slightly to the right and force it into the revolving stock until cutting begins. The beveled edge should be tangent to the cylinder. Then push the tool slowly toward the tailstock. Start the second cut several inches to the left of the first and continue in the direction of the first cut until both meet. When rounding off the material, do not take long cuts; large chips or slivers of wood are apt to fly off, which could cause injury to you and to the material.

After each cut, move the tool several inches more toward the headstock and repeat. When the cylinder is formed to within 2 inches of the headstock, twist the tool to the left, pushing it toward the headstock. At first the cutting will be done only on the edges, then gradually on the whole cylinder. It is easy to tell if the stock is round by laying a tool lightly against the revolving surface.

When making a roughing cut, do not attempt to shape the material to a perfect cylindrical form of the required dimension. When roughing, occasionally check the dimensions of the cylinder with the calipers. Continue to move the gouge back and forth from right to left on the tool rest until the entire piece of stock is cylindrical in form and approximately $\frac{1}{8}$ inch larger than the largest diameter of the turning. Then turn off the motor.

The next series of cuts, called sizing cuts, are made with a parting chisel. Move the belt to the proper pulley to obtain the proper speed (see page 99). Readjust the position of the tool rest to $\frac{1}{8}$ inch from the cylinder and tighten in place. Adjust the calipers to a diameter $\frac{1}{16}$ inch greater than that required for the finished work. This allowance has to be made for the finishing cuts and final sanding.

With the calipers held in the left hand and the parting chisel in the right (Fig. 8·6) start the lathe. Using the parting tool, cut a narrow groove in the stock several inches from dead center. Take light, thin shavings and do not exert too great a pressure on the chisel. As the work progresses, check the depth of cuts made with the calipers. Stop cutting when the leg of the calipers passes over the cut without any pressure. Repeat the operation at intervals of approximately one inch over the entire length of the work. These grooves are sizing or parting cuts.

Smoothing and cutting the cylinder to the required dimension is the final operation. This is called the finishing cut. When making this cut on the lathe by the scraping method, use a large skew or a square-nosed chisel (Fig. 8·7*A*). Use the recommended speed for this job. Hold the cutting edge parallel to the cylinder and force it into the stock until the scraping begins. Then move it from one side to the other. Always start the scraping some distance in from the ends to prevent the tool from catching and splitting the wood. Check occasionally with an outside caliper until the finished size is obtained.

For the cutting or paring method, use a large-size skew. Place the skew on its side with the cutting edge slightly above and beyond the cylinder. Start at a point 2 to 3 inches in from the end. Hold the side of the tool firmly against the tool rest. Slowly draw the skew back until the cutting edge is over the cylinder at a point about halfway between the heel and toe (Fig. 8·7*B*). Keep the edge at an angle of about 40 to 60 degrees with the axis of the work. Be careful not to catch the toe of the tool in the revolving cylinder. Tip the skew slightly until the cutting edge can be forced into the wood.

Then push the skew along toward the tailstock, taking a shearing cut. Reverse the direction and cut toward the headstock.

The major difficulty of the beginner is that he holds the tool at too great an angle to the work, thus making the tool dig in; or he holds it in one position too long, resulting in too small a diameter.

Cutting a Shoulder. When the stock has been turned to a perfect cylindrical form of the required dimensions, it is ready for turning or forming to any desired shape or combination of shapes that constitutes a finished turning.

Make a full-size dimensional drawing of the desired turning. Then determine the points where the shoulder or sizing cuts are to be made and mark them on the drawing. With a pair of dividers, transfer these points from the drawing and locate them on the cylinder. Place the point of a pencil on each of the marks made by the dividers and revolve the cylinder by hand to mark the entire circumference. Adjust the calipers for a diameter $\frac{1}{16}$ inch larger than required, as shown in the drawing or pattern, at the point where the first shoulder or sizing cut is to be made.

Place the narrow edge of a parting chisel on the tool rest, with the point above the line of the centers. Locate the

Fig. 8·7A   **Fig. 8·7B**

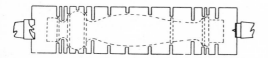

Fig. 8·8

point on one of the pencil marks on the turning, start the lathe, raise the handle of the parting chisel, and push the point into the stock. Check the accuracy of the sizing or shoulder cut by holding the previously adjusted calipers in the groove that has been cut. Continue cutting until the calipers slip easily over the stock. Adjust the calipers for each of the subsequent shoulder cuts and proceed in the same way. A typical turning with the necessary shoulder cuts is illustrated in Fig. 8·8.

To cut a shoulder when using the cutting method, hold the small skew on edge with the toe down and the heel up. Hold the skew at a slight angle so that one bevel is at a right angle to the cylinder. Force the skew into the wood a little at a time; then remove it and cut a half V groove until the smaller diameter is reached (Fig. 8·9A). Rough-cut the smaller diameter with a small gouge. Then place the skew on its side and trim to the smaller diameter. Use the heel of the skew to cut to the corner (Fig. 8·9B).

Cutting a Long Taper. The gouge or round-nose chisel is used to make taper cuts by the scraping method. Cut from the larger to the smaller end of the taper. With the tool, cut it down to within about ⅛ inch of the entire depth of the shoulder cuts previously made with the parting or sizing chisel, using the same procedure as described for forming the stock to cylindrical form. Finish with a skew or square-nose chisel. As the cutting progresses, check the work with the calipers set from the full-size drawing.

The skew chisel is used to make taper cuts by the cutting method. Place this chisel on the tool rest at an angle of approximately 60 degrees to the surface of the stock and slightly above it. After starting the lathe, draw the chisel back just a little, until the heel starts the cut, then draw it slightly farther down and back to the original position. Repeat this procedure until the actual cutting is being done by the heel of the chisel. The entire taper cut can be made with the heel.

Cutting Large Rectangular Recesses. First, turn the cylinder to the largest finished diameter as previously discussed. Then hold a rule on the tool rest and mark the location of the recesses. With a parting tool cut a groove at the end of each recess to the desired diameter about

Fig. 8·9A   **Fig. 8·9B**

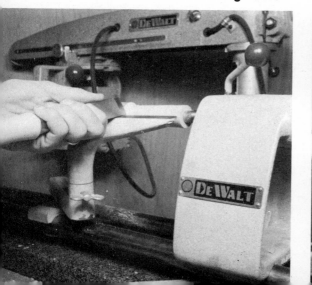

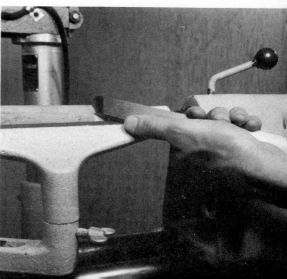

$\frac{1}{32}$ to $\frac{1}{16}$ inch inside the layout line.
Scrape the recess to size, using a gouge,
and trim the shoulders of the recesses
with the toe of a skew. Finish the recesses
with a skew chisel.

Cutting a Line. The simplest ornament
for a spindle turning is an incised line.
After the cylinder has been cut, set the
tool rest about level with the lathe center,
touch a lead pencil against the revolving
work. Rest the skew on its edge with the
toe down and the handle lowered. Lift the
handle until the point digs in and there is
the incised line. A shallow line can be
made when the cylinder is scraped with
a diamond-point chisel laid flat on the
tool rest.

Enlarged, the line becomes a V groove.
Simply hold the diamond-point tool flat
and force it into the wood until the desired width of the V is obtained (Fig.
8·10). As the V angle on this tool is
rather blunt, you may want to grind a
sharper angle—possibly 90 or 80 degrees
—which will also enable you to work in
close quarters when scraping ends of
spindles or shoulders. Of course, a scraped
V groove can be blunted by swinging the
handle from right to left, care being taken
to prevent scoring opposite sides with the
point.

To cut a V by the paring method, mark
the center and edges of the V cut with a
pencil. Hold a skew on edge with the heel
down; then force the skew into the stock
at the center of the V cut. Use a slight
pump-handle action (Fig. 8·11). Work
from one side of the V, using the heel of
the skew to do the cutting. Continue to
force the skew into the center of the cut
and cut one side of the V to the correct
depth. Then cut the opposite side in a
similar manner.

Cutting Coves. The round-nose chisel
is used to make cove or concave cuts by
the scraping method. After making the
parting or shoulder cuts on the cylinder,

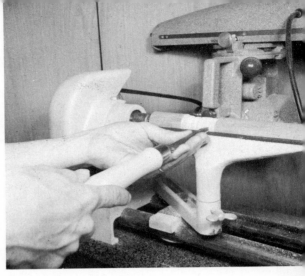

Fig. 8·10

and checking dimensions with the calipers, place the round-nose chisel flat on
the tool rest with the bevel side down.
Hold the tool slightly above the center of
the work at a right angle to its axis. Start
the lathe and begin the cutting at the top.
Complete the cove cut by using light cuts
with the chisel. Work down on each side
of the cut previously made by the parting
tool, to within $\frac{1}{16}$ inch of the required
depth. The remaining stock can be removed by smoothing cuts with the chisel.
Swing the tool from one side to the other,
using the tool rest as a fulcrum point, until the desired depth is reached.

A gouge is used for making cove cuts
by the cutting method. Hold the chisel in
a horizontal position with the hollow part
up. Start the cut at the top. Roll and push
the tool forward simultaneously to the
right and down toward the bottom of the
cut. Start the cut from the high point in
the design and work to the lowest point.

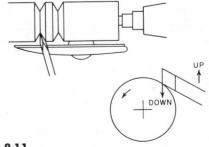

Fig. 8·11

Then reverse the position of the tool and start the cut at the top of the other side. The bottom of each side must then be cut alternately, with the cutting chisel repeatedly shifted from right to left until the desired shape of the cove cut has been made.

Cutting Beads. Either the spear-point or parting chisel is used for bead or convex cutting by the scraper method. Mark the location of the beads on the cylinder previously described (page 101). With either chisel make the cut to the required depth. Hold the spear-point chisel at a slight angle to the work to round out the corners of the bead. The parting tool can be used instead of the spear-point chisel when the beads on the turning are not close together.

In the cutting method, which is more popular than the scraping method for this operation, a skew is used to cut the beads. Mark the position of each bead with a line indicating the ends and centers of the beads. Begin the cut as you would a V cut, using the toe of the skew to start it, with the heel doing most of the cutting. You should start quite high on the cylinder at the center of the bead and turn the tool in the same arc as the bead, at the same time drawing it backhand and moving it to a vertical position. If the tool is not turned as the cut is made, the heel will dig into the next bead. When one side of the bead is complete, reverse the chisel procedure to cut the other side of the bead.

Cutting Reverse Curves. Reverse curves can be treated as combinations of beads and coves. The skew chisel, in turning the convex parts, is rolled on its edge and then rolled back to the flat position as the curve flows into the cove. Use the heel of the skew to clean the angles against isolated beads and shoulders, and the point in narrow places. A parting tool is useful for dressing narrow fillets and small coves.

Square Sections. When the turning has a square section such as a table leg, the stock must be accurately centered, since any error will show at the shoulder where the round meets the square. The fingers must be kept out of the way of the flying corners, and the tool rest must clean them at all times. Square the ends with the small skew chisel, toe down, using light cuts to prevent splintering the face of the square. Then cut the square beads, with the toe thrust in at a slight angle with the axis and the handle swung gradually to the right angle.

Cutting Stock to Length. After the cylinder is worked to the correct diameter, mark the length with a pencil.

When using the scraping method, force a parting tool into the stock exactly at the layout line at the tailstock and cut to a ⅛-inch diameter. Repeat at the headstock end. If you wish to cut the end off completely at the headstock, hold the parting tool in your right hand and place your left hand loosely around the revolving stock. Continue to force the parting tool into the wood until the cylinder drops off. Remember to allow enough wood at the headstock end to keep from hitting the spur center. (This procedure can also be done with the small skew held on its side as shown in Fig. 8·12.) Never cut the stock off at the tailstock end, as the work might be thrown.

For the cutting method, hold a small skew on edge with the heel up and with the toe down. Then turn it at an angle so that one bevel is parallel to the cut to be made. Force the skew in slowly; then back it out and cut a half V in the waste stock. It is of the utmost importance to keep one cutting edge of the skew parallel to the wood, since it is easy for the tool to "hog in" and damage the stock.

Make this cut at both ends. With either method, trim off the waste stock on the ends with a saw and sand smooth.

You can remove a live center by driving a dowel or a soft metal rod through the spur center. The dead center is removed simply by backing off the tailstock wheel until the center is loosened and can be taken out of the cup center of the tailstock.

Making a Turning. Any spindle turning legs, lamp bases, and similar objects is simply making a combination of the individual cuts previously described. The work is roughed with the gouge to a maximum-size cylinder and is then given one running cut with the skew to make it smooth enough to take pencil marks. The required dimensions along the turning are set off with a pencil and ruler. If the pencil marks are made about half an inch long, they will be visible when the work is at top speed. Marking can also be done while the work is rotating, using rule and pencil, scratch marker, or crayon.

Templates are useful when you must make identical turnings such as table legs. They can be made of sheet metal, cardboard or, as shown in Fig. 8·13, thin plywood, cardboard, or hardboard. (Some craftsmen make use of a plywood pattern by manipulating the chisel directly over the pattern to produce the required shape.) The spacing of the different sections is marked on the straightedge of the plywood template with brads. By pressing the edge with the brads against the rough-turned rotating piece, all divisions can be marked at once.

FACEPLATE TURNING

When the work to be turned cannot be held between the live and the dead center, a faceplate is used. All cutting in faceplate work is done by scraping; any attempt to use a cutting technique on the edge grain of large work will result in a hogging, gouging cut which may tear the chisel out of your hands. The work is held to the faceplate by means of screws.

Mounting the Work. Before attaching the faceplate, remove all surplus wood from the material by drawing a circle on it slightly larger in diameter than desired for the finished work. Cut this circle out with the saber saw. Make sure that there are no checks or defects in the wood which will crack or split during the turning. Center the work accurately when screwing it to the faceplate. If the material is hardwood, drill small holes in it to start the screws. Use short, heavy flatheaded screws that will enter the work not more than $\frac{3}{8}$ to $\frac{1}{2}$ inch. Make sure

Fig. 8·12   **Fig. 8·13**

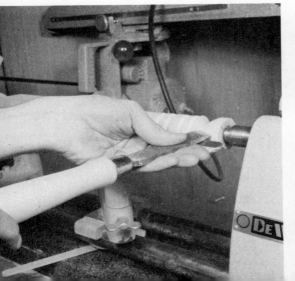

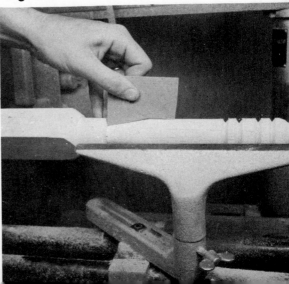

that the work is securely fastened to the faceplate and that the ends of the screws will not come in contact with the cutting chisel.

When the shape of the finished piece is such that contact with the screws cannot be avoided, the work must be backed up with a disk of the same size. Bore and countersink the holes for the screws at points where they will not come in contact with the chisel. Screw this extra disk or backing plate on the work and attach it to the faceplate (Fig. 8·14).

Place the faceplate on the headstock spindle and tighten the setscrew. Move the tool rest so that its top edge is about ⅛ inch above the center of the revolving turning; then lock the adjusting wrench.

Simple Turning. With the lathe rotating at a slow speed, use a square-nose, skew,

or gouge cutting tool to true the face. Hold it on its side with the cutting edge parallel to the front of the cylinder. Start at the center and take a scraping cut toward the outside nearest yourself (Fig. 8·15). Take several cuts until the stock is the correct thickness. Hold a rule or square against the face surface and make sure that it is true.

Locate the center of the stock. Adjust the dividers to half the largest diameter that must be turned and mark a circle around the face of the work. Readjust the tool rest until it is parallel to the edge of the stock. Use the same tool to turn the edge until it is the correct diameter (Fig. 8·16).

With the dividers mark the location of the recess or bead on the face surface of the cylinder. Readjust the tool rest across the face and turn to shape, using various kinds of tools (Fig. 8·17). For a simple recess, a round-nose tool is usually preferred. For cutting a bead, choose a square-nose or skew. Sometimes the tool rest must be readjusted at an angle to the work to do certain kinds of turning. A spear-point chisel is often used to cut a sharp shoulder on the face of the work (Fig. 8·18).

Deep Boring. The deep boring required for bowls, boxes, and similar faceplate

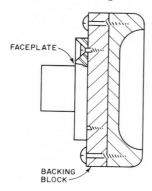

FACEPLATE

BACKING
BLOCK

Fig. 8·14 (above)   Fig. 8·15 (below)   Fig. 8·16

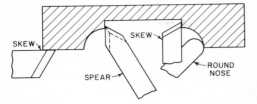

Fig. 8·17

Fig. 8·18

work is not difficult, but it is slow. To speed up this operation, rough out the recess by drilling a series of holes to the required depth with a drill. If this is not done, drill a center starting hole at least. The cutting tools used for deep boring are the skew, round-nose, and spear-point chisel. The skew is used for sliding down the edge of the hole and can also be used with a series of jab contacts to rough the wood at the bottom of the recess. For the bottom cuts, use a round-nose chisel, starting at the center, with overlapping short strokes directed toward the center. The tool rest should be positioned at an angle into the hole to provide maximum support to the chisel. The accuracy of the boring can be checked with a combination square held against a parallel edge spanning the work opening. The final finish cuts down the side should be made with a skew. Any shoulders on the deep boring can be made with the spear-point chisel.

Turning Both Sides of the Stock. Many faceplate jobs require that both sides of an object be turned—for example, a simple bowl. For work of this type, it is generally objectionable to have the screw hole in the stock. Therefore, cut a piece of stock slightly larger than the finished bowl. Cut another piece of scrap stock thick enough to fasten screws into. Glue these two pieces together with a piece of paper between them for easy separation. Next fasten the stock to the faceplate, installing the screws in the scrap piece. Then place the faceplate on the headstock spindle and tighten the setscrew.

Turn the front or top and the edge of the bowl. When this is complete, do all the sanding operations necessary to finish the top. If mineral oil is to be used as a finish, apply this now (see page 108 for application instructions). Then separate the scrap stock from the finished piece by driving a sharp chisel between them.

In order to hold the bowl on the face side, make a simple wood chuck. Cut a piece of scrap stock slightly larger than the diameter of the bowl. Fasten this to the faceplate. Turn the cylinder and cut a recess in this scrap stock so that the bowl will just fit, with a tight pressed fit.

Press the stock into the chuck and turn to the back side. The bottom side should be finished in the same manner as the top side. The work can usually be removed by pulling it out. If necessary, the recessed edge can be cut away to release the bowl.

FINISHING LATHE WORK

There are several methods of finishing turned parts. Often the parts are removed from the lathe and the finish is applied as a part of the completed furniture or other work.

Sanding Turnings. To sandpaper turnings on the lathe, medium, fine, extra fine, and very fine sandpaper are usually used. Cut strips of sandpaper about 1 inch wide.

These must be held in both hands, with the right hand above and the left below the turning. To avoid cutting grooves, keep the sandpaper in motion while the work is turning in the lathe. Fold the sandpaper and use the edge of the fold to get into the bottom of a V-shaped cut. Always remove the tool rest and adjust the lathe to a high spindle speed. Never wrap the paper around the work. For sanding the inside of a bowl, hold the pad of paper over your fingers and follow the contour of the bowl.

Frictional Polish. A handful of fine shavings taken from the work is cupped in the hand and pressed against the revolving spindle. This will bring out some measure of shine on the work, but it is usually done only as an initial step before some other form of finishing.

Oil Finish. This entails the use of hot boiled linseed oil as the only polishing medium. The oil is brushed on and the surface thoroughly rubbed with a soft cloth as the lathe revolves. Considerable rubbing is necessary to dry the oiled surface entirely.

For small bowls and accessories used for food, mineral oil should be substituted for the linseed oil.

French Polishing. Mix equal quantities of 4-pound commercial shellac and wood alcohol. Make a pad of cheesecloth about 2 inches square. Dip this into the diluted shellac and then put several drops of a good grade of machine oil on the pad. Hold the pad lightly on the revolving turning, keeping it in contact with all parts of the work and in motion all the time. The heat generated by friction will harden and glaze the shellac so that it becomes necessary from time to time to redip the pad. Each time the pad is dipped into the shellac, additional oil must also be dropped on the pad. Continue in this way until the desired finish is obtained.

Wax Finish. Apply paste wax to the work with your fingers or a cloth. Allow about 10 minutes for the wax to flat out. To polish, run the lathe at low speed and hold a piece of soft cloth against the revolving spindle. A second coat can be applied 1 hour after the first. Harder waxes can also be used—beeswax, paraffin wax, or carnauba wax. These are in lump form; apply them by pressing the lump against the revolving spindle so that the wax will become soft and adhere to the turning. After the piece is evenly coated, rub with a soft cloth. If a higher polish is desired, repeat the entire operation.

To finish turnings with stain or any of the commercial varnishes or paints, see Chapter 14.

CHAPTER 9

Disk, belt, and drum-sander operations

COMPARING power sanding with hand sanding is like comparing a new car with a horse and buggy. Both of them will get you where you are going, but the power sander, like the car, does the job a lot faster and easier.

With the versatile radial arm, you have a choice of three major types of power sanders—disk, belt, and drum. Each type has its advantages and uses. But unlike ordinary sanders, the attachments shown in Fig. 9·1 allow you to take full advantage of the maneuverability and flexibility of the radial-arm machine. Attached directly to the motor arbor, they can be tilted, swiveled, or elevated, and absolute accuracy is always possible.

ABRASIVES

When choosing the proper abrasive, there are five things to consider: type of abrasive material, grit size, backing, type of coating, and form.

Types of Abrasives. For power sanding there are four types of abrasive materials to choose from: flint, garnet, aluminum oxide, and silicon carbide.

Flint, the oldest of modern abrasives, is a soft, yellowish natural quartz mineral. It is cheap but has little efficiency as compared to other abrasives. Flint paper is good for removing old paint and for other jobs requiring quantity rather than quality.

Garnet, a rubylike gemstone, is the hardest of natural abrasives. It is rated at 6.5 to 7.5 on the Mohs hardness scale, where the diamond rates 10. Garnet paper is used in most home workshops as the basic paper for finishing wood.

Aluminum oxide is a synthetic abrasive made from bauxite, coke, and iron filings in an electric furnace. It is very hard (8.8 to 9 on the Mohs scale) and tough. Aluminum oxide paper is fast becoming the most widely used all-around paper. It is gray-brown in color.

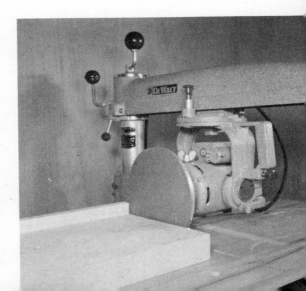

Fig. 9·1A

Fig. 9·1B **Fig. 9·1C**

Silicon carbide, another synthetic made of coke and sand, is the hardest of all abrasives manufactured today—rated at 9.5 to 9.9 on the Mohs scale. But it is very brittle and can be used only in certain applications (see page 111). Silicon carbide paper appears dark gray to black.

Grit Size. This is determined by the number of grains which, end to end, equal 1 inch. Until recently, grain sizes were referred to by a complicated numbering system. To simplify this situation, many manufacturers label their papers as fine, medium, coarse, etc. The table below

lists the numbers and equivalent names.

Backing. Paper-backed abrasives are generally used for hand sanding. Of the six weights of paper available, the only one suitable for machine sanding is the heaviest weight—Type E. This is satisfactory for disk, spindle, or drum sanders, but should never be used on any form of power-driven belt sander.

There are two weights of cloth backings available to the home craftsman. The heaviest (Type X) is drill or twill, a linen or cotton fabric with a diagonal weave. An abrasive with this backing is

Name designations, all types of paper	Numbering system—types of paper		
	Aluminum oxide or silicon oxide	Garnet	Flint
Superfine	10/0—400	10/0—400	
Extra fine	9/0—320	9/0—320	
	8/0—280	8/0—280	
	7/0—240	7/0—240	
Very fine	6/0—220	6/0—220	4/0
	5/0—180	5/0—180	3/0
	4/0—150	4/0—150	2/0
Fine	3/0—120	3/0—120	
	2/0—100	2/0—100	0
Medium	0 — 80	0 — 80	1/2
	1/2— 60	1/2— 60	1
Coarse	1 — 50	1 — 50	1 1/2
	1 1/2— 40	1 1/2— 40	2
Very coarse	2 — 36	2 — 36	2 1/2
	2 1/2— 30	2 1/2— 30	3
	3 — 24	3 — 24	

recommended for the belt sander. A lighter-weight cloth backing (Type J), which is jean, is preferable to a heavy-weight paper backing for disk, spindle, or drum sanders when used on a production basis. It is also suitable for light work on the belt sander, particularly if the sanding requires a pliable backing.

Type of Coating. There are two types of coating—closed and open. Closed-coat papers have tightly packed abrasive grains that cover the entire surface. The grains on open-coat papers cover 50 to 70 per cent of the surface, leaving open spaces between the grains.

Closed-coat papers are durable and fast cutting, but have the disadvantage of clogging under certain conditions. Open-coated abrasives are not so durable, but they are useful for finishing certain surfaces such as soft or gummy woods, paint and other finishes, and soft metals and plastics where the abrasive dust tends to clog the disk or belt.

Forms of Abrasives. Abrasive-coated materials can be obtained in sheets, rolls, disks, drums, and belts.

The most common *sheet* form measures 9 by 11 inches and is generally used for hand sanding. It can also be cut into disk form for use on power-driven sanding disks.

ABRASIVE SELECTION CHART
FOR POWER SANDERS

| Abrasive | Use | Grit | | |
		Rough	Medium	Fine
Aluminum oxide	Hardwood	2 1/2–1 1/2	1/2–1/0	2/0–3/0
	Aluminum	1 1/2	1/2–0	2/0
	Copper	1 1/2–1	0–2/0	2/0–3/0
	Steel	3–2 1/2	1/2–0	2/0
	Ivory	1/2–0	2/0–3/0	2/0–8/0
	Plastics	1–0	3/0–5/0	7/0
Garnet	Hardwood	2 1/2–1 1/2	1/2–1/0	2/0–3/0
	Softwood	1 1/2–1	1/0	2/0
	Composition board	1 1/2–1	1/2	1/0
	Plastics	1–0	3/0–5/0	7/0
	Horn	1 1/2	1/2–0	2/0–3/0
Silicon carbide	Glass	1–1/2	2/0–3/0	4/0–8/0
	Cast iron	3–2 1/2	1/2–0	2/0
	Ceramics	1/2	3/0	4/0–8/0
	Gemstones	1–1/2	0–3/0	4/0–8/0
	Steel	3–2 1/2	1/2–0	2/0
	Plastics	1–0	3/0–5/0	7/0
Flint	Removing paint or old finishes	3–1 1/2	1/2–1/0	

Grit Equivalents

8/0—280	5/0—180	2/0—100	1—50	2 1/2—30
7/0—240	4/0—150	0— 80	1 1/2—40	3—24
6/0—220	3/0—120	1/2— 60	2—36	

Abrasives are also obtainable in *rolls* of various widths, but these are seldom used by the home craftsman except for cutting disks.

For power-driven sanding disks, most abrasive manufacturers can supply *pre-cut disks* in diameters from 1 inch upward. These can be obtained with paper or cloth backing coated with aluminum oxide, garnet, or silicon carbide. Flint-coated abrasive can be obtained in paper-backed disks only.

Abrasives in *belt* form for the belt sander are available in both paper and cloth backing coated with garnet, aluminum oxide, or silicon carbide. Because of the constant flexing of belts as they travel over the drums, a cloth backing will stand up much better than paper.

Spindle or drum sanding machines require a *sleeve* of a diameter equal to that of the spindle over which it is slipped. Sleeves or drums are available in the same abrasives and backing as belts.

BASIC RULES OF POWER SANDING

1. Always select the grade of abrasive carefully for the job you want. See Abrasive Selection Chart, page 111.

2. Always sand with the grain of the wood.

3. Do all the cutting operations before sanding. Except for special jobs, the sander is designed to finish the surface of the work, not to shape it.

4. Apply enough pressure to complete the work. The tendency of the beginner is to press too hard and attempt too big a pass, thus cutting scratches in the surface.

5. At frequent intervals clean off the abrasive paper or cloth with a brush.

6. Always sand surfaces square. The tendency in sanding is to round all edges and surfaces. Do not spoil the accuracy of your work by careless sanding.

7. "Break" all edges slightly to prevent splintering. The corners should be rounded to about the diameter of the lead in a pencil.

MOUNTING THE DISK SANDER

Remove the safety guard, saw blade, arbor nut, and two arbor collars from the arbor shaft. Replace the two arbor collars (⅜-inch one first and recessed sides together), then place the disk plate on the shaft. Place a wrench on the flat of the arbor shaft to hold it, and tighten the disk plate by turning it counterclockwise (Fig. 9·2).

The abrasive disk must be cemented or glued to the plate. Any good glue may be used. Spread glue on the metal plate, then set the abrasive disk against it. When glue is used, a wood disk of ¾-inch stock the same diameter as the plate will have to be placed over the abrasive so that clamps may be applied. The clamps should remain in place until the glue has set.

There are two types of special adhesives that can be used to secure abrasive disks to the metal plate. These eliminate the need of clamps and permit immediate use of the disk. The first type comes in stick form and is applied to the disk while it is warm. First, place a piece of softwood firmly against the disk as it is turning and keep it in place about 30 seconds. The friction-generated heat is enough to melt the adhesive. Hold the adhesive stick against the revolving disk (Fig. 9·3), moving it from the edge to the center until a smooth, even coat has been

Fig. 9·2

applied. After the metal has been coated, stop the machine and press the abrasive against the metal disk, using hand pressure or a roller.

The second type of adhesive, a viscous liquid, is applied directly from the can to the disk. Spread it smoothly over the entire surface. Then apply the abrasive material to the plate and press it tight with hand pressure or a roller.

The ease with which an old disk can be removed depends on the adhesive you used. If the stick or liquid adhesive was used, just pull off the old abrasive sheet from the plate. A new sheet may be applied by renewing the adhesive coating, but it is good practice to clean the disk first. Remove stick adhesive by dampening with alcohol. The cement can be rubbed off cleanly with the fingers. If other types of adhesive were used, the major portion of the disk can be removed by working the blade of a knife between the disk and the metal, then pulling off the disk. The surface of the metal should be cleaned of all traces of glue and backing material.

OPERATING THE DISK SANDER

The abrasive used on the disk sander will depend upon the work. Garnet can be used for all types of woods (both soft and hard), while aluminum oxide is rec-ommended for hardwood and metals (see page 111). Since the disk sander is commonly employed for edge work, the abrasive can be somewhat coarser than that used for surfacing. A 1/2 or 1/0 disk cuts rapidly to a fairly smooth surface. Fine woodworking, however, requires final sanding with a 2/0 or 3/0 disk so that abrasive scratches will not show.

Sanding on the disk sander is usually done freehand, the work being held flat on the auxiliary table (Fig. 2·25) and projected into the sanding disk. A smooth, light feed should be practiced. Avoid heavy pressure. The best results on curved work can be obtained by going over the work two or three times with light cuts. Sanding should be done on the "down" side of the disk (Fig. 9·4). Although it is permissible to sand small pieces on the "up" side, and while it is necessary to use both sides of the disk when sanding end grain on wide work, the surface produced will not be quite so smooth as that sanded only on the side of the disk going down. But with the versatile tilting-arbor disk sander, it is possible to sand large areas with only the down-side portion of the disk.

Surface Sanding. To position the machine for general-surface sanding, elevate the radial arm until the motor with disk

Fig. 9·3   **Fig. 9·4**

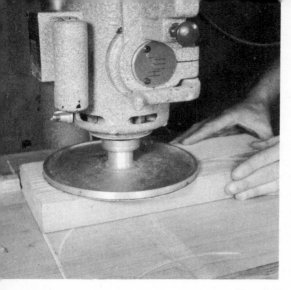

Fig. 9·5

attached can be tilted to the vertical position. Then move the motor out on the arm until the disk is directly above the path the material will follow along the guide fence, and lock it in position with the rip clamp. Place the stock to be sanded on the table and lower the arm until the disk fits snugly against the top surface of the board. Push the board from right to left along the fence (Fig. 9·5).

For extra-fine sanding, raise the motor from the 90-degree bevel position 1 or 2 degrees (indicated as 89 or 88 on the bevel scale). In this position, the sanding will be done on the down-side portion of the disk.

Straightedge Sanding. Swing the radial arm 60 degrees to the left and place the motor so that the front of the disk sander is parallel to and along the guide fence; this is achieved by adjusting the swivel-clamp handle and the swivel-latch assembly. Lock the motor in position with the rip clamp. Lower the radial arm until the disk is within 1/16 inch of the top of the fence. To raise the material above the surface of the table, the simple auxiliary table used for horizontal sawing (Fig. 2·25) is ideal. Replace the standard guide with the auxiliary table jig.

Place the material to be sanded on the auxiliary table against its fence and push the material past the disk. If fine sanding is desired, swivel the motor 1 to 3 degrees to the left so that the material contacts the disk on the down rotation only (Fig. 9·6).

Butt Sanding. Place the motor in the crosscut position and set the auxiliary-table jig in place of the guide fence. With the material tight against the fence of the auxiliary table and making contact with the disk, pull the motor past the material (Fig. 9·7) in the same manner as when crosscutting.

For fine butt sanding, swing the arm 1

Fig. 9·6

Fig. 9·7

to 3 degrees to the left for the down-rotation operation.

Bevel Sanding. With the arm in the crosscut position, place the motor at the desired angle of bevel and locate the auxiliary table in place of the guide fence. Position the stock on the jig so that it contacts the sander and pull the disk across the beveled end of the board (Fig. 9·8). As in butt sanding, swinging the motor 1 to 3 degrees to the left will produce a finer job.

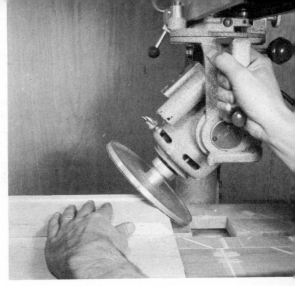

Fig. 9·8

Miter Sanding. With the motor in the crosscut position, locate the arm at the desired miter angle and replace the guide fence with the auxiliary table. Position the material on the table so that it contacts the abrasive and pull the motor across the miter end of the board (Fig. 9·9). If finer sanding is required, swivel the motor 1 to 3 degrees to the left.

Sanding Circles. Sanding circles and curves to accurate size and true radius can be done on the disk sander with the aid of a fixture. (This jig is the same as the one detailed on page 91.)

Start with a perfectly square board; find the exact center by using the diagonal method; then cut the square down to the approximate circumference of the circle on the saber saw. Place the stock to be sanded on the center pin of the sliding strip of the jig and place the motor in the crosscut position. Lower the motor to the proper height and lock it in place directly in front of the jig. Turn on the machine and slowly rotate the stock on the center pin (moving it closer to the disk from time to time) until it is perfectly round and uniformly smooth (Fig. 9·10).

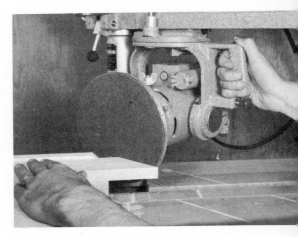

Fig. 9·9

Rounding Corners. The sanding of corners is allied to circular work in that the edge being worked is part of a true circle. Most work of this nature can be done freehand, sweeping the corner of the work across the face of the sanding disk two

Fig. 9·10

or three times until the desired round is obtained (Fig. 9·11). The motor is placed in the crosscut setup and locked into position by the rip lock.

Pointing Dowels. Drill a hole the same diameter as the dowel stock through a scrap piece of wood which is located on the auxiliary table and set the disk at the required angle, as shown in Fig. 9·12. Push the work through the hole until it contacts the sanding disk; rotate it to finish the point.

Sanding Metals and Plastics. Finishing metals and plastics on the disk sander is the same as similar operations on wood, with the exception that the proper abrasive should be used. Generally, the feed with these materals should be less and the pass made more slowly.

MOUNTING THE BELT SANDER

Before attaching the belt sander to the radial-arm motor, a mounting board must be made. It is made of 3/4-inch plywood and the lower projection on it fits into the slot normally occupied by the guide fence. When the spacer-board clamp screws are brought up tight, your 4-inch sander will be in place.

Remove the safety guard, arbor nut, saw blade (or other tool), and arbor collars from the motor shaft. Place the pulley on the motor shaft (hub toward the motor) and tighten the setscrew. Replace and tighten the arbor nut.

Now swing the radial arm left until you read approximately 60 degrees on the miter scale. Swivel your motor and extend it out on the radial arm until it is parallel and in line with the pulley on the belt sander. Slip the belt on both pulleys and readjust the motor by extending it farther on the arm or swinging the radial arm right or left a few degrees until the belt is tight. Lock the motor in place by means of the rip clamp. Turn on the machine to check the alignment of the pulleys and the tension on the belt. The belt sander is used mainly for flat work, though with-the-grain edges can be sanded square, beveled, or chamfered.

BELT-SANDER ADJUSTMENTS

The belt sander is provided with two drums over which the abrasive belt travels. The powered drum, the one on which the power pulley is placed, is covered with a rubber sleeve to give traction to the belt. The other drum, which is the idler, is provided with an adjusting device as shown in Fig. 9·13, which produces the belt tension and keeps the belt tracking. This device consists of four knurled nuts, two at each end of the idler drum.

Fig. 9·11   **Fig. 9·12**

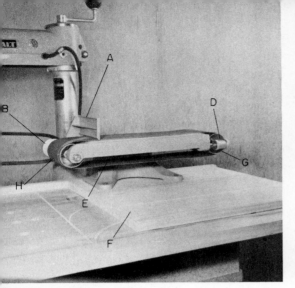

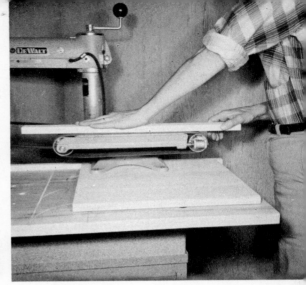

Fig. 9·13

A. Work Guide   E. Sanding Belt
B. Pulley   F. Mounting Board
C. Motor Belt   G. Idling Drum
D. Tension Adjuster   H. Driving Drum

When placing a belt on the sander, loosen the two inside nuts, releasing all tension, and slip the belt over the pulleys. (Be sure the arrow on the inside of the belt points toward the guide fence.) Tighten both adjustments back to the original position so that there will be sufficient tension for the belt to move when the power pulley is turned over by hand.

Turn the power pulley over several times to determine if the belt is tracking properly. If the belt shifts to the right when doing this, slightly loosen the right outside nut and tighten the right inside nut; this throws the belt to the left. If this does not solve the problem, slightly loosen the left side inside nut and tighten the left outside nut; this will help to throw the belt to the left. Alternate until proper tracking of the belt has been secured. But remember—*loosen lightly not radically*—as adjustments are sensitive.

If the belt is tracking to the left, reverse the procedure given in the previous paragraph. Do not start the machine until you are certain that the belt is tracking on the center of the pulleys.

When the machine is started, it may be

Fig. 9·14

necessary to adjust the tension on the belt. To increase the tension, loosen the outside knurled nuts about a quarter turn and tighten the inside nuts until the assembly is forced against the outside nuts. Sometimes it may be necessary to adjust the tension on one side or the other to prevent the belt from shifting to the right or left.

To decrease tension, reverse the instructions given in the preceding paragraph. Too much tension will act as a resistance to your motor and will shorten the life of the abrasive belt.

Occasionally apply a few drops of oil on each end of the drive shaft to lubricate the self-lubricating bronze bearings. Every 4 to 6 months, remove the abrasive belt and the screw in the center of the idler pulley. Place a few drops of SAE 30 or 40 oil in the hole. Replace the screw and belt.

OPERATING THE BELT SANDER

Work on a belt sander is generally done freehand—that is, the material to be surfaced is simply placed on the table. Use a light but firm pressure to keep the piece in the proper position (Fig. 9·14). Avoid excessive pressure, since it will scratch the surface being sanded.

End Sanding. The belt sander is provided with a fence which extends across the face of the belt as shown in Fig. 9 13.

The fence may be set at any angle from 90 degrees, or square to the belt, to 45 degrees. This permits the sanding of long edges or ends at any angle. The work is pushed down alongside the fence until it contacts the surface. Figure 9·15 shows how beveling is done on the edge of the stock. Chamfering can be done in the same manner.

For all operations in which the fence is used, feed the wood against the direction in which the belt is traveling; otherwise the stock will be pulled from your hands.

Sanding Long Work. To sand the surface of long pieces, remove the fence (two screws on the side of the machine). Start the work at one end, moving it back and forth, and gradually advance it with the grain as the belt runs under it, keeping a light but even pressure on it. With-the-grain edges can be sanded square in the same way.

The use of a diagonal feed, as shown in Fig. 9·16, permits the surfacing of work considerably wider than the 4-inch capacity of the belt. The angle at which the work is fed across the belt should be kept as slight as possible so as to hold to a minimum the scratches that may appear on the surface from diagonal sanding. A belt with a fine abrasive will also help to reduce scratches.

Fig. 9·15

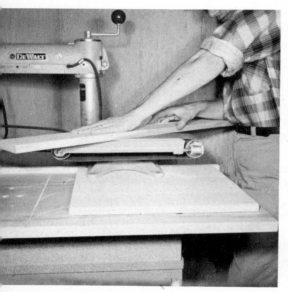

Fig. 9·16

Small flat stock can best be sanded with the fence set across the belt as shown in Fig. 9·17. When the table is in this position, it acts as a stop for the material being sanded.

Sanding Inside Curves. Inside curves (concave sanding) can be sanded on the end drum, as shown in Fig. 9·18.

MOUNTING THE DRUM SANDER

Small sanding drums come in a range of sizes from 1 to 3 inches in diameter. The most popular is the 3-inch size.

Both the drums and abrasive sleeves

Fig. 9·17

are inexpensive and very efficient for edge-sanding curved work.

To mount the 2-inch drum, remove the safety guard, saw blade (or other cutting tool), arbor nut, and arbor collars from the arbor shaft. Replace the two arbor collars ($\frac{3}{8}$-inch one first and recessed sides together); then place the drum on the shaft. Place a wrench on the flat of the arbor shaft to hold it, and tighten the drum by hand, turning it counterclockwise. The 3-inch drum sander may be used in either the horizontal or vertical position, depending on the operation.

Directions for replacing sleeves are shown in Fig. 9·19. Cut a 9- by 11-inch sheet of garnet sandpaper of the proper grit into three 3- by 11-inch strips by tearing it against a metal straightedge or hacksaw blade. (Never cut the sandpaper

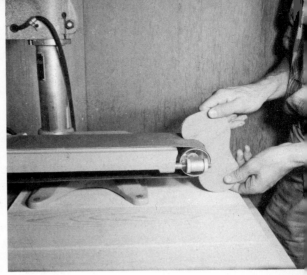

Fig. 9·18

with scissors or a knife, as this will damage the cutting edge of the tool.) Bend the ends of the sleeves by the use of a board as shown. The board must be measured accurately and cut square. Then wrap the sleeve around the drum approximately $\frac{1}{4}$

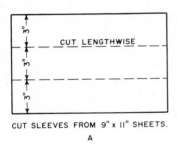

CUT SLEEVES FROM 9" x 11" SHEETS.

A

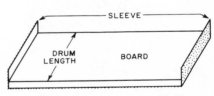

BEND ENDS OF SLEEVES BY USE OF BOARD AS SHOWN. BOARD MUST BE MEASURED ACCURATELY AND CUT SQUARE.

B

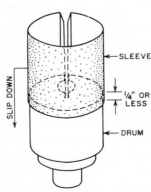

WRAP ABOUT ¼" OF DRUM OR LESS. THEN SLIP ON DOWN OVER DRUM. USE TALCUM POWDER IF NECESSARY TO MAKE SLEEVE SLIP EASILY.

C

SQUEEZE HARD TO GET SLACK OUT OF SLEEVE AND ENDS DOWN INTO SLOT. THEN INSERT TUBE AND TURN WITH KEY. OVAL TUBE SHOULD FIT SNUGLY. DO NOT FORCE. IF TOO TIGHT PUT IN VISE AND SQUEEZE EDGE. IF TOO LOOSE SQUEEZE FLAT SIDE OF TUBE.

D

Fig. 9·19

Fig. 9·20A

Fig. 9·20B

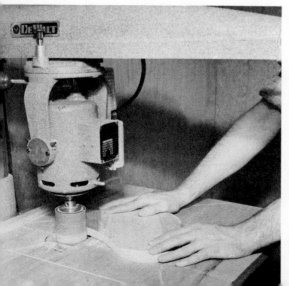

inch down on it and slip the ends in the slot. Now slip the sleeve on down over the drum. A little talcum powder on the soft-rubber drum will make the sleeve slip on more easily. Squeeze hard to get the slack out of the sleeve and push the ends down into the slot. Then insert the tube that comes with the drum and turn it with a key. The oval tube should fit snugly; do not force it. If it is too tight, put it in a vise and squeeze the edge; if too lose, squeeze the flat side of the tube.

To mount the 1-inch drum, remove all items from the arbor shaft and replace the two arbor collars ($\frac{3}{8}$-inch one first and the recessed sides together). For this drum operation, use the same adapter as the one used for boring and place it on the shaft. Place a wrench on the flat of the arbor shaft to hold it and tighten the adapter by turning it counterclockwise. The sanding drum is held in place with an Allen-head setscrew in the arbor. The 1-inch drum sander can be used in a horizontal position only. One-inch sleeves are purchased ready made and are slipped over the drum with the help of a little talcum powder.

VERTICAL OPERATION OF THE DRUM SANDER

When using the 3-inch drum sander in the vertical position, locate it over the shaper cutter hole in the table top. The back edge of the guide fence should be notched out for straightedge sanding (Fig. 9·20A). The jointer fence can also be used and be positioned with a $\frac{1}{64}$-inch offset between the infeed and outfeed edges (Fig. 9·20B).

With the radial arm raised to its fullest extent, place the drum in the shaper hole and, with the motor in the vertical position, bring the arbor shaft over the drum shaft. Lift the drum and mount it as previously described. Tighten the rip clamp on the arm. With the sander in this

Fig. 9·21

position, the lower edge of the drum will be a little below the surface of the auxiliary table so that the entire edge of the stock being finished will come in contact with the abrasive.

When using a drum sander, the material being finished should be kept constantly in motion to prevent overheating and scorching the wood. Wire-brushing the sleeve occasionally will prolong its useful life. Ordinarily, this is most effective if done while the machine is running.

Curved Sanding. When sanding curved work where the width dimension is not extremely important, move the work past the drum from right to left as shown in Fig. 9·21. When sanding uniform curves, and especially when rounding corners with a drum, follow the procedure shown in Fig. 9·22 for smooth sanding results. Figures 9·23A and B show internal sanding of curved surfaces.

Straight Sanding. Although nearly all drum sanding is done freehand, straight work usually requires a guide fence or the use of the jointer fence. With the motor at the rear, bring the sander forward into the shaper slot on the table. Locate the sander so that its leading edge is in a straight line with the outfeed side of the fence and tighten the rip clamp on the radial arm. Place the material against the infeed side of the fence, start the motor, and push the stock past the drum sander.

In sanding straight work, the work must be kept moving at a uniform rate past the drum (Fig. 9·24). If the work is stopped at any point while in contact with the rotating drum, it may be scored or burned. Uneven feed can produce scoring at intervals along the length of the stock. On short work, such as that pictured in Fig. 9·25, it is possible to make the sanding stroke with one sweep of the arms without removing either hand from the work. On longer stock it will be necessary to shift

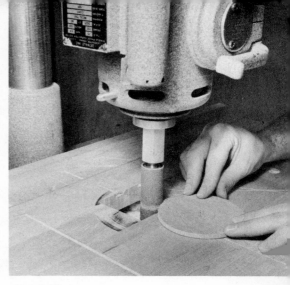

Fig. 9·22

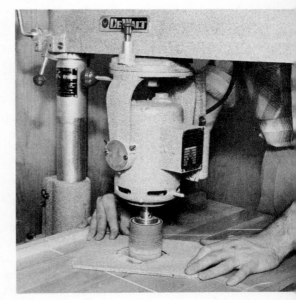

Fig. 9·23A

Fig. 9·23B

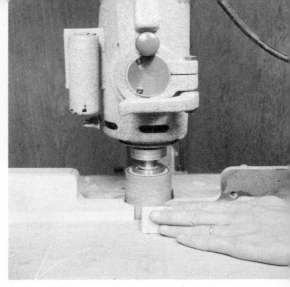

Fig. 9·24

Fig. 9·25

the hands alternately. Here the trick is to maintain uniform pressure and rate of feed with one hand while the other is being shifted. In some cases an overhand movement gives satisfactory results.

HORIZONTAL OPERATION OF THE DRUM SANDER

In the horizontal position, the drum sander will do an effective job of surfacing narrow work when used as shown in Fig. 9·26. For this operation, use either the auxiliary or stationary table. With the motor raised to its full extent, set the motor shaft in a horizontal position. Place the material tight against the fence, and lower the radial arm until the abrasive hits the start of the stock. Withdraw the stock, turn on the motor, and feed the work against the rotation of the drum. If more smoothness is desired, keep lowering the arm a quarter turn at a time.

Wider boards may be handled in the same manner except that several passes will have to be taken with the sander at the same height. Remember—in any surface sanding operation do not attempt too deep a bite in one pass; two or more passes will result in a better job.

Sanding Rabbets and Similar Cuts. Sanding the inside corners of rabbets and similar cuts can be easily executed with the drum sander as shown in Fig. 9·27. The rabbeted stock is set against the auxiliary-table guide fence, and the drum is set to fit in the corner. Then feed the work forward past the drum to make the cut. For operations like this, the sleeve should be mounted so that it projects about $\frac{1}{32}$ inch beyond the bottom of the drum, allowing the inside corner to be finished cleanly.

Fig. 9·26

Fig. 9·27

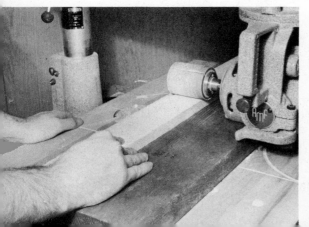

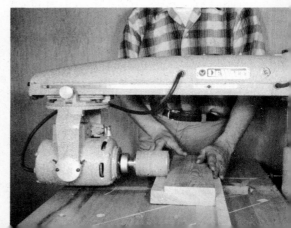

CHAPTER 10

Grinding, buffing, and polishing wheel operations

NO WORKSHOP is complete without a grinder. You will find many uses for it. With the versatile radial-arm machine, you can use a grinder, wire brush, or buffer simply by adding these attachments to the motor shaft.

It is that simple. To mount any of the three, all you have to do is remove the safety guard, arbor nut, cutting device, and arbor collars. Replace the ⅜-inch collar, place the desired wheel on the shaft, followed by the small arbor collar, and tighten them on the shaft with the arbor nut. You are now ready to carry on the operation desired.

SAFETY RULES

The grinder must be handled with care, and the following general safety precautions should be kept in mind when using these attachments.

1. Always wear goggles when grinding or wire brushing and be sure they cover the eyes properly

2. Stand to one side out of the line of the wheel when it is starting up.

3. Let the wheel warm up before using it heavily; feed the work gradually. Using too much pressure or striking the wheel suddenly may cause it to break.

4. Keep the tool-rest jig (page 124) approximately ⅛ inch from the grinding wheel. Too

much clearance may cause the tool being sharpened to jam the wheel and break it.

5. Never use a wheel if it has a lower rated speed (3,425 rpm for the radial-arm saw) than the speed of the arbor shaft.

6. Do not set the tool rest while the machine is in motion, and wait for the wheel to stop after the power has been shut off. Do not attempt to stop the wheel with your hands.

7. Do not treat a cloth buffer turning at 3,425 rpm lightly. A loose thread on the buffing wheel can give you a badly cut finger. Wear goggles or your regular glasses to protect your eyes, and it is a good idea to wear gloves.

OPERATION OF THE GRINDING WHEEL

The most important use of the grinding wheel is to sharpen tools. Sharp tools promote accuracy, reduce finishing operations and accidents. The radial-arm grinder can be used for sharpening plane irons, wood chisels, lathe tools, screwdrivers, and drills.

For most uses, the grinder is generally fitted with either a medium-grain or a fine-grain abrasive wheel. The medium wheel should be used to rough off a metal surface where smoothness is not too important. The fine wheel is usually used when close tolerance is required or for sharpening. When a considerable amount of metal is to be removed or when a deep cut is to be made, the work can be speeded by using the medium wheel first and then finishing with the fine wheel. There are two types of wheels suitable for the radial-arm machine—cup wheels and disk wheels.

For most sharpening operations, the motor shaft should be in a horizontal position and swung to the left (standard crosscut setup). In this position, the grinding

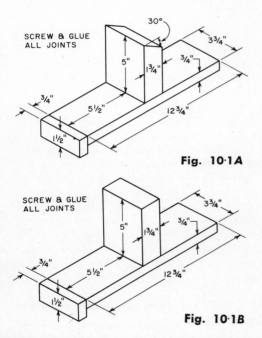

SCREW & GLUE ALL JOINTS

30°
3¾"
5"
1¾"
¾"
¾"
5½"
12¾"
1½"

Fig. 10·1A

SCREW & GLUE ALL JOINTS

3¾"
5"
1¾"
¾"
¾"
5½"
12¾"
1½"

Fig. 10·1B

wheel will run toward you, which will help to eliminate the formation of a wire edge.

For most grinding, use a tool-rest jig such as the one shown in Fig. 10·1A and locate it in place of the standard guide fence. A level tool rest should be about ¼ inch below the center line of the axis of the grinder for general work. Work ground in this position, or in any other position in which the work points to the center of the wheel, will be finished with a square edge. Work located in any position other than pointing to the wheel center will be ground more or less at a bevel.

The grinder wheel should be adjusted so that it is as close as possible to the tool rest and locked into position with the rip clamp on the arm. Freehand grinding, without the use of a rest, should always be done on the lower quarter of the wheel (Fig. 10·2).

Sparks given off by a grinding wheel indicate different grades of steel or iron. High-carbon tool steel explodes in bright white sparks and travels only a short distance from the wheel. Wrought iron gives off a reddish-yellow spark which will extend quite a distance. Cold-rolled steel and mild steel fall somewhere between these two. High-speed steel produces a bright yellow spark that stops abruptly a few inches from the wheel.

When Are Tools Dull? Beginners are apt to use dull tools without knowing why they cut so poorly. Dullness will show in a thin bright line along the cutting edge. Another test is to feel the edge with your thumb or fingers. If the edge feels smooth and as though some pressure would be necessary to cause it to cut, the tool is dull.

A dull tool does not, of course, always mean that both grinding and whetting are necessary. Grinding is required only when the edge is nicked or the bevel is out of shape.

Fig. 10·2

If tools are not abused, little grinding should ever be necessary; but not so for whetting or honing. No sharp-edged tool can be used long without needing this touching up. Do not begrudge the time you spend on tools with your oilstone.

Wood Chisels and Plane Irons. Wood chisels and plane irons are sharpened similarly, since they both are hollow ground. Check the cutting edge for squareness with a try square. To square edge or remove nicks, project the chisel straight (Fig. 10·3). Then hold the blade at a 30-degree angle, working it squarely across the face of the wheel. (Worked on the face of the wheel, the bevel will have a slight hollow, making it easy to hone to a perfect edge several times before regrinding again becomes necessary.) To hold the blade at this angle, use a jig as shown in Fig. 10·1*B*. Move the blade from side to side, grinding until a burr appears on the upper edge (Fig. 10·4). Dip it in water often to cool.

Fig. 10·3

To remove the burr, use either an aluminum oxide or a silicon carbide oilstone. The stone should be well oiled— use thin oil or kerosene—so that the metal particles will not become embedded in the stone. The burr is removed by turning the tool on its flat side and lightly stroking it diagonally backward and forward. Repeat the honing process until the burr disappears. Avoid any bevel on this side.

Turning Tools. Wood-turning tools are ground on the side of the grinding wheel to obtain perfectly flat bevels. They should

Fig. 10·4

not be hollow ground because hollow grinding destroys the fulcrum action of the bevel. For correct grinding angles for wood-turning tools, see Fig. 10·5.

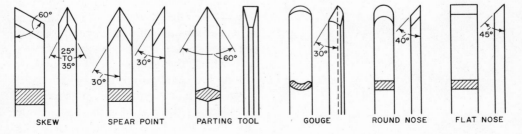

SKEW   SPEAR POINT   PARTING TOOL   GOUGE   ROUND NOSE   FLAT NOSE

Fig. 10·5

Fig. 10·6

Fig. 10·7

The bevel of the *skew chisel* is ground to an angle of 25 to 35 degrees. The chisel can be held freehand, but better results will be obtained with a simple jig as shown in Fig. 10·1A. Swing the radial arm to the 15-degree right-hand miter position. The skew is held in the jig against the side of the grinder, with the point upward, for the first grinding operation (Fig. 10·6). The second cut is made with the point down. The skew should be dipped in water frequently to prevent drawing the temper. In honing or whetting, follow the same procedure as for wood chisels, but be sure to maintain the proper bevel.

The *flat-nose chisel* is sharpened either freehand or with a guide as in Fig. 10·1B, except that the angle should be 45 degrees. Honing is the same as for wood chisels.

The *spear-point chisel* is sharpened either freehand against the side of the grinding wheel or, for better results, with the aid of a jig (Fig. 10·1A). The spear-point tool is held flat against one bevel side of the jig, then the other, until sharpened. The radial arm should be swung to the 30-degree right-hand miter position. The point should be maintained on the center line of the grinder.

The *parting tool* may be sharpened freehand or in the jig shown in Fig. 10·7. The radial arm should be swung to the 30-degree right-hand miter position. As in the case of the spear-point tool, the point should be kept on the center line.

The simplest method of sharpening the *gouge* is to use the cup wheel, rotating the chisel inside the wheel as shown in Fig. 10·8. The curved surface of the cup wheel lessens the amount of rolling necessary and makes grinding easy. Lacking a cup wheel, the gouge can be ground by rolling the bevel on the face of the wheel (Fig. 10·9) or on the side of the wheel. In all cases the roll must be just a little less than that of a full half-circle. The

Fig. 10·8

Fig. 10·9   Fig. 10·10

internal surfaces of the gouge are properly honed by using a special curved slipstone. The type most commonly used is hollow on one side for honing the bevel and rounded on one edge for removing the wire edge (Fig. 10·10).

The *round-nose chisel* is sharpened in the same way as the gouge except that the burr resulting from the grinding is removed on the flat of an oilstone.

Screwdrivers. While the term "sharpening" may not be correct for screwdrivers, the edge must be maintained so that it will be a good fit in the slot of a screw head. The edge should be square and flat. To obtain this, hold the screwdriver on the tool-rest jig and advance it directly into the wheel (Fig. 10·11*A*). The side

bevel can be ground by placing it flat against the side of the grinder (Fig. 10·11*B*).

Drills. The angle of most drills is approximately 59 degrees; and this should be maintained when sharpening them. The easiest way to do this is to set the radial arm in the 59-degree right-hand miter position and use the level tool-rest jig shown in Fig. 10·1*A*. With the drill held straight and against the side of the wheel (Fig. 10·12), give it a slight twist and at the same time drop the end. Try it several times, using a properly ground drill and a motionless grinding wheel to get the feel of the procedure. Keep the drill straight as you twist and drop it. At the end of each stroke, the point of the drill

Fig. 10·11A   Fig. 10·11B

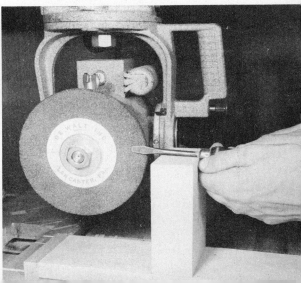

Fig. 10·12

should be down, flat against the grinder wheel.

As the point of the drill is ground down and resharpened, the web becomes thicker. If allowed to remain thick, more force would be required to pull the drill through the work. While this can be done better on a special round-edge wheel, it also can be done on a square-faced wheel by grinding the back of the lips. The grind is carried up to the center of the point on each side (Fig. 10·13).

Care of Grinding Wheels. Grinding wheels require relatively little attention to keep them in good condition. All that is necessary is to keep the face of the stone flat and clean. Narrow tools are apt to wear grooves in the surface if held in one position while grinding. The tool should be moved slowly back and forth across the stone. Should the face become irregular or the pores become clogged with particles of metal, the wheel must be

dressed or trued. A diamond dresser, a genuine diamond set into the end of a suitable holder, is preferred, but is fairly expensive. Therefore, the common disk-type dresser, which contains a replaceable set of star- or gear-shaped sharp, pointed, hard pieces of metal, is usually used. These disks revolve freely and rapidly when held in contact with the moving face of the wheel and dig in to remove the small particles of metal and bits of the grain that have clogged the wheel. It will also quickly true up the stone. Give the stone an occasional cleaning with gasoline to keep the wheel in good shape.

WIRE-BRUSH OPERATION

The wire-brush wheel is mounted in the same way as the grinding wheel. The wire wheel may be used to give a beautiful brushed effect on soft-metal projects. It may be used also for removing dirt, grease, or oxide from the surface of metal in preparation for brazing or soldering. It will remove rust and corrosion in preparation for refinishing or repainting, too.

You can usually hold the work against the brush by hand (Fig. 10·14*A*). Take it easy and do not force the work into the wire brush as it will scratch the metal. Also do not try to remove paint or scale of any kind from wood since the stiff

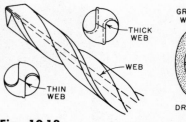

Fig. 10·13

Fig. 10·14A

wire bristles will mar the wood. But if you wish a striated effect, the wood may be pushed past the wire brush as shown in Fig. 10·14B. If metal surfaces should become scratched when wire brushing, buffing will take the scratches out. Always wear goggles when wire brushing.

BUFFING OPERATION

The process of restoring a gleaming finish to a pitted or badly tarnished metal surface can be performed easily on your radial-arm machine. To buff a metal surface, mount the cloth buffer on the motor shaft. Place the ⅜-inch arbor collar on first, the cloth buffer next, and then the ¼-inch collar and the arbor nut. The motor shaft should be in a horizontal position and swung to the left. If the object is badly pitted, you will have to cut the entire surface down to the level of the deepest pit, using emery composition which comes in a tube or stick.

To charge the buffer, hold the tube to the face of the running buffer and let the heat of friction melt the binder so that it will flow on the wheel. The face of the wheel will turn black when it is well charged. To smooth it down, hold a piece of scrap metal against it with downward, passing strokes.

After the entire metal surface is uniformly clean, put on another wheel and charge it with tripoli. Go over the metal very lightly, using the same downward strokes. The scratch lines left by the emery polishing will smooth out and blend into each other.

Although the object will have a good finish now, it is usually desirable to give it a really fine finish by a final buffing, or coloring, with a buffer wheel charged with jeweler's rouge (Fig. 10·15A and B). Final color buffing will show up imperfect work in the preliminary stages. If you find such spots, go back over them with tripoli. Protect the final finish with a coat of lacquer, after first cleaning the article

Fig. 10·14B

Fig. 10·15A

Fig. 10·15B

with carbon tetrachloride. The charged wheels may be used several times before recharging is necessary.

Buffing wheels charged with suitable compounds are used for polishing bare wood, lacquered surfaces, plastic, etc. Such easily obtained abrasives as pumice, rottenstone, and rouge will usually do the job. Benzene or wood alcohol will remove any film of compound left on the work after buffing.

Grinder-Buffer Wheel. Some jobs will require more metal removal than can be done by buffing. A solid grinding wheel will do this, of course, but it cannot follow contours. You can make a wheel for flexible grinding, as follows. Take a buffer wheel and roll it in good liquid glue which has been poured on wax paper. Coat the face uniformly with the glue and smooth the coating with your fingers or a stick. Then hang the buffer on a nail to dry for 12 to 24 hours. After it has dried, place the wheel on the motor shaft and mark an arrow on the side of the wheel to show the direction of rotation (be sure always to put it back on the shaft the same way). Run the wheel and sand its face lightly with coarse or medium sandpaper to smooth the surface. Roll the wheel in the glue preparation again and then roll it in a flat pile of abrasive which you have spread out on the waxed paper. Let the weight of the wheel provide the pressure. Allow an hour for drying. Repeat the treatment and then allow 12 to 24 hours to dry. The following day, scrape any loose grains from the sides of the wheel and crack the face by flexing it with your thumb or pressing it with a blunt tool. The face should now have hundreds of small cracks. Mount the wheel on the motor shaft and break it in by polishing a piece of scrap metal lightly. Be very careful of this wheel, as it cuts fairly rapidly.

POLISHER

To convert the radial-arm tool into a polishing machine suitable for such operations as polishing wood and metal surfaces and even your shoes (Fig. 10·16*A*), all that is required is the sanding disk plate and a lamb's-wool bonnet or pad. The lamb's-wool bonnet is secured to the metal disk plate by means of a draw string provided in the bonnet. Then mount the plate on the arbor shaft as described on page 112.

Use an electric-tool wax (available at most hardware stores) when polishing either wood (Fig. 10·16*B*) or metal surfaces. The standard waxes do not work

Fig. 10·16A   **Fig. 10·16B**

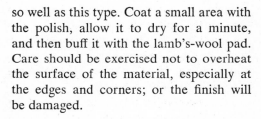

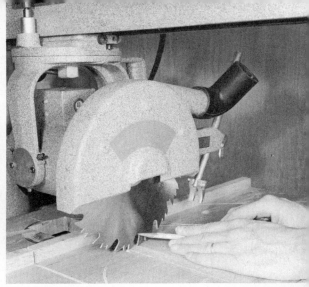

| Fig. 10·17 | Fig. 10·18A |

so well as this type. Coat a small area with the polish, allow it to dry for a minute, and then buff it with the lamb's-wool pad. Care should be exercised not to overheat the surface of the material, especially at the edges and corners; or the finish will be damaged.

GENERAL SHARPENING METHODS

Several of the cutting tools used on the radial-arm machine cannot be sharpened on the grinder—notably the saw blades, boring bits, and shaper and jointer blades. However, they must be kept sharp, and this can be done without too much difficulty.

Saw Blade. The sharpening operation of your radial-arm saw blade may be divided into four parts: jointing, gumming, setting, and filling. All these operations, however, need not be done every time a saw needs sharpening.

Jointing means bringing the point of every tooth to exactly the same distance from the center or arbor hole in the saw. This is generally not required until the blade has been filed several times, and the length of the teeth may be unequal.

To joint a blade, lay a flat oilstone against the guide fence on the crosscut kerf and bring the saw forward from the column until it is over the stone. Lower the blade until it just touches the stone (Fig. 10·17), then push it back against the column. Turn on the machine and pull the saw across the stone. This causes plenty of sparks to fly, indicating that the points of the teeth are being ground down. Stop the saw after a few seconds and examine the points of the teeth while revolving the saw by hand. When every tooth has a bright spot on its point, the jointing operation has been completed. If some of the teeth have not been touched by the sharpening stone, lower the blade a little and repeat the process.

Gumming means increasing the depth of the gullets between the teeth so that the sawdust can be carried away. It is usually necessary to do this after a blade has been jointed, since that operation shortens the teeth and makes the gullets shallower.

Mark a pencil line on the side of the saw so that all the gullets may be filed to the same depth. To do this, turn the blade around by hand if the pencil is held as shown in Fig. 10·18A. The file to be used is a 7-inch file with one or two rounded edges. Since a mill file is a single-cut flat type, teeth or serrations should be cut in one direction only. Never file the gullets with an ordinary square-edge flat file because cracks are likely to develop.

Before starting to file, clean the gullets with a rattail file or the tang of another

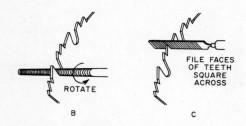

Fig. 10·18B and C

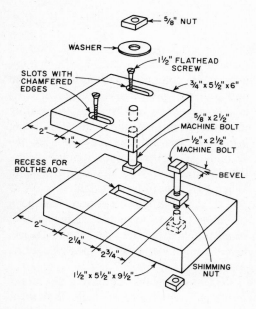

Fig. 10·19A

file (Fig. 10·18B). Holding the rounded edge of the file down, file the gullets to the depth of the line. File the front or face of each tooth square (Fig. 10·18C), too. The angle of the front of each tooth, called the rake, must be maintained when gumming a saw. To find the rake: mark a circle on the saw blade halfway between its center and its edge, and draw a line from the front of any one of the teeth tangent to this circle.

Setting a saw means to bend every other tooth to one side and the rest to the opposite side. All blades except those which are hollow ground and those which are swazed must be set. When a saw is properly set, it cuts a kerf or groove wide enough for the blade to go through without binding. In other words, the saw cuts "freely" without binding.

To accomplish this, a setting jig (Fig. 10·19A) should be made, as follows. Use a ⅝-inch bolt to fasten the blade to a block of wood screwed to a base block that holds the anvil. The anvil is also a bolt with half of its head beveled to the angle of set. To set a ripsaw blade, adjust it so that each tooth projects one-third over the beveled part of the anvil. Mark a tooth that has been bent away from you with a piece of chalk, place it on the anvil, hold a flat-ended punch on it, and strike a blow with a hammer (Fig.

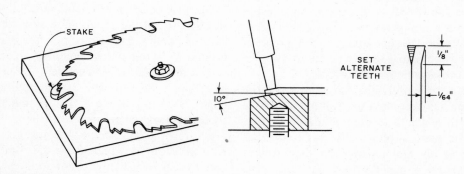

Fig. 10·19B

10·19*B*). Skip the next tooth, but set the following one as before and continue setting every other tooth until the one with the chalk mark has been reached. Now reverse the saw on the setting jig and set those teeth which were skipped before. Be sure not to set more than one-third the length of the teeth, because a saw can cut itself free only with the points of its teeth. Also, if the teeth are set too much, the saw offers resistance to the wood and does not cut well.

Filing, the final operation, is done while the saw is held in a special filing vise (Fig. 10·20*A*). To make this vise, use a 1- by 6-inch board rounded at one end and bored to admit a ⅝-inch bolt. Make a short front jaw, boring it to match and hinging it to the first board. With a blade held between the jaws by the bolt, the vise can be clamped against any suitable support or in a bench vise while the blade is filed. Be sure the saw vise is held rigidly enough to prevent chatter during filing.

To file a ripsaw, begin by filing the front edge of each tooth square to its sides. (If the saw his just been gummed, this operation will have been done in the gumming process.) Then file the top edges of the teeth. Start on a tooth set away from you and file it so that its top edge is in line with the seventh tooth back. File the teeth straight across. If a good deal of material has to be filed away after a joining operation, go over the saw twice to be sure that all the flat points have disappeared.

A *miter* or *hollow-ground blade* has groups of four crosscut teeth with a rip or raker tooth between. The raker is filed square 1/64 to 1/32 inch shorter than the others and is not set. As the fronts and backs of the teeth must be filed separately, a cant file—a triangular file with two sides longer than the third—should be

used. If an ordinary taper or blunt saw file must be used, be careful to press only on the tooth being sharpened. Test the saw after filing it by making a shallow cut across the grain of a piece of waste wood. If the cut is not smooth, the raker teeth are too long. When the cut is right, it should be flat on the bottom, but two fine parallel lines should be scored by the crosscut teeth.

A *combination blade* is filed in the same way as a hollow-ground blade except that the crosscut teeth are beveled on alternate sides, the fronts 18 degrees, the backs 12 degrees, with the fronts radial.

The outside cutters of a *dado head* resemble the hollow-ground blade and are filed in the same manner. The inside cutters are swaged; that is, their ends are spread out to a chisel point by hammering them. These cutters may be sharpened by light filing.

Cleaning a Saw Blade. Saw blades that are used for cutting woods containing a considerable quantity of resin and pitch have the gullets and sides of the teeth

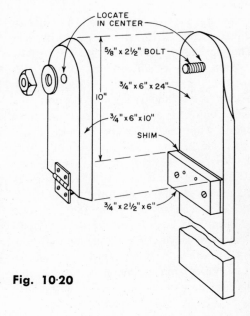

Fig. 10·20

Fig. 10·21 **Fig. 10·22**

filled with sawdust that adheres tenaciously to the metal. Using a blade in this condition not only results in overloading the motor but may be the cause of a burned blade. The pitch and hardened sawdust can be removed readily by immersing the blade in a container of solvent such as kerosene or turpentine. Allow the blade to remain in the liquid for 8 to 12 hours; then when the sawdust has softened, it can be removed with a brush. If the first treatment is not sufficient, repeat.

Boring Bits. An auger-bit file and a slipstone are used to sharpen a boring bit. The specially designed file is small, tapered, and double-ended so that the narrow portion can be used on small-diameter bits and the wider portions on larger bits. One end is made with the sides uncut, while the other end has cut edges.

In sharpening a boring bit, file both the lips and the nibs of the spurs (Fig. 10·21). The uncut section of a boring-bit file makes it easy to file either the nibs or the lips without damaging any of the adjacent surfaces. To maintain the proper clearance, file the lips of the bit only on the top surface of the cutting edge. To keep the original diameter of the bit, file the nibs only on the inside. To help main-

tain its original bevel, it is best to hold the bit in a vise. After completing the filing, use a slipstone to remove any wire edge.

Shaper and Jointer Cutters. Shaper and jointer cutters must be kept as sharp as possible. This is done with several special sharpening stones. A flat Arkansas oilstone approximately 2 by 6 inches or a slipstone made of the same material about 4 inches long and tapering from $\frac{1}{8}$ to $\frac{3}{8}$ inch in thickness, with rounded edges, is needed. Also, one about 4 inches long and $\frac{1}{4}$ inch square and another 4 inches long, 2 inches wide, and $\frac{3}{8}$ or $\frac{1}{2}$ inch thick should be available. Another convenient oilstone to have is a triangular sectional one with each face $\frac{1}{16}$ inch wide and 3 inches long. With this collection of oilstones it is possible to sharpen almost any cutter used on the shaper or jointer.

The action of the cutters when shaping or jointing wears the cutting edge. To renew this, remove as little metal as possible and keep the cutting angle of the edge the same.

Select the oilstone that fits the curve or shape of the cutter. Rub the stone lightly, holding it flat against the back of the cutting edge (Fig. 10·22). To remove the wire edge that will result from sharpening, lay the cutter flat on a flat oilstone and with a back-and-forth motion rub it over the surface until it is removed.

TOOL STORAGE AND RUST PREVENTION

Every tool with your radial-arm machine should have its proper storage place. Tools that are most often in use should be kept at hand on a tool rack such as shown in Chapter 15. Plans and directions for building a work bench and tool-storage cabinet are also given in Chapter 15.

Tools that are not used frequently should be stored in tool drawers or in the boxes in which they were originally packed. During the damp spring and summer months, each tool should be coated with a film of grease or oil to prevent rust. When tools are to be stored for an extended period of time, it is a good idea, in addition to coating, to wrap them in heavy paper or cloth for protection from dust and moisture. The cutting edges of tools should be protected at all times.

When rust forms on tools, it should be removed immediately. There are several rust-removing solutions on the market that are fairly successful; they must be used according to manufacturer's directions. Another satisfactory method of removing rust from tools is with fine emery cloth. Place the emery cloth on a felt surface and rub the tool on it. After the rust has been removed, rub the tool clean with a dry cloth and coat it with a film of oil or grease.

CHAPTER 11

Shop safety

WHEN USING the radial-arm machine and its attachments, or any other power tool, the first consideration of every operator should be SAFETY! In the preceding chapters, safety rules were stressed for each type of operation. But as a review and because of their importance, they are listed here again in the form of do's and don'ts. It is wise to read them over very carefully and keep them in mind always.

DON'T wear a necktie or loose-fitting clothes in the shop.

DON'T forget to think before doing—this eliminates most accidents before they can happen.

DON'T clutter the work surface of your machine with unnecessary objects.

DON'T attempt to stop the saw by forcing a piece of wood against it or into it.

DON'T fail to ground the machine properly.

DON'T start a cut or move the material unless the motor and yoke are fully back against the column. (For ripping, of course, the motor is first positioned in front of the guide fence to the desired width of rip.)

DO keep work area clean and uncluttered always.

DO use the proper tool for the job. Be sure the equipment is adequate for the purpose intended.

DO keep tools clean and sharp. Also keep the worktable clean. No loose material should be left on top so that the saw blade may catch and throw them as the saw travels forward.

DO keep the hands from getting in the path of the saw.

DO place stock firmly against the guide fence for all cutting operations. The action of the blade will help you keep it in this position.

DO lock all adjustment clamps firmly

DON'T force the cut. Use a light, steady pull for crosscutting, a firm steady push for ripping.

DON'T change the position of the cutting member until the blade has completely stopped.

DON'T hesitate to use a pusher stick when ripping or when cutting with the shaper if there is any doubt of finger clearance.

DON'T force the dado head into its cut. Because more stock is being removed, only a very slight pull is required. When crosscutting heavy stock, or cross-dadoing, tools will have a tendency to climb-cut or move forward without pulling. You may have to hold back.

DON'T forget—the motor rotation is clockwise. Mount all tools accordingly.

DON'T cross your arms when making any kind of cut so as to be in the path of the saw or cutting tool. If crosscutting material from the left side of saw, hold the material with the left hand approximately 12 inches to the left of the saw blade travel, and pull the yoke handle with the right hand. If cutting from the right side, hold the material with the right hand, and pull the yoke handle with the left hand.

DON'T use cracked saw blades or defective tools on high-speed equipment.

DON'T remove the stock from the table until the saw is returned to the rear of the table.

DON'T allow your workshop to become cluttered with scraps and shavings. Clean floors are essential; you need firm footing and good balance at all times.

DON'T let children gather near the machine. Ban them from your shop.

DON'T do work in cramped quarters.

after making changes in the machine position.

DO properly position the guard for ripping. The infeed end is lowered to $\frac{1}{8}$ inch above the surface of the stock. Anti-kickback fingers are lowered to $\frac{1}{8}$ inch below the surface of the stock. Be sure the rip lock is drawn up snugly before starting to cut. Always feed material from the opposite end of the guard where the anti-kickback is mounted, also use a caution tag which reads "Do not rip or plough from this end." Never stand in back or in the direct line of the saw and the material when ripping, shaping, or planing.

DO draw up all cutting tools snugly on the arbor—use both wrenches provided when tightening the arbor nut —before starting the motor.

DO position the rubber dust spout so that dust and chips are directed away from the operator.

DO use the guard at all times when dadoing. The procedure is the same as when sawing.

DO use the shaper-jointer guard at all times, if inexperienced or unfamiliar with these operations.

DO get in the habit of always removing the key from the switch on the arm when changing tools or making adjustments.

DO use only saw blades tensioned for the high speed of the motor used.

DO keep the machine in good alignment and adjustment, to prevent excessive vibration, which will cause inaccurate cutting and could cause the saw to grab or creep.

DO wear goggles or a face shield if there is danger of flying splinters—especially when grinding.

Have plenty of room to work in and you will avoid accidents. Have a box for scraps, and dispose of them as they accumulate.

DON'T look into the shaper or planer cutter as the board passes through.

DON'T let your mind wander when working on a power tool. Keep it on the work at all times.

DO provide maximum support for the work. Handle all larger-than-average work as explained.

DO remember, above all, never to trust the machine. It will not think for you.

DO mount all attachments according to the instructions given in this book.

DO make sure that the stock or jig is properly clamped whenever clamping is necessary.

ADDITIONAL SAFETY EQUIPMENT

As previously stated, the radial-arm machine is the safest of all shop tools. Built-in safety features include a removable ignition-type starting-switch key, a rubber dust spout which directs the stream of chips away from the operator, a saw-blade guard with attached anti-kickback device, an eye-easy Plextone finish of a soft safety-green color, vivid red plastic control knobs which quickly direct the operator's eye to the adjustment handles for fast, safe changes of positioning; and, of course, the basic machine design which places all moving parts above the work surface in easy view of the operator.

In addition to the standard features just mentioned, a variety of other safety devices are available as optional accessories. Among these are an automatic safety guard, a special splitter and anti-kickback device, a power brake, and a shaper guard.

Automatic Safety Guard. The unique safety guard (Fig. 11·1) with "free-floating" action is a practical, yet absolutely safe, solution to the long-time problem of enclosing the lower half of the saw blade on a radial-arm woodworking machine. The two circular safety rings, completely free to adjust automatically for depth and angle of cut, protect the operator at all times from the cutting member and moving parts of the machine. The guard in no way detracts from the versatility of

the machine nor from the maneuverability of the cutting member through all normal woodworking operations. Although designed primarily for use with a wood-cutting saw blade, the new "free-floating" guard (like the standard model) can also be used for dado work, accommodating a full-width head as determined by the length of the motor shaft on each individual model.

The new "free-floating" guard is mounted on the end belt of the direct-drive motor in much the same fashion as the standard safety guard. The only deviation from the mounting of the conventional guard lies in the placing of the inside ring in position before installing the saw blade and arbor nut on the motor shaft. Complete instructions are packed with each guard.

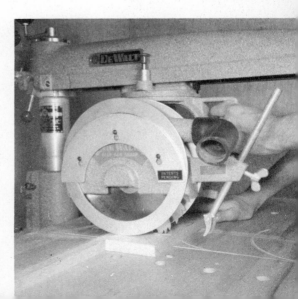

Fig. 11·1

Special Splitter and Anti-kickback Device. This safety device (Fig. 11·2) consists of the standard anti-kickback fingers plus a splitter. The splitter holds the saw kerf open; it prevents kickbacks; it takes some of the strain off long overhangs; it prevents long ripped work from falling to the floor at the end of the cut. It mounts in the safety guards and is used in the same manner as the standard anti-kickback fingers.

Power Brake. The power brake (Fig. 11·3) stops the rotation of the cutting tool at the instant the current is cut off from the motor. Because the direct-drive motors of radial-arm machines are equipped with high-quality ball bearings, the cutting tool on the motor shaft normally continues to revolve for a considerable length of time after the motor is shut off. This drift time ordinarily varies from 3 to 5 minutes, depending on the size and weight of the tool being used. The efficiency of the power brake can be attested to by the fact that a 9-inch blade, with a normal drift time of 3 to 4 minutes, comes to a complete stop from an operating speed of 3,425 rpm in just 5 to 7 seconds when the brake is used.

The power brake can be easily installed; it is entirely automatic and is operated from the same power source which supplies the motor of the machine. Complete mounting instructions are given with the purchase of the unit.

Shaper Guard. With the shaper guard shown in Fig. 5·6 it is virtually impossible for the operator to come into contact with any of the moving parts of the machine. For mounting and operational detail, see page 62.

Fig. 11·2   **Fig. 11·3**

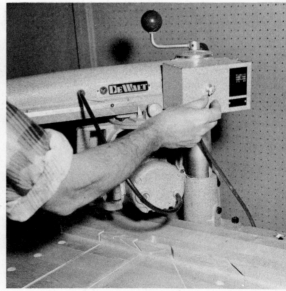

CHAPTER 12

Facts you should know when buying wood

THE TWO MAIN classifications of lumber are hardwood and softwood. Hardwoods are the deciduous trees like oak, maple, and hickory, which lose their leaves in the fall. The softwoods are the evergreens or conifers like pine and spruce. These terms are slightly misleading, since you will run across hardwoods that are relatively soft and softwoods that are hard.

Hardwoods are more difficult to work with but are more durable than softwoods. They also have more attractive grains and take finishes better. They should be used where appearance and sturdiness are important factors. The common hardwoods used in home workshops are walnut, mahogany, cherry, oak, birch, and maple, in descending order of working ease, maple being the most difficult to work.

The softwoods most frequently used are pine, cedar, fir, and redwood. For general utility indoors, use white pine and sugar pine. Sugar pine is softer and more expensive than white pine. Poplar (frequently called whitewood) and gumwood, though considered hardwoods, will work almost as easily as white pine. Other softwoods, because of their large, riotous grain, often cause difficulties in painting and staining.

All wood contains hundreds of small cells called pores. In some hardwoods these pores are very pronounced. Mahogany and oak, for example, have very noticeable pores and are called open-grain woods. Birch and maple, on the other hand, have small pores and are referred to as close-grain woods. (See page 166 for wood-grain characteristics.)

Wood can be cut in three distinct planes with respect to the annual rings. The end of a piece of wood shows a cross section of the annual layers or rings of growth. This end or transverse surface shows the size and arrangement of the cells better than any other surface or plane. When wood is cut lengthwise through the center, or pith, of the tree, the exposed surfaces are called radial or quartered surfaces. A longitudinal surface that does not pass through the center is called a tangential surface. Lumber classified as plain-sawed is tangentially cut.

Plain-sawed lumber is cut with less waste and generally costs less than quarter-sawed. In some types of wood, ash, chestnut, or elm, and in all the coniferous species, plain-sawed lumber has a figure or grain superior to that of quarter-sawed.

Despite its usually higher cost, quarter-sawed lumber has certain advantages that must be considered. It shrinks less in width and is less subject to twisting or checking. In many hardwoods, such as oak, walnut, and mahogany, quarter-sawed lumber has a much more attractive grain, and for that reason is preferable to plain-sawed in spite of its higher cost. Quarter-sawed lumber also is known as edge-grain, rift-grain, and comb-grain.

GRADES AND SIZES OF LUMBER

Lumber is sold according to grade and size. For commercial purposes it is standardized under two codes, one for softwoods, the other for hardwoods.

Softwood Grades. Yard lumber is classified as Select and Common. Each of these, in turn, is graded according to quality—that is, freedom from knots, blemishes, or defects.

Select lumber is generally clear or contains only minor defects which can be covered by paint or other finishes. It is graded A, B, C, and D. Generally speaking, C Select will prove the best buy for you in Select lumber.

Common lumber contains numerous defects and blemishes which prevent its use for finishing purposes, but it is suitable for general utility or construction. It is graded as Nos. 1, 2, 3, 4, and 5. The best buy, No. 2 Common, will keep your waste at a minimum.

Under a new grading rule, certain types of softwoods have name markings instead of the old numbering system. They are as follows:

No. 1 is now Construction Grade.
No. 2 is now Standard Grade.
No. 3 is now Utility Grade.
No. 4 is now Economy Grade.

Hardwood Grades. Hardwood grades are based on the percentage of clear cuttings that can be obtained from a piece of lumber. The system is much more difficult to understand than that of softwood. Numbered gradings are not com-

CHART OF GRADE REFERENCE FOR BUYING SOFTWOODS

Select: Lumber of good appearance and finishing qualities
Suitable for natural finishes:
   Grade A   Practically free from defects
   Grade B   Allows a few small defects and blemishes
Suitable for paint finishes:
   Grade C   Allows a limited number of small defects or blemishes that can be covered with paint
   Grade D   Allows any number of defects or blemishes which do not detract from a finish appearance, especially when painted

Common: Lumber containing defects or blemishes which detract from a finish appearance, but which is suitable for general utility and constructional purposes
Lumber suitable for use without waste:
   No. 1 Common   A sound and tight knotted stock. Size of defects and blemishes limited. May be considered watertight lumber.
   No. 2 Common   Allows large and coarse defects. May be considered graintight lumber.
Lumber permitting waste:
   No. 3 Common   Allows larger and coarser defects than No. 2 and occasional knotholes
   No. 4 Common   Low-quality lumber admitting the coarsest defects, such as decay and holes
   No. 5 Common   Must hold together under ordinary handling

parable between different woods. For example, the fourth grade of mahogany is a much better wood than the fourth grade of hickory. The essential grading information is given in the chart on page 143; however this chart is not complete nor absolutely accurate, but it can be taken as a general guide for the purchase of hardwoods.

To save money, always buy the lowest

HARDWOOD GRADES

General grading—Indicates decrease in quality

Hardwoods	1st and 2d Grades	3d Grade	4th Grade	5th Grade	6th Grade
Alder, ash, beech, birch, maple, oak, sycamore	Firsts and seconds	Selects	No. 1 Common	No. 2 Common	Sound Wormy
Cherry	Firsts and seconds	Selects	No. 1 Common	No. 2 Common	No. 3A Common
Chestnut	Firsts and seconds	Selects	No. 1 Common	Sound Wormy	No. 2 Common
Elm, hickory	Firsts and seconds	No. 1 Common	No. 2 Common	No. 3A Common	No. 3B Common
Mahogany, walnut	Firsts and seconds	Selects	No. 1 Common	No. 2 Common	No. 3 Common
Poplar	Firsts and seconds	Saps	Selects	Stained saps	No. 1 Common

Firsts: $91\frac{2}{3}$ per cent clear both sides
Seconds: $83\frac{1}{3}$ per cent clear both sides
Firsts and seconds: Not less than 20 per cent firsts (best commercial grade)
Selects: 90 per cent clear one side

No. 1 Common: $66\frac{2}{3}$ per cent clear face
No. 2 Common: 50 per cent clear face
No. 3A Common: $33\frac{1}{3}$ per cent clear face
No. 3B Common: 25 per cent clear face
Sound Wormy: No. 1 Common with wormholes

grade of lumber that will fill your needs. If, for example, you are buying one-by-two strips for furring, shelf cleats, or garden stakes, it is foolish to buy B and Btr lumber.

Sizes of Lumber. Manufactured lumber as shipped from the mill to the lumberyard is classified as (1) rough, (2) surfaced, and (3) worked. *Rough lumber* is furry and splintery. It is generally sold to factories or large woodworking shops that can dress their own lumber. *Surfaced lumber* is dressed by running it through a planer machine which leaves the wood smooth. It may be surfaced on one side (S1S), two sides (S2S), one edge (S1E), two edges (S2E), or a combination of sides and edges (S1S1E or S1S2E). The number you will normally use will be dressed four sides (S4S). *Worked lumber* is cut into moldings. Many kinds, shapes, and sizes are stocked by the average lumberyard.

Lumber comes from the saw in nominal sizes such as two-by-four, one-by-six, and so forth. In this form it is classified as "rough" or nominal size. When run through the planer, the surface dwindles in size by the amount of wood removed. A nominal two-by-four surfaced on four sides (S4S) thus shrinks to $1\frac{5}{8}$ by $3\frac{5}{8}$ inches in cross section, a one-by-six board to $\frac{25}{32}$ by $5\frac{5}{8}$ inches (actual size). A "five-quarter" board, nominally $1\frac{1}{4}$ inches thick, actually comes to $1\frac{1}{8}$ inches when dressed. Refer to the chart on page 144 for nominal and average actual sizes of stock lumber. In some areas of the coun-

NOMINAL AND ACTUAL SIZES OF LUMBER
(Inches)

Nominal thickness	Softwood	Hardwood
	Average actual thickness	
½	⁷⁄₁₆	½
1	²⁵⁄₃₂	⅞
1¼	1⅙	1⅛
1½	1⁵⁄₁₆	1⅜
1¾	1½	1⅝
2	1⅝	1¾
3	2⅝	2¾

Nominal width	Average actual width	
1	²⁵⁄₃₂	⅞
2	1⅝	Usually sold
3	2⅝	to nearest
4	3⅝	nominal
6	5⅝	size at ran-
8	7½	dom widths
10	9½	with edges
12	11½	left rough

try, the actual sizes may be slightly larger.

Moisture and Shrinkage. Freshly cut lumber contains a good deal of moisture. As the moisture disappears, the board shrinks somewhat. When the moisture content of a board drops to about 20 per cent, the lumber is considered seasoned. For furniture and cabinet use, only stock with 6 to 12 per cent moisture content should be used. This seasoning is generally speeded by placing the wood in an oven, a process called kiln drying. Lumber with a high moisture content is difficult to work with, and when the project is finished and the lumber begins to dry out, it will shrink and may open up glued joints and seams and may even crack. For this reason, store lumber in a warm, dry place. Do not let the lumber sag, or it will warp and twist out of shape.

If you want to test wood for moisture content and shrinkage, saw off a piece 1 inch long and exactly 6 inches across the grain. Weigh it carefully. Bake in the oven at 212 degrees Fahrenheit for at least 4 hours. Then measure it or compare it to an undried piece of the same stock. To determine the moisture content, find the difference between the wet and dry weight, and divide the difference by the dry weight. Example: A piece weighing 16 ounces originally weighs 12 ounces after drying (difference 4 ounces), dividing 4 by 12 gives ⅓, or a moisture content of 33⅓ per cent.

Lumber Defects. Several defects must be avoided in the selection of lumber:

1. Knots are places at which the branch of a tree has caused a fibrous, woody mass to form. Sometimes, when knots are solid, this wood is in demand for such things as knotty-pine paneling, but most often knots are a defect that must be removed from furniture lumber.

2. A split is a large break in a board.

3. Check is a slight separation lengthwise in a board. This is often found at the end of the board and must be trimmed off before cutting stock to length.

4. Warp is a curve across the grain which occurs during the drying process.

5. Wind is a longitudinal twist in a board.

6. Decay is rotted area in the wood which causes a soft spot.

7. A shake is a separation of wood along the annual ring.

8. Insect damage causes small holes in the wood surface.

9. Molds and stains cause discoloration of the wood surface.

PLYWOOD

"Plywood" and "home-craftsman projects" have become almost synonymous. It is important, therefore, for you to know something of the qualities and potentialities of this relatively new material.

Plywood is much stronger than wood of comparable thickness, and the large-size sheets eliminate the need for many joints and seams that would be necessary if regular boards were used. There is practically no shrinkage, expansion, or contraction, and the panels possess rigidity and strength in all directions. If well secured, they will not warp.

The production of plywood is normally divided between veneer construction and lumber-core construction. In veneer construction the faces run parallel to the length of the panel, with alternating plies at right angles; an odd number of plies (three, five, seven, etc.), is used. Lumber-core plywood has a comparatively thick middle layer of solid wood, with a $\frac{1}{16}$-inch layer on each side and a very thin face veneer ($\frac{1}{28}$ inch thick) outside. While more expensive than veneer-core plywood, it is ideal for projects like furniture, which call for doweled, splined, or dovetail joints.

Plywood is made with a moisture-resistant binder in the interior grades, while the exterior grade is waterproof. An almost endless variety of woods, from common fir to rare imported species, is used as the face or top veneer. The cost of the panel naturally depends upon the type of wood used as a face surface. Thicknesses range from $\frac{1}{8}$ to 1 inch, the most common being $\frac{1}{4}$, $\frac{3}{8}$, $\frac{1}{2}$, $\frac{5}{8}$, and $\frac{3}{4}$ inch. The standard sheet of plywood is 4 by 8 feet, but it is possible to obtain smaller or larger sheets when required.

The chart at the right shows the grade designations and descriptions of hardwood plywood as set forth in the commercial standards agreed upon by the U.S. Department of Commerce and the hardwood-plywood manufacturers.

In order to show hardwood-plywood face-veneer grades at a glance, the information given in the chart has been greatly oversimplified. Any grade combination of face and back veneers in the standard grades may be obtained in hardwood plywood. The combinations most

HARDWOOD PLYWOOD STANDARD GRADES
(Commercial Standard 35–49)

Grade	Face veneer	Allowable defects
1	Good-Matched for pleasing effect	Burls, pin knots, mineral streaks, discolorations, and patches in limited amounts
2	Good-Unmatched	Same as grade 1, plus filled wormholes, pin wormholes, and open joints not exceeding $\frac{1}{64}$ inch
3	Generally sound (with some cutting and/or repairs)	Same as grades 1 and 2 plus sound knots up to $\frac{3}{4}$ inch, open knots up to $\frac{3}{8}$ inch, wormholes up to $\frac{1}{8}$ inch, and splits
4	Reject	May contain any type and number of defects which do not destroy the strength and serviceability of the veneer for backs, crating, etc.

commonly found in dealers' stocks are 1–1, 1–4, 1–2, 1–3, 2–4, and 2–3.

Douglas-fir plywood is manufactured in strict accordance with government standards. The Douglas Fir Plywood Association has registered certain grade trademarks which are used by the manufacturers to designate different grades of plywood. These trade-marks are well known by lumber dealers. However, it is not necessary to order plywood by these widely used trade-marks, if you describe the grade you want by the letter system.

There are four basic grades of veneer, classified as A, B, C, and D.

Grade A is the highest standard-quality

veneer. Panels with an A face are smooth and paintable. Also, by selecting panels with similar patterns and appearance, A-face plywood is suitable for modern light stain and glaze finishes. Veneer may be of more than one piece, well joined and reasonably matched. Neatly made repair

patches, but no open defects, are permitted, as are shims, streaks, and sapwood.

Grade B is smooth and paintable, similar to Grade A veneer, but also permits circular plugs, the edges of which may be slightly rough. Also permitted are

GRADES OF EXTERIOR-TYPE DOUGLAS-FIR PLYWOOD *

Grade and reg. trade-mark	Face	Back	Width,† feet	Length,† feet	Thickness,† inches
EXT-DFPA A-A	A	A	2½, 3, 3½, 4	5, 6, 7, 8, 9, 10, 12	$3/16$, ¼, ⅜, ½, ⅝, ¾, ⅞, 1, 1⅛
EXT-DFPA A-B	A	B	2½, 3, 3½, 4	5, 6, 7, 8, 9, 10, 12	$3/16$, ¼, ⅜, ½, ⅝, ¾, ⅞, 1, 1⅛
EXT-DFPA Plyshield	A	C	2½, 3, 3½, 4	5, 6, 7, 8, 9, 10, 12	$3/16$, ¼, ⅜, ½, ⅝, ¾, ⅞, 1, 1⅛
EXT-DFPA Utility	B	C	2½, 3, 3½, 4	5, 6, 7, 8, 9, 10, 12	$3/16$, ¼, ⅜, ½, ⅝, ¾, ⅞, 1, 1⅛
EXT-DFPA Sheathing	C	C	4	8, 9, 10, 12	$5/16$, ⅜, ½, ⅝
EXT-DFPA Plyform	B	B	4	8	⅝, ¾

GRADES OF INTERIOR-TYPE DOUGLAS-FIR PLYWOOD *

Grade and reg. trade-mark	Face	Back	Width,† feet	Length,† feet	Thickness,† inches
Interior A-A	A	A	2½, 3, 3½, 4	5, 6, 7, 8, 9, 10, 12	$3/16$, ¼, ⅜, ½, ⅝, ¾
Interior A-B	A	B	2½, 3	5, 6, 7, 8, 9, 10, 12	$3/16$, ¼, ⅜, ½, ⅝, ¾
Plypanel	A	D	2½, 3	5, 6, 7, 8, 9, 10, 12	$3/16$, ¼, ⅜, ½, ⅝, ¾
Plyscord	C	D	2½, 3, 3½, 4	8, 9, 10, 12	$5/16$, ⅜, ½, ⅝
Interior	B	B	4	8	¼, ½, $9/16$, ⅝, ¾

* All grades are sanded both sides except EXT—DFPA sheathing and Interior Plyscord, which are unsanded; ⅜-inch and thinner panels have a minimum of three plies; ½- to ¾-inch are five-ply minimum, ⅞-inch and thicker are seven-ply minimum.

† About three-fourths of all fir plywood is of panels 4 by 8 feet; all sizes shown are standard, but the volume of panels of dimensions other than 4 by 8 feet is small. The great majority of fir plywood is of panels ¼ to ¾ inch thick.

knots up to 1 inch if sound and tight, tight splits, and slightly rough grain.

Grade C is principally used for inner plies and backs (some grades) of exterior type. It permits knotholes up to 1 inch, small borer holes, splits $\frac{3}{16}$ inch or less, tight knots up to $1\frac{1}{2}$ inches, and various repair patches.

Grade D is used only for interior-type panels. It permits knotholes up to $2\frac{1}{2}$ inches, pitch pockets, limited splits, and various repair patches.

If you look at the stamp on a sheet of plywood, you may find that it is, for example, Grade A-A. This means that both surfaces are of the very highest quality. Grade A-B, of course, means that one surface is of high quality and the other is not quite as fine but is still suitable for applications where it will be seen.

The standard types of plywood with their trade names are given in the table opposite.

When ordering plywood, therefore, be guided by the following questions:

Do you want veneer or lumber-core plywood?

What thickness will you need?

What panel size will be most economical?

Will you need one or both surfaces finished? Armed with the answers to these questions, you are ready to order plywood intelligently.

HOME-WORKSHOP WOODS

Within the space of this book, it would be impossible to list in detail the qualities of all woods used in the home workshop. White pine is, of course, the wood most commonly used for general inside work such as bookcases and shelves, and it may also be used for furniture units when the outside finish is to be painted or stained. For finer furniture and woodworking, the native hardwoods such as birch, maple, oak, or walnut are much in demand,

while mahogany has always been the most generally used of the imported woods.

In choosing a wood for a particular project, you should be guided by several qualities of the wood: ease of working, the grain and the finish the wood will take, its susceptibility to warpage, its hardness and resistance to the wear and tear of normal usage, its availability, and finally, its price.

The chart on page 148 lists some of the properties of the more common woods available for home and furniture purposes. Most of these woods can be purchased either in solid or plywood form.

HARDBOARD

Various compressed wood-pulp or hardboard products appear under many different trade names. These boards may often be used for the bottoms or backs of furniture or for the bottoms of drawers. Available in 4- by 8-foot sheets, $\frac{1}{8}$ to $\frac{3}{8}$ inch thick, hardboard is a dense, hard, grainless material, rich brown in color. It can be cut, nailed, and treated like any large thin wood panel. The sheets, composed of finely pulverized wood fibers mixed with a binder, are submitted to tremendous pressure to form a tough, moisture-resistant material. Hardboard takes a paint or wax finish very well.

ESTIMATING MATERIALS AND COSTS

Lumber is measured in various ways, depending upon the type of wood and its width and thickness. Lumber more than 4 inches wide and $\frac{1}{2}$ to 2 inches thick is measured in board feet. A board foot is a square foot of lumber 1 inch thick. To figure the total board footage, multiply the thickness (nominal) of the board in inches by its width (nominal) and length in feet, or

$$\text{B.F.} = \text{thickness in inches} \times \frac{\text{width in inches}}{12} \times \text{length in feet}$$

COMMON HOME-WORKSHOP WOODS *

Name of Wood	Hardness	Strength	Stability	Weight	Rot resistance	Split resistance	Working quality for hand tools	Shaping	Turning	Mortising	Planing and jointing	Nailing	Gluing	Sanding	Remarks
Alder	Med.	Weak	G	Light	F	F	G	F	F	F	G	G	G	F	A Pacific Coast favorite
Ash	Med.	Med.	E	Med. heavy	F	G	P	E	F	F	G	G	F	E	Interior trim, tool handles; wears well
Basswood	Soft	Weak	G	Light	P	E	E	P	P	F	G	E	E	P	Used as core stock
Beech	Hard	Med.	P	Heavy	P	G	F	F	F	G	F	P	G	G	Not durable outside; hard on hand tools
Birch	Hard	Strong	G	Heavy	F	G	P	E	G	E	G	P	F	F	Fine furniture, trim, flooring, and veneers
Butternut	Soft	Weak	E	Light	F	F	G	F	G	F	G	F	G	F	Furniture, sometimes called "White Walnut"
Cedar	Soft	Weak	G	Med.	E	P	G	P	P	F	F	P	G	P	Trim, chest lining, outside use
Cherry	Med.	Med.	G	Heavy	F	P	G	E	E	E	E	F	E	E	Furniture, joiner work, novelties
Chestnut	Soft	Weak	E	Light	F	P	G	G	E	G	G	G	E	E	Scarce; fine for turning
Cypress	Soft	Med.	G	Med.	E	F	F	P	P	P	G	F	F	F	Excellent for outdoor use
Elm	Med.	Med.	P	Med. heavy	F	G	F	P	P	G	P	E	F	G	Bends well; very durable under paint
Fir (Douglas)	Med.	Med. strong	F	Med. heavy	G	F	F	P	P	G	G	G	G	F	Common plywood veneer
Gum (Red)	Med.	Med.	P	Med.	F	G	G	F	E	F	F	G	E	F	Furniture; substitute for mahogany and walnut
Hickory	Hard	Strong	G	Heavy	P	F	P	F	G	E	G	P	G	E	Bends easily; furniture and sports equipment
Magnolia	Soft	Weak	F	Med.	F	G	G	G	F	P	G	E	E	G	Bends easily
Mahogany	Med.	Med.	E	Med. heavy	P	G	E	E	E	G	G	E	G		Excellent furniture wood and boats
Mahogany, Philippine	Med.	Med.	E	Med.	G	P	G	F	G	F	G	G	E	P	Furniture and boats
Maple, hard	Hard	Strong	G	Heavy	P	P	F	E	E	E	F	P	F	G	Excellent furniture wood, flooring, trim, fine for turning
Maple, soft	Med.	Med.	F	Med.	F	G	G	F	F	P	P	F	G	G	Difficult to machine smooth
Oak, red	Hard	Strong	E	Heavy	P	F	P	F	G	E	E	E	G	E	Substitute for white oak in less expensive work
Oak, white	Hard	Strong	E	Heavy	F	F	P	G	G	E	E	G	G	E	Excellent furniture wood, flooring, trim
Pine, white	Soft	Weak	G	Light	F	P	E	G	G	F	G	E	E	G	Best all-around soft wood
Pine, yellow	Hard	Strong	F	Heavy	G	P	F	G	P	G	G	F	F	F	Carpentry work
Poplar	Soft	Weak	G	Med.	P	G	E	P	G	F	G	E	E	P	Good for toys and carving
Redwood	Soft	Med.	E	Med.	E	G	G	G	F	P	G	G	E	P	Excellent for outdoor furniture
Sycamore	Med.	Med.	P	Heavy	F	G	G	P	G	E	P	E	G	P	Furniture and trim
Walnut	Med.	Strong	E	Heavy	G	F	G	G	E	E	G	F	E	E	Excellent for furniture, cabinetwork, trim

* E = excellent, G = good, F = fair, P = poor.

LUMBER CALCULATOR—BOARD FEET FOR VARIOUS LENGTHS

Size in inches	8-foot	10-foot	12-foot	14-foot	16-foot
1 $\times$ 2	$1\frac{1}{3}$	$1\frac{2}{3}$	2	$2\frac{1}{3}$	$2\frac{2}{3}$
1 $\times$ 3	2	$2\frac{1}{2}$	3	$3\frac{1}{2}$	4
1 $\times$ 4	$2\frac{2}{3}$	$3\frac{1}{3}$	4	$4\frac{2}{3}$	$5\frac{1}{3}$
1 $\times$ 5	$3\frac{1}{3}$	$4\frac{1}{6}$	5	$5\frac{5}{6}$	$6\frac{2}{3}$
1 $\times$ 6	4	5	6	7	8
1 $\times$ 8	$5\frac{1}{3}$	$6\frac{2}{3}$	8	$9\frac{1}{3}$	$10\frac{2}{3}$
1 $\times$ 10	$6\frac{2}{3}$	$8\frac{1}{2}$	10	$11\frac{2}{3}$	$13\frac{1}{3}$
1 $\times$ 12	8	10	12	14	16
$1\frac{1}{4}$ * $\times$ 4	$3\frac{1}{3}$	$4\frac{1}{6}$	5	$5\frac{5}{6}$	$6\frac{2}{3}$
$1\frac{1}{4}$ * $\times$ 6	5	$6\frac{1}{4}$	$7\frac{1}{2}$	$8\frac{3}{4}$	10
$1\frac{1}{4}$ * $\times$ 8	$6\frac{2}{3}$	$8\frac{1}{3}$	10	$11\frac{2}{3}$	$13\frac{1}{3}$
$1\frac{1}{4}$ * $\times$ 10	$8\frac{1}{3}$	$10\frac{5}{12}$	$12\frac{1}{2}$	$14\frac{7}{12}$	$16\frac{2}{3}$
$1\frac{1}{4}$ * $\times$ 12	10	$12\frac{1}{2}$	15	$17\frac{1}{2}$	20
2 $\times$ 4	$5\frac{1}{3}$	$6\frac{2}{3}$	8	$9\frac{1}{3}$	$10\frac{2}{3}$
2 $\times$ 6	8	10	12	14	16
2 $\times$ 8	$10\frac{2}{3}$	$13\frac{1}{3}$	16	$18\frac{2}{3}$	$21\frac{1}{3}$
2 $\times$ 10	$13\frac{1}{3}$	$16\frac{2}{3}$	20	$23\frac{1}{3}$	$26\frac{2}{3}$
2 $\times$ 12	16	20	24	28	32

* Sometimes referred to as five-quarter boards.

Thus a piece of lumber 1 by 6 inches by 10 feet would measure 5 board feet— $1 \times \frac{1}{2} \times 10 = 5$. Lumber of this size is always quoted at a specified price per M (thousand) board feet. To find its cost: for example, if it was quoted at $120 per M board feet, it would be charged for at the rate of 12 cents per foot, and would cost 60 cents. The number of board feet in lumber of various sizes and lengths is shown in the above Lumber Calculator.

Lumber less than 4 inches wide and of any thickness is ordered by the linear foot. Thus, an order for a board 10 feet long would specify 10 linear feet.

Plywood and hardboard are ordered in square-foot measurements. A piece of plywood 4 by 8 feet equals 32 square feet.

When you order lumber, make a list of the number of boards you need, their sizes, types, and ultimate uses. From this list, add all lengths of lumber of similar wood, width, and thickness to get the total footage needed for each type.

You can then estimate costs by multiplying the price per board foot, linear foot, or square foot by the total footage needed. Because yard lumber is usually sold only in standard lengths, 15 per cent should be added to the estimated cost for the additional footage you may have to buy.

CHAPTER 13

Woodworking techniques

IN THE first ten chapters of this book, the complete operation of the radial-arm saw and its many attachments was discussed in detail. This is important in the making of any project, but a knowledge of the basic elements of woodworking will be necessary to obtain the best results. This entails, among other things, a knowledge of fastenings, joints, hardware installation, etc.

BASIC PROCEDURES

In all woodworking projects you should follow these six major procedures:

1. Lay out the project by measuring, diagramming, and estimating the quantity of materials needed.

2. Mark the materials for length, width, and shape. Use a well-sharpened pencil, knife, or metal scriber for marking out lines. Be sure that the point of the pencil or scriber is as close to the edge of the rule or square as possible. The thickness of a blunt pencil point can often mean the difference between a good fit and a poor one.

3. Cut the material to the exact size required. Always make your cut on the outside, or waste side, of the line marked on the board. The blade of the saw has some thickness, and if you saw on the finish side, or inside, of the line or along the line itself, you may find that, in spite of your accuracy in measuring, the cut piece of wood is too short.

4. Join the cut parts into the desired assembly by nailing, screwing, or gluing and by using the most appropriate of the wide variety of joints available.

5. Prepare the surface for finishing.

6. Apply the finish material selected to give the project its final appearance.

To get the best results from any project, there are certain other fundamental principles that must be followed:

1. Be accurate when taking measurements and laying out work.

2. Lay out the job clearly by marking the different pieces—front, back, side, etc. Also mark all companion pieces where joints appear as 1 and 1, 2 and 2, etc.

3. Plan ahead as each step is completed.

4. Be orderly and neat. Take pride in turning out a fine job.

5. Use only the best materials. Since the difference in cost between good and cheap materials is small on a single project, it pays to buy the best.

6. All lumber must be squared, to find any deviation from a right angle, straight line, or plane surface, and it must be trued

to the required size before proceeding with the actual work. (See page 35 for details of this operation.)

7. Joints must be made to fit together; never make them too loose or too tight. Remember, your finished item is only as strong as its weakest joint.

8. Wherever possible, duplicate pieces should be laid out and cut at the same time.

9. Keep all tools in good condition. A sharp blade or cutter makes work easier, safer, and more accurate.

FASTENING TECHNIQUES

Nailing. The length, diameter, head size, and approximate number to a pound of the various penny sizes of common nails and finishing nails are shown in the charts on page 159.

A nail must be properly selected for the work it is to do so that it will not split the wood or distort the fibers. The type of nail that distorts the fibers of the wood the least will have the greatest holding power.

In fastening hardwoods, bore holes slightly smaller than the diameter of the nail and to a depth two-thirds of its length. In nailing a board end, blunt the tip of the nail to prevent it from splitting the end. A few staggered nails are stronger than a large number of nails in a row. If one of two pieces of wood to be joined is thin, use nails that will penetrate one-half to three-quarters of the second piece.

Corrugated fasteners, often called "wiggle nails," are used for holding two wood surfaces together side by side. They can be used for making window screens, screen doors, window frames, flower boxes, etc., and for tightening loose joints or cracks in woodwork. They are made with a plain edge for hardwoods and a saw edge for softwoods. They are gen-

erally used with glue for better holding power.

There is a trick in driving a corrugated fastener. Use a medium-weight hammer and strike light blows which are evenly distributed over the outside edge. It is essential that the pieces which are being fastened together rest on something solid while the fastener is driven in.

Another steel fastener, the clamp nail, is new in woodworking. These nails are used on miter joints only. The wide end of the clamp nail is driven into a saw cut $\frac{5}{16}$ inch deep on both edges of the miter, and the joint is held more firmly than with corrugated fasteners.

In fine work where the nailhead must not show or must be inconspicuous, it is driven well below the surface with a nail set. The hole in the wood over the nailhead can then be filled flush with the surface with putty, plastic wood, or sawdust mixed with glue.

Nail sets are made in several sizes, usually $\frac{1}{32}$, $\frac{2}{32}$, and $\frac{4}{32}$ inch, the size being indicated by the diameter of the small end of the tapered shank. The end of a nail set is often "cupped" or hollowed, which prevents it from "walking" or slipping on the nail. Use a nail set of a size which will not enlarge the hole made by the head of the nail.

Screwing. Screws have much greater holding power than nails. Another advantage: work held together by them is easily taken apart and put together again without damaging the pieces.

A little soap rubbed into the threads of a wood screw makes it easier to drive.

If a screw is driven in without first boring a pilot hole for the threaded part, the wood may split, and in some instances the screwhead may be twisted off. Bore holes for small screws with a small brad awl, for large screws with bits or twist drills. If the wood is soft (pine, spruce, basswood, etc.), bore the hole only about half as deep as the threaded part of the screw. If the wood is hard (oak, maple, birch, etc.), the hole must be almost as deep as the screw.

If the screw is large or if it is a brass screw, bore a pilot hole slightly smaller in diameter than the threaded part of the screw and then enlarge the hole at the top with a second drill of the same diameter as the unthreaded portion of the screw.

When two pieces of wood are to be fastened tightly together with screws, two sets of holes must be drilled. The holes are drilled so that the threaded portion of the screw "bites" or takes hold only in the under piece of wood. The piece on top is clamped to the lower piece by the pressure of the screwhead. There are five steps in the operation:

1. Locate the position of the screw holes and mark them with a brad awl. The awl mark will center the drill and prevent it from "walking" away with the spot.

2. Bore a pilot hole, slightly smaller in diameter than the threaded portion of the screw, all the way through the upper piece of wood and into the lower piece half the length of the threaded part of the screw.

3. Enlarge the pilot hole in the upper piece of wood by drilling it out to the same diameter as (or slightly larger than) the shank or unthreaded portion of the screw.

4. If flathead or ovalhead screws are to be used, countersink the clearance hole in the upper piece of wood to match the diameter of the heads of the screws. If roundhead screws or cup washers are used, do not countersink.

5. Drive all screws firmly in place and, after they are all in, tighten each of them.

Screws are sometimes set below the surface of the wood and concealed by a wooden plug. The planking on a boat is

BODY AND LEAD HOLES FOR WOOD SCREWS

Screw gauge	Body hole drill No.	Lead hole drill No.	Countersink drill No.
0	53	Unnecessary	32
1	49	Unnecessary	20
2	44	56	16
3	40	56	4
4	33	52	B
5	$1/8$	52	F
6	28	47	L
7	24	47	O
8	19	42	S
9	15	42	T
10	10	42	X
11	5	38	$7/16$
12	$7/32$	38	$29/64$
14	D	31	$33/64$
16	I	28	$37/64$
18	$19/64$	23	$41/64$

usually fastened to the frame in this manner. Wooden plugs of various diameters, cut from mahogany, oak, pine, white cedar, and cypress, can be purchased from dealers in boat supplies and at some hardware stores. Plugs should be cut from the same kind of wood as that in which they are to be inserted, and the grain should match as closely as possible. They should be cut so that the grain runs along the plug, not lengthwise. Sometimes dowels may be cut off for use as plugs.

First bore a hole at least $3/8$ inch deep with an auger bit the same size as the wooden plug. Then bore the proper pilot and clearance holes. Drive the screw in as far as it will go with a screwdriver. Select a suitable plug, put some glue on its sides, and insert it in the hole, with the grain on the end of the plug running in the same direction as the grain on the surface of the work. Drive the plug in as far as it will go. When the glue has dried, use a chisel or a plane to pare the plug off level with the surface.

Wood screws are sized according to diameter and length. The length is indicated in inches or fractions thereof; the diameter is indicated by a number. The smallest diameter is No. 0, and the largest common size is No. 24. The most generally used sizes are Nos. 3 to 16.

The length of a flathead screw is the over-all length, but the length of round- and fillister-head screws is measured from the point to the underside of the head. The length of an ovalhead screw is measured from the point to the edge of the head.

Standards for screws have been established by cooperation between the manufacturers and the U.S. Bureau of Standards so that standard screws of all screw manufacturers are alike.

Gluing. Glue is the neatest, most durable, and strongest wood fastener when properly used. Glues are classified as hot or cold, depending upon whether heat is necessary to prepare them. Hot glues come from animal parts, are strong, and set quickly with an even consistency. They come in dry sheets or flakes and are hard, transparent, and very brittle. Cold types are resin glue, from resin and chemicals, and casein glue, from milk and chemicals; both come in powder form. Regardless of type, be sure to mix according to the manufacturer's instructions. There are also all types of glues ready mixed for immediate use which may be applied by following the manufacturer's instructions on the container.

Before assembling or gluing any part of a project, carefully inspect each part to make sure that all sandpapering has been completed and that all joints fit properly. Put all the items together (without glue) to make sure that joints come together as they should and that the parts line up and are square and true. Then with a soft pencil clearly mark all companion pieces as 1 and 1, 2 and 2, etc.; then indicate front right, front left, etc. This is done so that the pieces will fit together quickly without further adjustment, for the time between spreading the glue and applying pressure should not exceed 15 minutes.

Now adjust all hand screws and clamps to the proper size. Carefully inspect the work, for it is not too late to trim a joint a little to make it fit better.

Gluing should be done in a warm, dry room, free from drafts. The glue is applied with a brush to only one of the surfaces to be bonded; this makes the bond between the wood rather than between two surfaces of glue. Apply plenty of glue; do not starve the joint. Now apply the clamps; remember to put blocks of scrap wood under the clamps to prevent their bruising the surface. Carefully test the job for squareness and alignment. Then scrape off all excess glue with a chisel. It will help greatly if you throw sawdust over the glue as it oozes out of the joint; the sawdust absorbs the moisture of the glue, which makes it easier to peel off later. Never wash off excess glue with a cloth and water, since this will coat the wood with a thin layer of glue which may show up when dry. Furthermore, the wetting of the wood will make it swell, and this is very undesirable. Once the clamps are in place and all parts have been tested, the project must not be disturbed for at least 2 to 10 hours, depending on the type of glue used.

When it is dry, carefully remove the clamps and start on the final cleaning job. Use a sharp chisel. Holding it with the bevel side up and cutting across the grain (where possible), remove all glue that still remains. Follow this with a thorough sandpapering of all such parts. Give a final sandpapering to all parts of the furniture with fine and then very fine sandpaper.

COMPARISON OF GLUES

	Animal glue	Liquid glue	Casein glue	Urea resin glue	Resoranal glue	Contact glue
Ready mixed	Both	Yes	No	No	No	Yes
Resists dampness	No	Yes	Yes	Yes	Yes	Yes
Water-proof	No	Yes	No	Yes	Yes	Yes
Stains	Yes	No	Stains certain woods	No	Yes	No
Pressure needed	Heavy	Slight	Medium	Heavy	Medium	None
Drying time	2–4 hr.	10–30 min.	4–5 hr.	3–6 hr.	4–10 hr.	1 hr.
Setting temperatures	Any above freezing	Any above freezing	Any above freezing	70° F. up	70° F. up	70° F. up
Gap filling	Yes	No	Yes	Yes	Yes	No
Special uses	General indoors	Repairs small articles	Heavy work. Oily wood. Furniture	Veneers. Furniture	Outdoor work. Oily wood	For holding laminated plastic
Home craftsman	Harder to use than most types	Handy for small jobs and quick applications	Easy to use. Long lasting	Easy to use	Fairly easy to use. Waterproof	Easy to use, but manufacturer's instructions must be followed

Doweling: Many types of joints—miter, edge, butt, and mortise and tenon—are greatly strengthened by installing dowels. Dowels are hardwood rods—generally maple or birch—and are available in diameters from ⅛ to 3 inches, with either a plain or grooved surface. The latter surface allows the glue to run more freely into the joint. (You can groove your own dowel sticks, see page 93.)

In selecting the size of dowel rod to use, a general rule is that the diameter should be no more than half the thickness of the stock. The depth of the hole will vary with the type of joint. The length of the dowel rod should always be cut about ¼ inch shorter than the total of the two holes. The ends of the dowel pins should be cut with a bevel.

For the proper method of locating and drilling dowel holes, see pages 78 and 79.

Splines. A spline is a thin strip of wood inserted in a groove cut in the two adjoining surfaces of a joint. It is a popular means of strengthening miter joints. The groove is cut with the radial-arm saw to a specific width and depth (page 44). A thin piece of stock is then cut to fit into this groove. This stock should be cut so that the grain runs at right angles to the grain of the joint.

WOODWORKING JOINTS

Properly constructed wood joints are essential for all good woodworking projects. All well-constructed joints not only add to the over-all appearance of a piece of furniture, but also provide strength and durability. Sharp cutting tools and accurate measurements and cutting are necessary to produce a really tight joint. Some of the more common joints are shown in Fig. 13·1 and their cuts are described in Chapters 2, 3, 4, 5, and 6. The joints may be nailed, screwed, or glued and can be strengthened by doweling or splining. For your convenience the page numbers for these joint cuts and others are cross-referenced by name.

EDGE-GRAIN TREATMENT FOR PLYWOOD

Plywood edges can be a problem. If care is not exercised, the finished job will be bonded with raw edges that resemble half-healed scars. First, check the design of the piece to be built. Even with plain butt joints, there are an astonishing number of ways to assemble a simple box, and each one makes a difference in the number or position of visible edges. By using rabbets and miters, a little thought at the design stage will reduce the edge problem. Consider also where the piece of furniture will be located, what surface will be exposed, and what finish you will use.

Possibly the best treatment for edge grain is shown in Fig. 13·2, detail *A*. Two 45-degree cuts are made from the underside, completely through the wood, the small piece is removed, and the end is bent as shown. By this method a continuous grain is shown even on the ends.

A solid piece of material—that is, solid hardwood—in the shape of a T in cross section can be forced and glued to the piece of plywood so that, when the edge is viewed, it will appear as solid lumber (detail *B*). The procedure shown in detail *C* is the same, except that the piece of lumber is triangular in cross section.

Cutting the edge at an angle, as shown in detail *D*, is a neat and cheap method; the edge grain may be painted or stained to match the panel.

It is also possible to bead the edge or to glue a beading strip or molding to the edge. A mitered framing strip, secured by glue and by brads that have been set and puttied, is a very effective treatment, especially for table and desk tops. Shaped molding made on your shaper is also good for the exposed top edges of a desk. Do not overlook common half- or quarter-round molding; its width may be greater than the edge width. Aluminum veneer cap molding may also be used, or thin veneer can be glued to the edge grain.

A new veneer tape, available in several wood grains, can be obtained. It consists of a precut ¾-inch strip of thin wood veneer with its own adhesive applied on

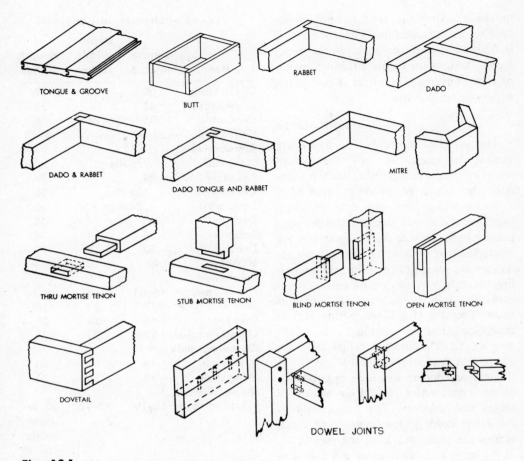

TONGUE & GROOVE

BUTT

RABBET

DADO

DADO & RABBET

DADO TONGUE AND RABBET

MITRE

THRU MORTISE TENON

STUB MORTISE TENON

BLIND MORTISE TENON

OPEN MORTISE TENON

DOVETAIL

DOWEL JOINTS

Fig. 13·1

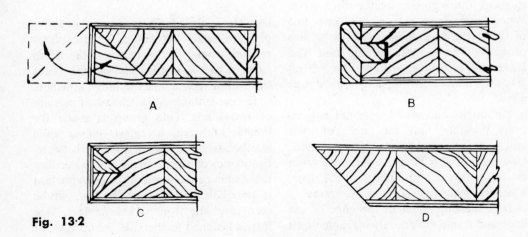

A

B

C

D

Fig. 13·2

the back. After the tape is applied according to manufacturer's instructions, it is finished exactly the same as the panel faces—with stain, varnish, lacquer, paint, or other finishes. The effect is that of an expensive solid panel.

HARDWARE INSTALLATION

The varieties of cabinet hardware are almost unlimited; so only the typical varieties used on furniture, kitchen cabinets, and similar pieces are covered here.

Full-mortise, loose-pin, and bullet-tip butt hinges are well designed for modern cabinetwork. Where two dimensions are given for butt hinges, the first always indicates the length of the joint, not including the tips; the second dimension indicates the full width when the hinge is open. The size of a hinge, within certain limitations, has no relation to its weight or strength. The latter depends upon the gauge and kind of metal used.

Drop-leaf hinges are used in good furniture construction for drop leaves of tables and cabinets. The longer half of the hinge must be long enough to reach across the joint and have the screws set in the drop leaf. The center pin is in line with one face of the hinge, so that it may be set without gaining or cutting out for the whole hinge; however, it is necessary to gouge out a groove for the hinge joint. When these hinges are set, the center line of the pin must coincide with the center of the arc which marks the rule joint. The leaves are, of course, first cut with a drop-leaf table cutter on the shaper (see page 67).

Although concealed hinges are not entirely invisible, only the edges of their thin joints show when the door is closed. One half of the hinge is set in a grain cut in the top or bottom edge of the door, while the other half is set in the frame.

Invisible hinges set in the edge of the door and frame are entirely invisible when

AVERAGE FURNITURE, DIMENSIONS

Item	Length, inches	Depth-width, inches	Height, inches
Dining table	60	42	29
Kitchen table	42	30	30
Card table	36	36	30
Coffee table	36–60	18–24	14–18
Coffee table (round)	36 diam.		15–18
End table	24	15	24
Drum table	36 diam.		30
Lamp table	24 diam.		30
Desk	48	24	30
Secretary	36	24	84
Lowboy	30	18	30
Highboy	36	18	60–84
Breakfront bookcase	48–60	18	78–84
Sofa	72	30	36
Love seat	48	30	36
Occasional chair	27	30	36
Occasional chair (armless)	24	30	30
Wing chair	30	30	36
Dining, desk, folding chair	15–18	15–18	30–36 (seat height 16–18)
Twin bed	78	39	20–24
Double bed	78	54	20–24
Dresser	42–60	22	32–36

the door is closed. They come in a variety of sizes, with the length of the plates ranging from 1 to 5 inches and the width from $\frac{3}{8}$ to $1\frac{3}{8}$ inches. The mortise is cut out with a router and the hinge attached.

Hinges suitable for kitchen cabinets are of two kinds. One group is made for lipped, rabbeted, or offset doors, while another group is intended for flush doors. Both kinds of hinges are available in either the visible or the semiconcealed type; that is, only half the hinge, or one leaf, can be seen from the front of the cabinet. One leaf is fastened to the stile, or upright, of the cabinet, while the other leaf is attached to the edge or to the back face of the door.

Catches. Probably the oldest and most common is the elbow catch, which is screwed to the back of the door. Most catches are spring catches which are released by pulling the door; the elbow catch must be manually released before the door can be opened.

A newer type is the friction catch. Some friction catches are easily applied, being simply screwed in place, while others must be set in holes that are bored for them. Magnetic catches are also available.

Drawer pulls and knobs are never applied to furniture until after the finishing is complete. This makes it easier to do the finishing, since they are not in the way. Without going into the possibilities of metal, or other manufactured pulls, the possibilities with wood alone are vast.

FURNITURE DIMENSIONS

Residential living spaces such as the living room, bedroom, or study are subject to definite requirements. So that you can carefully plan furniture accommodations in your new home or when remodeling your present home, and as a reference for designing and building workshop furniture projects and built-in furniture units, the furniture-dimensions chart on page 158 is presented.

COMMON NAILS

Size	Length	Diameter guage no.	Diameter of head	Approx. no. per pound
2d	1″	15	$\frac{11}{64}$″	830
3d	1¼″	14	$\frac{13}{64}$″	528
4d	1½″	12½	¼″	316
5d	1¾″	12½	¼″	271
6d	2″	11½	$\frac{17}{64}$″	168
7d	2¼″	11½	$\frac{17}{64}$″	150
8d	2½″	10¼	$\frac{9}{32}$″	106
9d	2¾″	10¼	$\frac{9}{32}$″	96
10d	3″	9	$\frac{5}{16}$″	69
12d	3¼″	9	$\frac{5}{16}$″	63
16d	3½″	8	$\frac{11}{32}$″	49
20d	4″	6	$\frac{13}{32}$″	31
30d	4½″	5	$\frac{7}{16}$″	24
40d	5″	4	$\frac{15}{32}$″	18
50d	5½″	3	½″	14
60d	6″	2	$\frac{17}{32}$″	11

FINISHING NAILS

Size	Length	Diameter gauge no.	Diameter of head gauge no.	Approx. no. per pound
2d	1″	16½	13½	1351
3d	1¼″	15½	12½	807
4d	1½″	15	12	584
5d	1¾″	15	12	500
6d	2″	13	10	309
8d	2½″	12½	9½	189
10d	3″	11½	8½	121
16d	3½″	11	8	90
20d	4″	10	7	62

CHAPTER 14

Wood-finishing facts

THE IMPORTANCE of a proper finish for your projects cannot be overemphasized. Whether that finish is varnish, shellac, lacquer, paint, or wax, it will provide the final professional appearance to make you proud of your work. If the wood grain has an attractive appearance, a natural finish may be used. The wood may be given a stain to match other pieces of furniture; or it can be bleached and given one of many attractive modern finishes. Sometimes paint may be more suitable when the wood is unattractive or when color fits into your decorative scheme. The chart on page 162 gives the characteristics of wood and the accepted finishes.

PREPARATION OF WOOD

Success in finishing depends largely on the choice and preparation of the wood. The pieces should be carefully matched as to grain and color, and surfaces must be clean and smooth. To obtain this smoothness, start the finishing process as the pieces are assembled. Sand each piece on the disk, belt, or drum sander as described in Chapter 9.

All marks left on the wood after construction must be removed. Rough edges left by the saw should be sanded until perfectly smooth. If they are very rough, touch them up with the jointer before sanding. Dents in wood can be eliminated by pricking the wood slightly with a sharp-pointed tool and then applying a few drops of water. The water will make the wood fibers swell back to the original shape. After the area is dry, sand the rough surface.

Joints that are not so tight as they should be can be filled with a wood filler. The seam should be cleaned and then packed with a filler such as plastic wood or spackle. As these fillers shrink slightly when dry, use a little more than required. An excellent homemade filler is wood glue mixed with sawdust; use the same sort of sawdust, when possible, as the wood to be filled. After the filler is dry, shave down the excess with a razor blade and then sand. Similarly, cracks in end grain and other spots should also be filled.

Nailheads should be punched below the wood surface and the resulting hole filled with wood filler. Screwheads that have been countersunk can be treated in the same manner. However, a more professional method is to glue a wood plug on top of the screwhead (see page 153).

GENERAL WOOD-CHARACTERISTIC AND FINISHING CHART *

Wood	Natural color	Grain figure	Stain Type	Stain Color	Filler Weight [1]	Filler Color	Natural finish	Bleach	Paint
Alder	Pink to brown	Plain or figured	Oil or water	Red or brown	None	None	Yes	Yes	Yes
Amaranth	Purple	Plain or stripe	None	None	8	Match wood	Yes	No	No
Ash	White to brown	Plain	Any	Any	1.5 to 2	White or brown	Yes	Yes	Yes
Aspen	Light straw	Plain or stripe	Water	Amber	None	None	Yes	No	Yes
Avodire	White to cream	Stripe	None	None	8	Match wood	Yes	Yes [2]	No
Basswood	Cream	Mild	Water	Red or brown	None	None	No	Yes [2]	Yes
Beech	White to brown	Mild	Water	Red or brown	8	Red or brown	No	Yes	Yes
Birch	Cream	Mild	Any	Walnut or mahogany	None or 7	Natural or brown	Yes	Yes	Yes
Bubinga	Pale red to flesh red	Plain to figured	Water	Red or brown	12 to 14	Red or brown	Yes	No	No
Butternut	Amber and cream	Like walnut	Water	Walnut or oak	12 to 14	Medium brown	Yes	Yes	No
Cedar	Red and cream	Knotty or stripe	None	None	None	None	Yes	No	No
Cherry	Red to brown	Fine	Water	Red or brown	6 to 8	Brown, red, or black	Yes	No	No
Chestnut	Gray-brown	Heavy grain	Oil [3]	Red or brown	15	Red or brown	Yes	Yes	Yes
Cypress	Brown and cream	Plain or figured	Water or oil [3]	Red or brown	None	None	Yes	No	Yes
Ebony	Dark brown to black	Plain or stripe	Water	Red or brown	None	None	Yes	No	No
Elm	Cream to brown	Heavy grain	Water	Red or brown	12 to 14	Dark brown	Yes	No	Yes
Fir (Douglas)	Cream	Wild	Oil [3]	Brown	None	None	No	No	Yes
Gaboon	Golden to pinkish tan	Plain or stripe	Water	Red or brown	None	None	Yes	No	No
Gum (red)	Cream and red	Plain or figured	Any	Red or brown	None or 4 to 6	Match wood	Yes	Yes	Yes
Hemlock	Light reddish brown	Plain	Water or oil [3]	Red or brown	None	None	No	No	Yes
Hickory	White to cream	Straight	Water	Red or brown	15	Brown	Yes	Yes	No
Holly	White	Mild	Water	Amber	None	None	Yes	Yes [2]	Yes
Kelobra	Brown	Plain or stripe	Water	Dark brown	12 to 14	Dark brown	Yes	Yes	No
Korina	Creamy gray	Plain or stripe	Water	Red or brown	12 to 14	Red or brown	Yes	Yes	No
Lacewood	Medium brown	Flake	Water	Oak	12 to 14	Dark brown	Yes	Yes	No
Locust	Golden brown	Wild	Water or oil	Brown	12 to 16	Brown	Yes	No	Yes

Wood	Natural color	Grain figure	Stain		Filler		Natural finish	Bleach	Paint
			Type	Color	Weight [1]	Color			
Magnolia	Light to dark yellowish brown	Plain	Water or oil [3]	Brown	None	None	Yes	Yes	Yes
Mahogany	Brown to red-brown	Stripe	Water	Red or brown	12	Red, brown, or black	Yes	Yes	No
Mahogany (Philippine)	Brown to red-brown	Stripe	Water or oil [3]	Red or brown	18	Red, brown, or black	Yes	Yes	No
Maple	Cream	Varied	Water or oil [3]	Maple	None	None	Yes	Yes	Yes
Oak (red)	Red to brown	Plain or flake	Water	Light green	15	Brown	No	Yes	Yes
Oak (white)	White to pale brown	Plain or flake	Water	Brown	15	Brown	Yes	Yes	Yes
Orientalwood	Light brown	Stripe	Water	Amber or brown	12	Brown	Yes	No	No
Padouk	Golden red to deep crimson	Stripe or mottle	None	None	14 to 16	Red or brown	Yes	No	No
Pine (white)	White to cream	Very mild	Water or oil	Brown	None	None	No	No	Yes
Pine (yellow)	Cream to brown	Mild	Water or oil	Brown	None	None	Yes	No	Yes
Poplar	White	Mild	Water or oil [3]	Red or brown	None	None	No	No	Yes
Prima Vera	White to yellow	Stripe	Water	Amber	12	Natural	Yes	Yes	No
Redwood	Red	Mild	Oil [3]	Red	None	None	Yes	No	Yes
Rosewood	Red to brown	Stripe to varied	Water	Red	12 to 15	Dark red to black	Yes	No	No
Sapeli	Medium brown	Stripe	Water	Red or brown	10	Dark brown	Yes	Yes	No
Spruce	White	Plain	Water or oil [3]	Amber or brown	None	None	No	No	Yes
Sycamore	White to pink	Flake	Water	Amber or brown	None	None	Yes	Yes [2]	Yes
Teakwood	Golden brown	Plain or figured	Water or oil	Brown	16	Natural or brown	Yes	Yes	No
Tigerwood	Golden brown	Stripe	Water	Dark brown	8 to 12	Dark brown	Yes	Yes	No
Tupelo	Pale to brownish gray	Plain	Water	Brown	None to 7	Brown	Yes	Yes	Yes
Walnut	Cream and dark brown	Varied	Water	Water	12 to 15	Brown to black	Yes	Yes	No
Zebrawood	Tan with brown stripe	Heavy stripe	Water	Light oak	12	Natural	Yes	No	No

* This chart is a general one and gives only the usual accepted finishes and uses of the wood.

[1] Weight designates number of pounds of filler plastic per gallon of thinner.

[2] Generally not necessary because of the light color of the wood.

[3] Penetrating oil stain may also be used. Non-grain-raising stains may be substituted for water stains throughout.

Check all joints to be sure they are solid. If they do not appear to be strong enough, additional nails or screws may be necessary. In some cases, metal angle irons or wood blocks may be required.

SANDING

When an assembly is completed and ready for finishing, go over the job carefully with at least three grades of sandpaper (see page 111 for abrasive data), using successively finer grits of garnet paper or cloth. If you do a good job when power sanding (Chapter 9), you will only have to go over it lightly by hand with fine-grade paper.

All sanding should be done in the direction of the wood grain. If the sanding is done by hand, make a sanding block with a felt pad attached to the underside. This does a better, faster job than if the sandpaper is pushed by hand alone.

BRUSHES AND BRUSHING

Brushing is the commonest method of applying finish materials. It is slow compared with the spray gun, but has advantages in simplicity of equipment and ease of application. With paint, varnish, and other brushing mediums, the quality of the brushed finish, as judged by durability and appearance, is equal and in some cases superior to the same finish applied by spraying.

The best all-purpose finishing brush is an XXX black China hog bristle, full chisel, about 2½ inches wide. Softer brushes, such as those made from goat, sable, badger, or nylon, can be used to advantage for flowing quick-drying materials. The most popular of the soft brushes is the fitch hair brush, excellent for flowing varnish. "XXX" on a brush means that the bristles are put up in three rows or thicknesses. Single-thickness and double-thickness brushes are proportionately thinner in body and are useful where flexibility is required, as for brushing around a turning.

Good brushes have flag ends. In cheap brushes, the bristles are commonly cut to length and do not have the paint-holding flags at the end of the bristles. Most finishers prefer a full chisel brush, one in which long and short bristles are arranged to form a true chisel edge. A cheap chisel edge is sometimes made by trimming the bristles. All brushes are made in varying bristle lengths. Wood finishers working on large areas prefer a long bristle because it holds more material. Better control is possible with the average or medium-length bristle.

The proper handling of a brush is largely a matter of common sense, coupled with a little practice. Use the tip or edge of the brush to work into corners or to make a line or edge. Cross-brush all large areas for good coverage and to eliminate any skilled places, or "holidays." Brush turnings round and round and then use light lengthwise strokes where possible. For general brushwork, the bristles should be dipped to a little over one-third of their length. Surplus paint or varnish should be wiped off on a strike wire or on the edge of the can.

Finishing materials are either brushed out or flowed on. Materials such as varnish and shellac should be flowed on and allowed to level off. In finishing flat surfaces, brush out toward the edges; this will prevent drips which invariably occur when a loaded brush is pulled over a sharp edge. When brushing stain, shellac, lacquer, and other materials where a uniform coat must be applied, exercise care to prevent double-coating any areas; start the loaded brush on bare wood and brush into the lap left by the previous brushful. This is good technique in applying any finishing material.

Immediately after use the brush should be cleaned with the proper solvent. Work the solvent well into the heel of the brush. Slap the brush over the edge of the hand to throw out the solvent and dirt; do not bang the brush over the edge of a board. Keep bristles straight by combing with a wire or fiber brush. Stain and shellac brushes should be wrapped in paper after cleaning; others can be kept in a brush keeper.

SPRAYING

In recent years, portable spraying equipment has been manufactured in the moderate-price range for the average homecraftsman. Since there are various types, it is necessary to check the manufacturer's instructions for proper technique and use of the gun.

ENAMELING

Before enameling, sand the wood very smooth and be sure it is clean and dry. Apply an enamel undercoater. (In the case of fir plywood, use a sealer first and, when dry, an undercoater.) This can be either flat white paint or a special enamel undercoater. If the finish is to be a color other than white, the undercoater can be tinted either by mixing in it some colors in oil or by adding a little of the enamel you plan to use as the finish coat. Allow the undercoater to dry at least 24 hours and then sand the surface with fine garnet or aluminum oxide paper. Remove all traces of dust with a clean cloth dampened in turpentine.

Enamel, unlike flat paint, is flowed onto the surface, and the action of the enamel removes the brush marks so that the surface dries completely smooth. Once the finish has been applied, do not go back over it for additional brushing as this may leave marks which will not flow out. Be careful of accumulations of enamel around edges. These must be removed at once before they dry. In most cases, one coat of enamel will be sufficient. If it is not, allow it to dry thoroughly, give it a light sanding and dusting, and apply a second coat.

STAINS AND STAINING

Staining is usually the first operation in applying a transparent or semitransparent finish to new wood if the natural color of the wood is not desired. There are many types of stains, but water stains and oil stains are the most common.

Water Stains. Water stains may be purchased in powder form in a variety of colors and mixed as needed by dissolving the powder in hot water. Water stain can be sprayed or brushed. Since the water in the stain raises the grain of the wood, a previous sponging with warm water is advisable.

Some workers prefer a small amount of dextrin in the sponging water to stiffen the wood fibers—2 ounces per gallon. Dextrin, also known as starch gum, can be obtained at any wallpaper store.

When the wood is dry, sand it with fine paper. Then apply the stain freely and rapidly. Better penetration is obtained if the stain is used warm. Brush on the stain in long, smooth strokes, with the grain. Wiping the end grain with a cloth will prevent darkening. Other methods used to prevent darkening of end grain include (1) previous treatment with a thin glue size, (2) sponging with water immediately before staining, and (3) using a separate light stain.

Water stain will dry overnight or in 12 hours. A wash coat of 7 parts alcohol to 1 part shellac can be applied when the stain is dry. A light sanding will then remove any remaining traces of raised grain.

Manufacturers have developed stains in which water-soluble powders are dissolved in a solvent other than water. Stains of this kind are known by various descriptive trade terms, such as non-grain-raising stain, fast-to-light stain, non-sand stain, etc. They are more expensive than regular water stains because of the solvent used, but offer one of the best stains for new work. Their rapid drying makes brushing difficult, but smooth coats are easily applied by spraying. They are nonbleeding and can be used under any type of finish coat. They dry in 10 minutes to 3 hours, depending on the type. Ready-mixed colors are numerous. Primary colors are available for mixing tints to suit individual tastes.

Oil Stains. The most commonly used oil stains are made from colors or pigments ground in linseed oil. Oil is nongrain-raising; therefore oil stains do not require previous sponging. They can be brushed or sprayed on. The main difference in technique between water and oil staining is that oil stain is dipped with a rag to remove the surplus and equalize the color. Wiping is done while the stain is wet, but time should be allowed to ensure good penetration. Immediate wiping of the end grain will eliminate darkening. Since oil stains will bleed into finishing coats of varnish and lacquer, always seal the stain with a wash coat of shellac. Avoid the use of oil stains on birch, maple, gum, cherry, or mahogany.

FILLERS AND SEALERS

A filler is used to fill the pores in coarse-grain woods before applying the final finish. A sealer is any liquid finishing material used as a first coat on close-grain wood or over the filler on coarse-grain woods.

Prepared paste filler is generally the best for homecraftsmen. It may be purchased in a number of colors; select a shade slightly darker than the color of your wood, for the wood will gradually turn darker as it ages. If the desired color cannot be obtained, get a light color and add colored pigment in oil.

Liquid filler is generally a cheap varnish

FILLER FOR VARIOUS WOODS

No filler needed	Liquid or thin paste	Paste filler
Cedar	Birch	Ash
Cypress	Cherry	Chestnut
Fir	Gum	Elm
Hemlock	Maple	Hickory
Pine	Redwood	Kornia
Poplar		Mahogany
Spruce		Oak
		Walnut

with a small amount of silex added. It is used on cheap work in medium close-grain woods. For a better grade of work a thin paste filler is more satisfactory. The accompanying table lists the various woods and the type of filler, if any, required for each.

Before using paste filler, thin it with a small amount of turpentine or naphtha until it is of the proper consistency to brush. Wood with coarse pores will require a thicker filler than wood with small pores. About 3 pounds of filler to 1 quart of solvent is correct for mahogany, while walnut can take a slightly thinner filler (about $2\frac{1}{2}$ pounds per quart of solvent).

To apply the filler, use a fairly stiff brush. Brushing is done with the grain, in order to pack the filler into the pores. In 5 to 20 minutes, the filler will start to lose its wet appearance. As soon as spots begin to flat out, take a piece of burlap or a handful of hair and pad the filler into the pores. Clean off the surplus by wiping across the grain; and finish wiping with clean rags, stroking with the grain. If the filler sets up too hard for easy wiping, moisten the wiping rag with benzine.

Inspect the entire project thoroughly. If the pores are not filled level, apply a second coat of slightly thinner filler immediately, wiping off in the same way. Paste filler should dry for 12 to 24 hours, unless it is a fast-drying type, which is ready in 3 to 4 hours. In any case, it is of the greatest importance that the filler be bone dry before any other coating is applied. The dry filler should be sanded lightly with fine or very fine garnet or aluminum oxide paper and wiped off with a rag moistened with benzine.

Whether or not to seal the filler is largely a matter of preference. The same applies to sealing the stain coat before applying the filler, except in the case of softwoods, such as fir, which must be sealed before staining. Generally, it is good practice to seal both stain and filler. A special resin sealer is best for the job, but for many people shellac is the old stand-by—white shellac for light finishes and orange shellac for browns and mahoganies. The shellac is reduced with alcohol (4 to 1 for filler sealer, 7 to 1 for stain sealer), after which the shellac is poured slowly into an equal amount or less of mixing lacquer. This mixture can be brushed on more easily than straight shellac, is almost waterproof, and dries to permit recoating in about 2 hours. Any type of sealer coat over the filler should be sanded with fine paper when dry, after which the work is ready for finishing coats of varnish or lacquer.

VARNISH FINISHES

Varnish makes an excellent transparent finish on wood, being unequaled for depth or build and possessing good durability and hardness. It brushes easily to a perfectly smooth film and dries to permit recoating in 24 to 48 hours. Varnishing should be done in a dust-free room, between 70 and 90 degrees Fahrenheit. Some craftsmen sprinkle the floor with water to settle the dust. Before applying the varnish, dampen a piece of lintless cloth in a little varnish and wipe the surface with it. The small amount of varnish in the cloth will pick up dust which would not otherwise be caught.

Spread the varnish on as it comes from the can—evenly with long strokes, first with the grain, then across the grain, and then with the grain. As varnish is slow-drying, thinned shellac is often used for a sealer coat. The shellac dries quickly and does not soak into the wood, thus speeding up the drying of the varnish.

A good varnished surface usually requires three or four coats. Rub each coat down with fine steel wool or extra-fine sandpaper, after letting the varnish dry for at least 48 hours. Remove all dust from the surface, after sanding, by rubbing with a lint-free cloth moistened with turpentine or a chamois dampened with water. Pumice and oil, followed with rottenstone and oil, will produce a finely polished surface.

SHELLAC FINISHES

Shellac makes a good finish for many pieces of furniture. It is hard, quite easy to apply, dries in a few hours, and does not require a dustproofer.

Since shellac dries very quickly, you must work fast with it, or it will become tacky and hard to handle. Never apply shellac over a damp surface, for the moisture will cause the shellac to become cloudy. Brush with the grain of the wood and do not brush too much. For best results, dilute the shellac with alcohol. It is easier to apply thinned shellac, and (unless you are experienced in applying it unthinned) you will generally get a better-finished surface. Several coats of thin shellac are best for a well-finished surface.

Standard shellac ordinarily dries hard in about 8 hours, although thinned shellac dries in 3 or 4 hours, ready for sanding. Go over each coat with fine sandpaper or 2/0 fine steel wool. Sandpaper with the grain of the wood. After each sanding, brush the surface and rub with a cloth dampened with benzine to remove the dust. The final rubbing or polishing should be done with FF pumice stone and rubbing oil, using a felt pad.

LACQUER FINISHES

Roughly speaking, lacquer can be divided into two groups—brushing lacquer and spraying lacquer. Lacquers dry very rapidly. Generally, spraying lacquers dry so rapidly that they cannot be applied with a brush.

The solvent used with the lacquer for thinning or as a cleaner for brushes or a spray gun is lacquer thinner. Thinners suitable for paint and varnish should never be used with lacquer. While paint and varnish can be applied over lacquer, lacquer should never be applied over paint or varnish because the solvent in the lacquer will soften these base coats.

Brushing Lacquer. To apply brushing lacquer properly, you must work with a good deal of speed. The lacquer should be flowed on and brushed out as little as possible. Use a large brush and let it carry as much lacquer as possible without dripping. Apply the lacquer in one direction only. If a second coat is required, it must be applied with even more speed, or the solvent in the second coat will soften the first coat.

Spraying Lacquer. By far the best method of applying lacquer is to use a spray gun, but this calls for good equipment.

RUBBING WITH PUMICE AND ROTTENSTONE

A fine finish for varnish, lacquer, and shellac is obtained by rubbing with pumice or rottenstone. Mix the pumice with either water or oil (paraffin or mineral), and use a felt pad to rub the paste over the finished surface. Rub with the grain. Use pumice with oil, not with water, on shellac finish, Rub until the desired finish is obtained. Rottenstone is much finer than pumice and is used in the same manner,

usually following a rubbing with pumice.

If water is used with either pumice or rottenstone, it makes the mixture cut faster and produces a duller finish. When rubbing edges, corners, and high spots, be very careful not to cut through the finish. Clean the surface thoroughly with a soft rag after rubbing.

WAX FINISHES

A wax finish has a pleasing eggshell gloss and is satisfactory for furniture as well as for floors and woodwork. Fill the wood and give a sealing coat of thinned shellac, lacquer, or varnish, and allow to dry. Sandpaper lightly before applying the wax.

Rub the wax on the surface, a little at a time, with a soft cloth. Allow to dry for about 20 minutes, and then rub hard with a soft cloth. Several coats are usually required.

BLEACHING OR "BLONDING"

Bleaching lightens the color of wood by means of chemicals. Apart from the bleaching process, the so-called blond finishes do not differ in any way from other finishes. Not all blond finishes are secured by bleaching. Maple, birch, and other light-colored woods are successfully blonded by the use of a pigmented undercoat. This subject is treated at the end of this chapter.

Simple homemade bleaches are 100 per cent effective on light-colored woods and will lighten any dark wood to a considerable extent. Typical of these is the simple oxalic acid bleach, which is inexpensive and easy to make. Three solutions are required: (1) 3 ounces of oxalic acid crystals dissolved in 1 quart of water, (2) 3 ounces of sodium hyposulfite (photo hypo) in 1 quart of water, and (3) 1 ounce of borax in 1 quart of water. These chemicals can be obtained from any drugstore at a small cost.

All solutions are made with hot water but are used cold. The oxalic acid solution is applied first, with a brush or rubber sponge. When this coat has partly dried, the second solution (hypo) is applied, after which the work should be allowed to dry thoroughly. If the color of the wood is not light enough, the process can be repeated. When the color is right, the surface should be flushed with the borax solution. Overnight drying should be allowed before sanding. The work is then ready for any kind of varnish or lacquer finish.

There are several prepared commercial bleaches which are high-powered enough to give nearly white tones on walnut and mahogany in a single application. The procedure for applying these bleaches varies with the brand, and the manufacturer's directions must be followed. After the work is completely dry, it should be sanded lightly with very fine sandpaper to remove any chemical residue and to clean up wood fibers lifted by the bleaching solution.

Wood is usually bleached a bit more than is required for the final finish. The color is brought back to the desired shade with a light application of non-grain-raising stain, applied in such a manner as to equalize any variations in color. The stain is followed by a wash coat of shellac or lacquer, after which the regular schedule of filler and top coat completes the finish.

Blond Sealers. Excellent blond finishes can be obtained without bleaching by using a surface color or blond sealer. This is a very satisfactory method of treating naturally light woods. Add white lacquer enamel to clear lacquer, or, if an amber effect is desired, add tan to clear lacquer. Blond sealers of this kind can be purchased ready mixed. A uniform, light coat of the sealer will produce a satisfactory blond color without obscuring the natural grain of the wood. This blonding technique is perfect on maple and birch and can be used on walnut and mahogany to produce a pleasing tone, a little lighter than the natural color of the wood. When overdone on dark-colored woods, it gives the wood a painted appearance and the effect is not pleasing.

FINISHING FIR PLYWOOD

Fir plywood needs a good sealer, because of the special character of the grain which is made up of alternate hard summer growth and softer spring growth. Without a sealer, the first coat of paint or stain penetrates unevenly, resulting usually in a "wild," overly conspicuous grain. To "tame" or quiet this grain, several special types of sealers are available; they allow the stain to soften the darker markings and deepen the lighter surfaces.

To obtain a light natural finish, sandpaper the wood with medium sandpaper, and then apply an even coat of resin sealer. Lightly sand when dry, and follow with a thin coat of pure white shellac; the shellac should be reduced to 2-pound cut. Sandpaper again when dry and apply either a satin-finish lacquer or a gloss varnish. If a flat finish is desired, a flat or dull varnish may be substituted. After it is thoroughly dry, steel-wool the surface and apply white wax.

A blond or pickled effect may be given to fir plywood by using a white plywood sealer or an interior white undercoater, thinned as follows: 6 pounds of flat undercoat, 3½ quarts of pure turpentine, and 1 pint of linseed oil. If the white sealer is used, it may be thinned 10 to 15 per cent with mineral spirits or turpentine. Paint the sealer on and allow it to set for 3 or 4 minutes. Then rub it into the pores and wipe clean, taking care not to leave a painted effect. Let it dry overnight, and next day lightly sand with very fine sandpaper. Apply a thin coat of pure white shellac, and sand when dry. Follow with a coat of lacquer or varnish. Steel-wool when dry, and wax.

An inexpensive but attractive finish may be given with a single coat of white sealer or interior white undercoater, pigmented to the desired tint and thinned sufficiently so that the grain of the wood will show through. A second coat of clear shellac or varnish will add to the durability of this finish and give it a deep luster.

For a painted surface on fir plywood, the sealer will provide a smooth, even base. For best results, the sealed surface should be sandpapered. Plastic and water paints may be used over the sealer, provided they are applied in accordance with the manufacturer's directions.

HARDBOARD

Practically any type of finishing material may be used on hardboard—oil paint, water paint, enamel, stain, lacquer, shellac, varnish, penetrating sealers, wax, and special finishes. By following the manufacturer's directions and applying the finishes in the same manner as on a hardwood surface, satisfactory results are obtained. The surface must be free of all dirt, grease, and other foreign material before a finish is applied. Dirt may be removed with water and a mild soap, grease with carbon tetrachloride or naphtha. Be sure the hardboard panel is dry before starting to finish it.

FINISHING JIGS

The jigs described for various woodworking operations should be made into a permanent shop fixture. Sand them smooth. Then a coat of shellac followed by a coat or two of machine gray enamel will make them last for a lifetime. Stencil their use—circle cutter, taper, etc.—on each jib with black enamel for quick reference.

CHAPTER 15

Workbenches for the radial-arm machine

FOR YOUR radial-arm machine, you must have a solid base. This may take one of several different forms: steel cabinets, saw horses, and built-in bench units.

Figure 1·7 shows the radial-arm machine mounted on a ready-made steel cabinet. The space under the machine can be used for storage of accessories. Placing the machine on a bench of saw horses is a good temporary setup. However, the ideal arrangement for your machine is to build it into and make it part of the workbench itself. As shown in Figs. 15·1 and 15·2 these two workbenches—one traditional, the other contemporary —are detailed completely in this chapter. They are both easy to construct and can easily be your first project with your radial-arm machine.

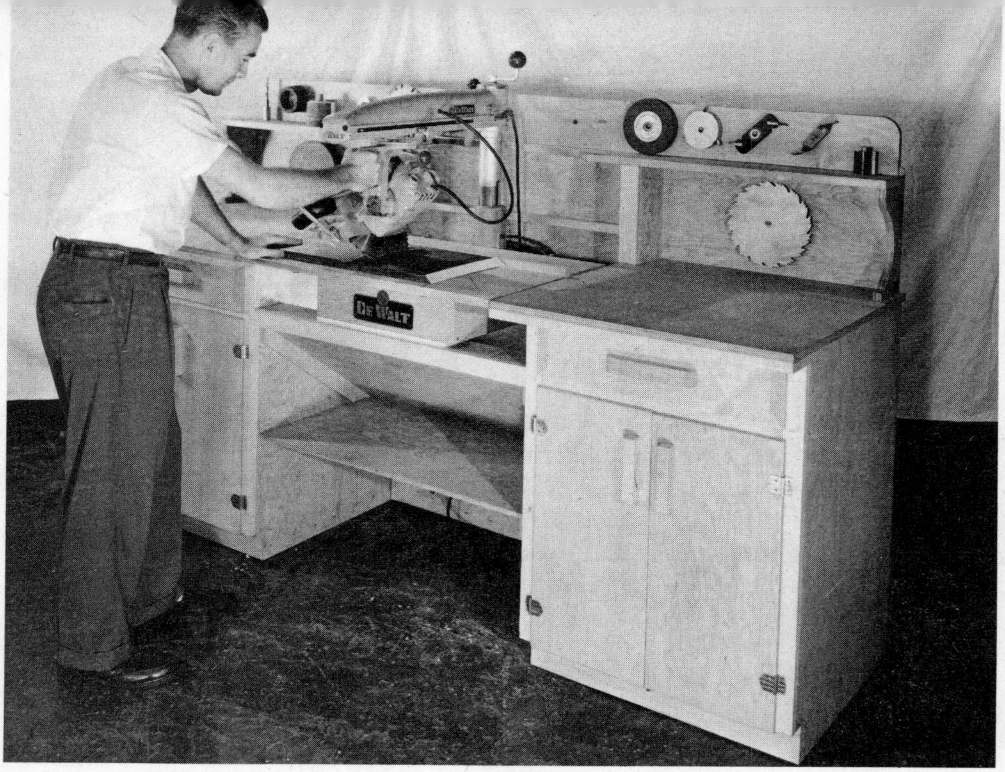
DeWALT

Fig. 15·1

CUTTING FOR 1/2" PLYWOOD 4'X8'

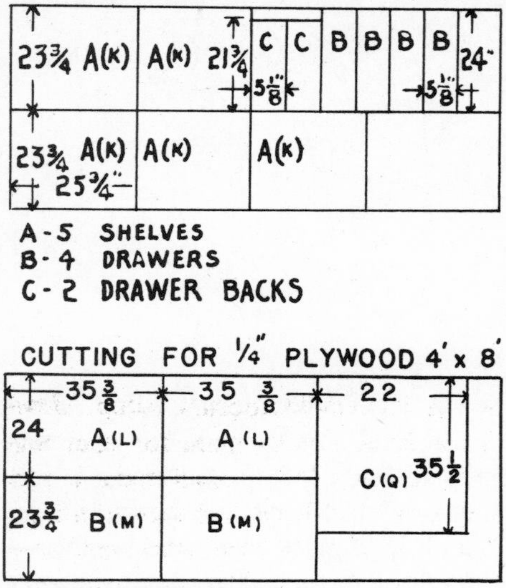
23 3/4 A(K)
A(K)
21 3/4
C C B B B B
5 1/8"
5 1/8"
24"
23 3/4 A(K)
A(K)
A(K)
25 3/4"

A-5 SHELVES
B-4 DRAWERS
C-2 DRAWER BACKS

CUTTING FOR 3/4" PLYWOOD 4'x8'

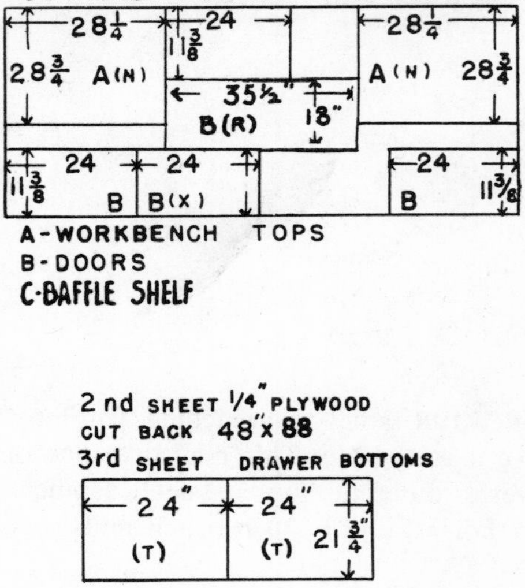
28 1/4
24
28 1/4
11 3/8
28 3/4 A(N)
A(N) 28 3/4
35 1/2"
18"
B(R)
24
24
24
11 3/8
B B(X)
B
11 3/8

A-WORKBENCH TOPS
B-DOORS
C-BAFFLE SHELF

CUTTING FOR 1/4" PLYWOOD 4' x 8'

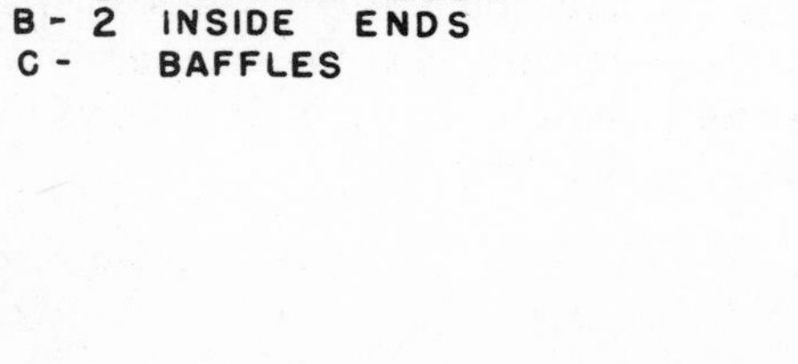
35 3/8
35 3/8
22
24 A(L)
A(L)
C(Q) 35 1/2
23 3/4 B(M)
B(M)

A- 2 OUTSIDE ENDS
B- 2 INSIDE ENDS
C- BAFFLES

2nd SHEET 1/4" PLYWOOD
CUT BACK 48"x 88
3rd SHEET DRAWER BOTTOMS

24"
24"
(T)
(T) 21 3/4

MATERIAL LIST FOR DE WALT MODEL MB POWER SHOP CABINET

Buy	No. required	Use	Part
FRAME (Pine)			
1 pc. 2" x 4" x 16'	2 pc.	$1\frac{3}{4}$ x $3\frac{5}{8}$ x $87\frac{1}{2}$	A
5 pc. 1" x 6" x 12'	8 pc.	$\frac{3}{4}$ x $5\frac{5}{8}$ x $35\frac{3}{8}$	B & C
	4 pc.	$\frac{3}{4}$ x $3\frac{1}{2}$ x $21\frac{3}{4}$	D
	6 pc.	$\frac{3}{4}$ x $1\frac{3}{4}$ x $23\frac{3}{4}$	E
	4 pc.	$\frac{3}{4}$ x $5\frac{5}{8}$ x $23\frac{3}{4}$	F
	4 pc.	$\frac{3}{4}$ x $\frac{1}{2}$ x $23\frac{3}{4}$	G
	2 pc.	$\frac{3}{4}$ x $5\frac{5}{8}$ x $28\frac{1}{4}$	H
PLYWOOD (Fir 1 side good)			
1 pc. $\frac{1}{2}$" ply. 4' x 8'	5 pc.	$\frac{1}{2}$ x $23\frac{3}{4}$ x $25\frac{3}{4}$" Shelves	K
	4 pc.	$\frac{1}{2}$ x $5\frac{1}{8}$ x 24" Drawer Sides	S
	2 pc.	$\frac{1}{2}$ x $5\frac{1}{8}$ x $21\frac{3}{4}$" Drawer Backs	U
	1 pc.	$\frac{1}{2}$ x 18 x $35\frac{1}{2}$" Baffle Shelf	R
1 pc. $\frac{1}{4}$" ply. 4' x 8'	1 pc.	$\frac{1}{4}$ x 48 x $87\frac{1}{2}$" Back	J
1 pc. $\frac{1}{4}$" ply. 4' x 8'	2 pc.	$\frac{1}{4}$ x 24 x $35\frac{3}{8}$" Outside Ends	L
	2 pc.	$\frac{1}{4}$ x $23\frac{3}{4}$ x $35\frac{3}{8}$" Inside Ends	M
	1 pc.	$\frac{1}{4}$ x 22 x $35\frac{1}{2}$" Baffle	Q
1 pc. $\frac{1}{4}$" ply. 2' x 4'	2 pc.	$\frac{1}{4}$ x $21\frac{3}{4}$ x $23\frac{3}{4}$" Drawer Bottoms	T
1 pc. $\frac{3}{4}$" ply. 4' x 8'	2 pc.	$\frac{3}{4}$ x $28\frac{1}{4}$ x $28\frac{3}{4}$" Workbench Tops	N
	4 pc.	$\frac{3}{4}$ x $11\frac{3}{8}$ x 24" Doors	X
CABINET FRONT TRIM (Pine)			
1 pc. 1" x 8" x 10'	2 pc.	$\frac{3}{4}$ x $1\frac{3}{4}$ x $21\frac{7}{8}$" Baffle Cleat	O
	2 pc.	$\frac{3}{4}$ x $1\frac{3}{4}$ x 18" Cleat	P
	4 pc.	$\frac{3}{4}$ x $1\frac{3}{4}$ x $31\frac{1}{8}$"	W
	2 pc.	$\frac{3}{4}$ x $1\frac{3}{4}$ x $22\frac{3}{4}$" Trim Above Drawers	Z
	2 pc.	$\frac{3}{4}$ x $5\frac{5}{8}$ x $23\frac{1}{2}$" Front of Drawers	V
	2 pc.	$\frac{3}{4}$ x $3\frac{1}{2}$ x $25\frac{3}{4}$" Kicks	I
CABINET TOP TRIM (Pine)			
2 pc. 1" x 6" x 8'	1 pc.	$\frac{3}{4}$ x $5\frac{5}{8}$ x $87\frac{1}{2}$" Shelf	Y
	4 pc.	$\frac{3}{4}$ x $5\frac{5}{8}$ x $10\frac{1}{2}$" Shelf Supports	Y-1
	2 pc.	$\frac{3}{4}$ x $2\frac{1}{2}$ x $10\frac{1}{2}$" Front Shelf Supports	Y-2

NECESSARY HARDWARE AND MISCELLANEOUS

36 flathead screws $1\frac{1}{4}$ in. (pcs. H & N)
1 lb. each 4d., 6. finish nails
1 lb. 6d. head nails for frame
4 pair brass butts $\frac{3}{4}$ in. x $2\frac{1}{2}$ in.
1 cabinet lock flush type
3 friction catches

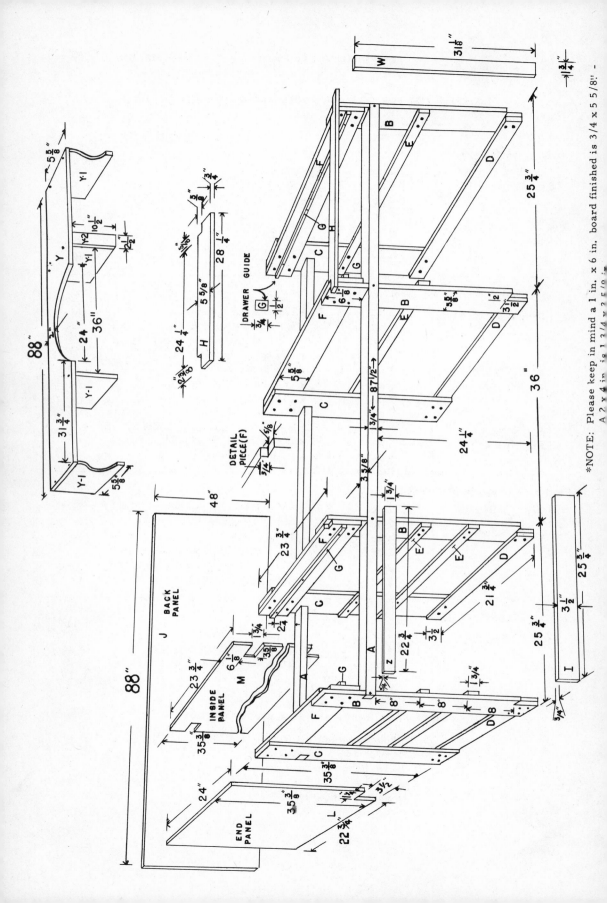

*NOTE: Please keep in mind a 1 in. x 6 in. board finished is 3/4 x 5 5/8'' –
A 2 x 4 in. is 1 3/4 x 3 5/8 in.

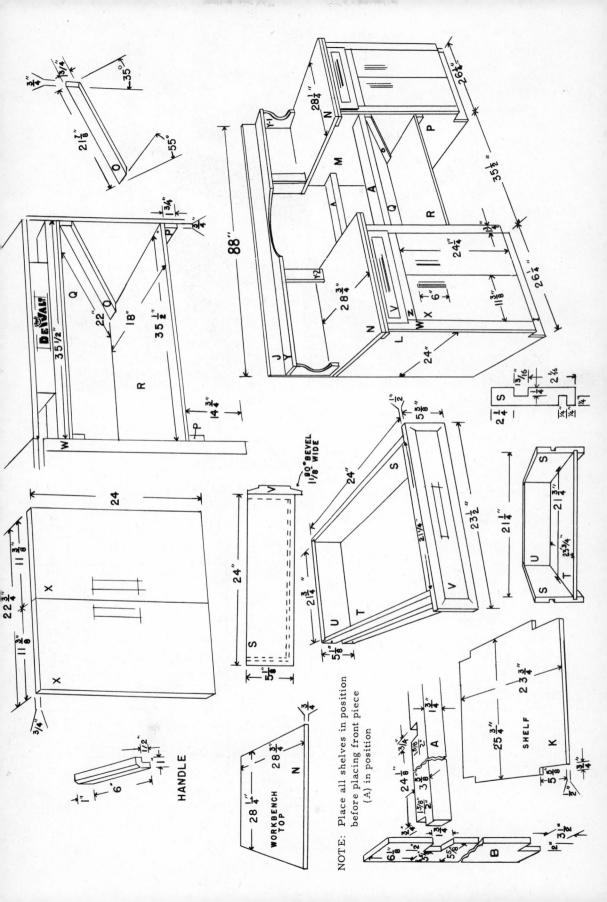

NOTE: Place all shelves in position before placing front piece (A) in position

HANDLE

WORKBENCH TOP

SHELF K

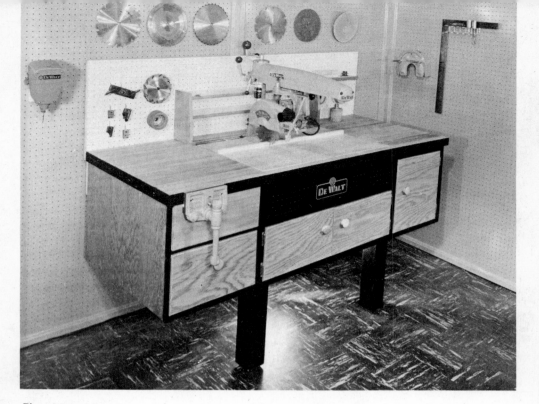

Fig. 15·2

CUTTING DIAGRAMS

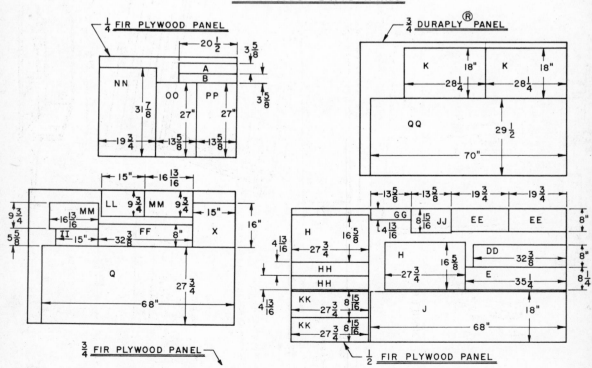

¼ FIR PLYWOOD PANEL

¾ DURAPLY® PANEL

¾ FIR PLYWOOD PANEL

½ FIR PLYWOOD PANEL

MATERIAL LIST *

Buy	No. required	Use	Part
PINE			
2 pc. 1″ x 2″ x 12′	2 pc.	$\frac{3}{4}$ x $1\frac{1}{8}$ x $27\frac{3}{4}$	I
	1 pc.	$\frac{3}{4}$ x $1\frac{3}{8}$ x $50\frac{1}{4}$	S
	2 pc.	$\frac{3}{4}$ x $1\frac{3}{8}$ x $68\frac{1}{4}$	R
	2 pc.	$\frac{3}{4}$ x $1\frac{1}{2}$ x $16\frac{5}{8}$	L
1 pc. 1″ x 3″ x 7′	1 pc:	$\frac{3}{4}$ x 2 x $4\frac{7}{8}$	U
	1 pc.	$\frac{3}{4}$ x 2 x 9	V
	1 pc.	$\frac{3}{4}$ x 2 x $15\frac{1}{4}$	W
	2 pc.	$\frac{3}{4}$ x 2 x 18	J
	1 pc.	$\frac{3}{4}$ x $2\frac{1}{4}$ x $7\frac{3}{8}$	F
1 pc. 2″ x 2″ x 5′	1 pc.	$1\frac{1}{8}$ x $1\frac{1}{4}$ x $27\frac{3}{4}$	M
	1 pc.	$1\frac{1}{8}$ x $1\frac{3}{4}$ x $27\frac{3}{4}$	N
PINE MOULDING			
1 pc. $\frac{3}{8}$″ Q.R. x 7′	2 pc.	$\frac{3}{8}$″ Quarter Round x $4\frac{7}{8}$	CC
	2 pc.	$\frac{3}{8}$″ Quarter Round x $32\frac{1}{2}$	BB
1 pc. $\frac{1}{4}$″ x $\frac{1}{4}$″ x 7′	2 pc.	$\frac{1}{4}$″ x $\frac{1}{4}$″ x $4\frac{3}{8}$	Z
	2 pc.	$\frac{1}{4}$″ x $\frac{1}{4}$″ x $32\frac{1}{2}$	Y
FIR			
1 pc. $1\frac{1}{2}$″ x $1\frac{1}{2}$″ x 4′	6 pc.	1 x 1 x 6	Handles
1 pc. 2″ x 4″ x 10′	2 pc.	$1\frac{5}{8}$ x $3\frac{5}{8}$ x $20\frac{1}{2}$	G
	1 pc.	$1\frac{5}{8}$ x $3\frac{5}{8}$ x $35\frac{1}{4}$	C
	1 pc.	$1\frac{5}{8}$ x $3\frac{5}{8}$ x $35\frac{1}{4}$	D
2 pc. 4″ x 4″ x 6′	4 pc.	$3\frac{5}{8}$ x $3\frac{5}{8}$ x $33\frac{1}{2}$	O, P
PLYWOOD MATERIAL			
1 pc. $\frac{1}{4}$″ x 3′ x 4′		Fir Plywood	
1 pc. $\frac{1}{2}$″ x 4′ x 8′		Fir Plywood	See cutting
1 pc. $\frac{3}{4}$″ x 4′ x 6′		Fir Plywood	diagrams
1 pc. $\frac{3}{4}$″ x 4′ x 6′		Duraply ®	for details
1 pc. $\frac{1}{8}$″ x $4\frac{7}{8}$″ x $32\frac{1}{2}$″		Perfowood ®	

MISCELLANEOUS		MATERIAL LIST: BACK
2″ Angle Brackets	6 pc.	1 pc. 1″ x 10″ x 6′ Pine
1″ Angle Brackets	4 pc.	1 pc. $\frac{1}{8}$″ or $\frac{1}{4}$″ x 16″ x 70″ Perfowood ®
$\frac{3}{8}$″ Offset Cabinet Hinges	6 pc.	2″ Angle Brackets (2 required)
Friction Catches	2 pc.	Wood Screws
Wood Screws		Nails
Nails		

* Note—All sizes in USE COLUMN are finish sizes

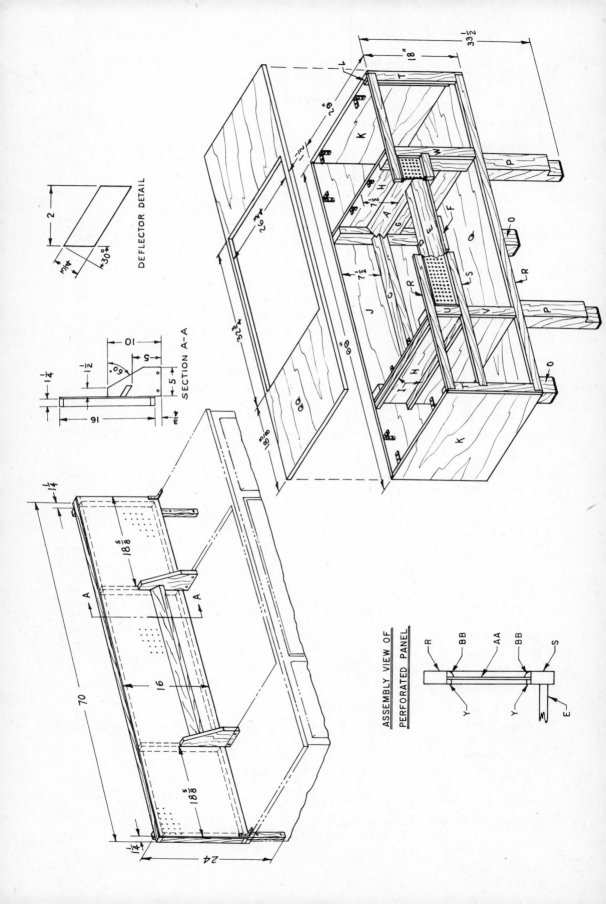

DEFLECTOR DETAIL

2

30°

SECTION A-A

$1\frac{1}{4}$

$\frac{1}{2}$

60°

10

5

5

16

$\frac{3}{8}$

A
A

$18\frac{5}{8}$

16

$18\frac{5}{8}$

70

24

$\frac{1}{4}$

$1\frac{1}{4}$

$\frac{1}{4}$

ASSEMBLY VIEW OF
PERFORATED PANEL

R
BB
AA
BB
S
Y
Y
E

$33\frac{1}{2}$

18"

2

10

26

$32\frac{1}{2}$

$18\frac{5}{8}$

68"

$7\frac{1}{2}$

$7\frac{1}{2}$

T
K
W
H
A
G
D
E
F
Q
O
R
S
U
V
J
C
I
H
T
O
P
P
O
K
DD

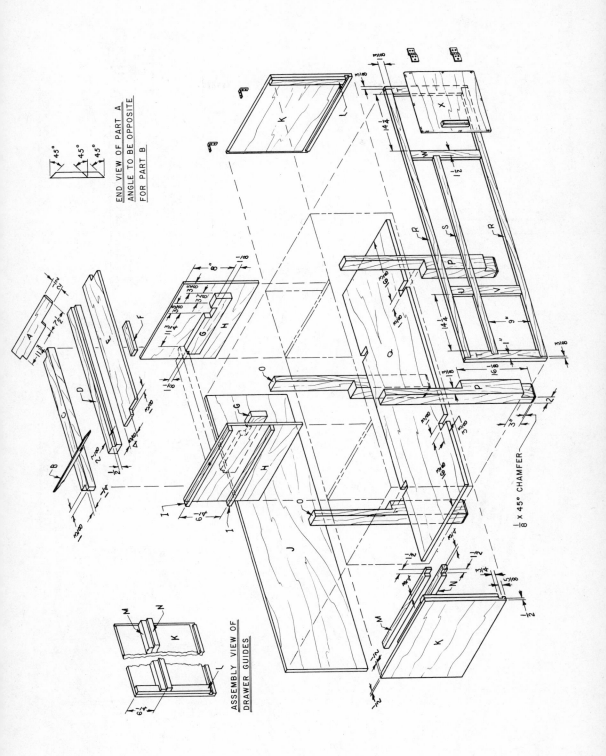

END VIEW OF PART A
ANGLE TO BE OPPOSITE
FOR PART B

45°
45°
45°

ASSEMBLY VIEW OF
DRAWER GUIDES

1/8 x 45° CHAMFER

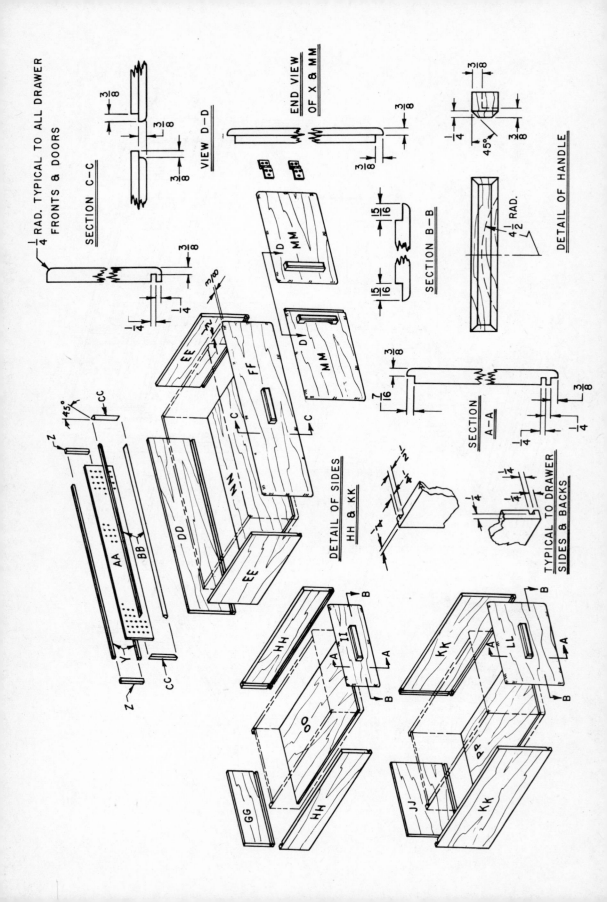

INDEX